Money Talks

Money Talks
Media, Markets, Crisis

Edited by
Graham Murdock and Jostein Gripsrud

intellect Bristol, UK / Chicago, USA

First published in the UK in 2015 by
Intellect, The Mill, Parnall Road, Fishponds, Bristol, BS16 3JG, UK

First published in the USA in 2015 by
Intellect, The University of Chicago Press, 1427 E. 60th Street,
Chicago, IL 60637, USA

A catalogue record for this book is available from the
British Library.

Part of the Changing Media, Changing Europe series

Series ISSN: 1742-9439
Electronic ISSN: 2043-7803

Cover designer: Holly Rose
Copy-editor: MPS Technologies
Production manager: Tim Mitchell
Typesetting: Contentra Technologies

Print ISBN: 978-1-78320-405-2
ePDF ISBN: 978-1-78320-412-0
ePUB ISBN: 978-1-78320-413-7

Printed and bound by Hobbs, UK

Contents

Introduction

Financial speculations: Contested constructions of markets and crisis

Graham Murdock

The commercial world is very frequently put into confusion by the bankruptcy of merchants, that assumed the splendour of wealth only to obtain the privilege of trading with the stock of other men, and of contracting debts which nothing but lucky casualties could enable them to pay; till after having supported their appearance a while with tumultuary magnificence of boundless traffic, they sink at once, and drag down into poverty those whom their equipages had induced to trust them.

Dr Samuel Johnson 1752 (quoted in Atwood 2012: 9)

I'm forever blowing bubbles, pretty bubbles in the air. They fly so high, nearly reach the sky. Then like my dreams, they fade and die.

(Chorus of a popular song first released in 1918)

Recent years have seen talk about the centrality of money and finance move to the centre of public and private life. Discourses around debt and credit, consumption and austerity, increasingly pervade discussion, from debates on the politics of national accounting to anxieties over personal living standards. This resurgence of interest has been prompted in large part by the financial crisis of 2007–2008 and the continuing attempts of governments across the advanced capitalist world to manage its consequences. It is against this background of crisis and response that the contributions to this volume address the ways that economic and financial affairs have been talked about and represented across a range of social sites and media genres.

As the French political economist Thomas Piketty has argued, journalists, commentators and citizens need to 'take a serious interest in money' since 'those who have a lot of it never fail to defend their interests' (Piketty 2014: 577). The response to crisis throws into sharp relief both the limits of the information and interpretive frameworks offered to the public and the resilience of the narratives generated by those benefitting most from the restoration of business as usual.

The discussions presented here, originated in a series of seminars on the contemporary public sphere, organized as part of the 'Changing Media, Changing Europe' programme funded by the European Science Foundation, pays particular attention to Europe. But since the crisis originated in the United States, involved financial institutions with global reach, and has been explored in feature films and documentaries with international distribution, consideration of talk about its causes and consequences inevitably escapes national and regional boundaries.

To understand constructions of the current crisis and reactions to it, we need to return to an earlier moment of crisis, in the 1970s. The policy and ideological responses that crystalized then laid the essential foundations for the crash of 2007–2008 and its continuing aftermath, setting in motion both the dynamics that would create it and the prevailing discourses though which it would be represented and understood.

Gathering storms

As Wolfgang Streeck has noted, it is now generally accepted that '[t]he late 1960s and early 70s' marked 'a watershed in the history of post-war democratic capitalism' (Streeck 2012: 28). Consumer demand for the mass-produced standardized goods that had fuelled the long boom was stagnating. The competitiveness of the core capitalist economies was increasingly challenged by emerging economic powers, led by Japan. Profits were further squeezed in 1973–1974 by a four-fold hike in the price of oil. Corporations moved to tackle their increasing costs. Unemployment increased. Retail prices rose, and by 1974 inflation in the world's largest economy, the United States, had reached 10%, over triple the 3% rate for 1966.

This 1970s' crisis of accumulation precipitated a radical break with the post-war intellectual consensus on the nature of advanced capitalism and how best to manage it. The styles of state management, public investment and regulation associated with Maynard Keynes were increasingly replaced by market-oriented views. The new thinking was underpinned by three assumptions:

First, the expanding services sector of the economy was seen as displacing manufacturing as the principle engine of recovery and competitiveness in the advanced capitalist economies. Routine assembly jobs were moved 'offshore' to low-wage economies. The key industries of the future would be those that traded in information, cultural goods, communication and intangible assets. The financial services provided by banking, investment and insurance rapidly emerged as pivotal to visions of this new 'weightless' economy and were enthusiastically promoted in dominant rhetorics. Within the financial sector this fostered both a sense of separation from the declining industries of the 'real' economy and an assumption that future economic growth required new, innovative financial products.

Second, within both government and the financial industries, the rapidly increasingly processing power offered by advanced computing, and the mathematical modelling of markets it facilitated, came to be seen as the solution to the problems posed by managing a more complex financial environment. As one leading enthusiast of modelling has noted, 'When computers first made economic modelling feasible, the mystique of the machine raised expectations that models built with it would prove as infallible as the machine's arithmetic' (Clopper 2012: vi). This belief was buoyed up by the successful manned moon landing in 1969. But economic modelling was not rocket science. Its utility depended on the assumptions about human behaviour that underpinned it.

The dominant models factored out any consideration of the vicious circle of debt-financed investment that Dr Johnson had warned against in the quotation that heads this Introduction. 'He was talking about merchants, but substitute banks and large corporations, and it's much the same story' (Atwood 2012: 9). The financial industry and mainstream economics failed dismally to predict either the coming collapse of the 'tumultuary magnificence of boundless traffic' in new financial products or its dire consequences for public services and ordinary people's living standards. Their assumptions were based firmly on the belief that market behaviour was governed by rational calculation in the pursuit of personal advantage. They took little or no account of collective enthusiasms and panics. As David Freedman has argued, 'It was the supposed strength of risk models that gave investment firms the confidence to leverage their bets with massive sums of borrowed money' adding that 'in no area of human activity [was] so much faith placed in such flimsy science' (Freedman 2011: 76). It was a delusion shared by both those working in the finance industries and those responsible for overseeing their operations. As Alan Greenspan, Chair of the US Federal Reserve from 1987 to 2006, later admitted, it led him to preside over a crash that he 'never saw coming' (Greenspan 2013: 90). Attributing a central role to the failures of computer systems, however, all too easily allows the core economic actors in the crisis to evade responsibility and ignores the key role played by neo-liberal ideology in shaping their actions.

By undermining the credibility of the dominant post-war style of political economic management based on extensive regulation of corporate activity and, in Europe, public ownership and operation of key infrastructural sectors, the crisis of the 1970s opened the way for a 'solution' based on privatizing state assets and relaxing regulatory oversight. The financial services sector was a major beneficiary of this new market-friendly turn.

In 1933, in the wake of the 1929 Wall Street stock market crash, the US government had passed the Glass-Steagal Act separating retail banking from investment banking. This regulatory wall was designed to protect the routine, but essential, business of accepting deposits and making loans to domestic and business customers from the risk of losses incurred in speculative investment ventures. In 1999, the Financial Services Modernisation Act removed it. The inclusion of 'Modernisation' in the title is telling. Only a deregulated market in which financial companies had maximum freedom of movement was seen as fit for the purpose of generating growth at hoped-for levels. In many ways, however, the act was an exercise in running to catch up and ensure that Wall Street was able to compete effectively with the City of London that had been extensively deregulated over a decade earlier, in 1986, in a cluster of measures known as the 'Big Bang', one of the cornerstones of the Thatcher Government's market-driven agenda. This more open playing field offered new opportunities to the investment vehicles operated by Hedge Funds and Private Equity Funds, which because they were closed to regular investors and only open to carefully selected institutions and high-wealth individuals, were subject to even less regulation than established players.

The rebalancing of Anglo-American capitalism, from manufacturing to services, and from extensive to minimal state intervention, was one response to the 1970s crisis. The other was a major push to expand consumption by moving from mass to segmented markets in which carefully engineered symbolic differences between brands were promoted as primary vehicles of self-expression and the assertion of social distinction. The turnover of styles accelerated. Objects became obsolescent and 'unfashionable' more rapidly inviting continuous replacement and updating. As corporations sought to rebalance the redistribution of profits in favour of shareholders and executives, however, real wages began their long relative decline. Consequently, expanded personal consumption had to be funded by a substantial extension of personal credit. Credit cards and store cards proliferated, and loans were extended to increasing numbers of those on low incomes, who might never be in a position to pay back the money borrowed. This was a dynamic that culminated in the growth of the sub-prime mortgages in the United States that were instrumental in precipitating the financial crisis of 2007–2008.

The renewed ethos of possessive individualism that informed the new climate of financial dealing and credit-fuelled consumption was memorably encapsulated in Mrs Thatcher's two most-quoted sayings, that 'there is no alternative', to market-driven growth, and 'there is no society, only individuals and their families'. She was reflecting a growing consensus. As Patricia Greenfield's (2013) analysis of the frequency with which particular words occur in English-language books printed in the United States demonstrates, whereas mentions of 'get' increased sharply from the mid 1960s onwards, mentions of 'give' declined. This shift to possessiveness and self-enclosure is supported by Jean Twenge and her colleagues. Using the same database as Greenfield, the Google Books Ngram viewer, they found mentions of the personal pronouns 'I' and 'me' increasing by 42% between 1960 and 2008 and mentions of the collective pronouns 'we' and 'us' dropping by 10% (Twenge, Campbell and Gentile 2012). These figures signal an imaginative shift in which making individual choices in the market with a view to maximizing personal advantage eclipses shared responsibility for the quality of collective life. The persona of the consumer elbows out the identity of citizen.

In the wake of the 2007–2008 crisis people are once again being exhorted to contribute to generating economic recovery by restoring and extending their commitment to consumption. At the same time, in the United States, the United Kingdom, and across Continental Europe, they are also being asked to accept swingeing cuts to welfare provision as the necessary cost of addressing the deficit in the public account, a shortfall largely created by the massive transfers of public money needed to shore up the financial system and bail out failing banks. In the dominant narrative, economic 'recovery' is identified with the return of consumer-fuelled growth and 'business as usual', including the business of operating financial services with only the minimum of regulatory oversight.

This discourse transfers the social costs of pursuing this strategy to those whose living standards and life chances have been most severely damaged by the continuing economic crisis. As a consequence, the corridors of economic decision-making are haunted by demonized 'others'; the unemployed who fail to devote enough time to looking for work that may not exist; the welfare recipients who submit false claims; the citizens of Spain, Portugal and Greece who have enjoyed the indolent lifestyle of the South and now expect to be bailed out by the hardworking citizens of Northern Europe.

Ranged against this construction of events is a counter narrative encapsulated in the Occupy Movement slogan 'We are the 99%', which lays the blame for crisis firmly at the door of the irresponsible and sometimes criminal actions of the bankers, the governments who gave them unprecedented freedom of action and the mainstream economists who furnished them with intellectual rationales and justifications. In place of calls for austerity and the restoration of business as usual, it advocates a variable basket of measures. These include; redressing the growing income and wealth gap by raising more taxes from corporations and the rich and closing the loopholes that allow then to evade payment; renationalizing key resources; reintroducing tougher regulation of corporate behaviour; and more, generally, privileging social justice and ecological sustainability over economic growth as the measure of economic success.

The analysis of this contested discursive field offered in the chapters that follow is divided into four sections, each dealing with a particular discursive space.

'Insider talk' explores the ways money is imagined and discussed by traders and dealers working inside major financial institutions and by politicians who promoted the policies that constructed the business environment within which they operated.

'News talk' looks at how the preoccupations and world views of financial and political insiders are repackaged as news and comment for consumption by a range of audiences, differentiated by their varying relations to the economic system (as investors, workers and taxpayers) and their media preferences, and explores the spaces available for counter conceptions.

'Screen talk' analyses representations of money and finance in two major media forms, documentary and feature films, both of which potentially release investigation, representation and storytelling from the formal and time constraints of news and allow for more flexible engagements with contexts, causes, motivations, blame and responsibility.

'Everyday talk' draws on the findings of a major survey across six European countries to explore the different ways the causes of the continuing crisis in the Eurozone and its possible solutions are understood by citizens in different economic and life situations.

Insider talk

Sherman McCoy, the bond dealer, in Tom Wolfe's iconic 1987 novel of Wall Street, *Bonfire of the Vanities*, imagines himself and his colleagues as 'Masters of the Universe', a group apart, with an unshakeable sense of entitlement.

Among the fund managers and other financial professionals based in the City of London interviewed by Aeron Davis for the opening chapter of this collection, this sense of 'cultural cohesion and outsider exclusion' is cemented by intersecting circuits of insider talk. The continual buzz of conversation and gossip that flows between trading rooms and favoured bars, eateries and social venues reinforces a powerful sense of being members of a thoroughly contemporary elite, occupying its own distinctive spaces and networks and operating according to its own rules on the basis of privileged information and analysis. As Peter Thompson confirms, from his interviews with traders working in the foreign exchange (forex) market in New Zealand, this 'insider' identity is not confined to the core centres of financial power. It extends to every node in the global digital dealing networks. As markets close in one time zone, others open in other zones, generating an unbroken chain of potential transactions encouraging participants to see themselves as runners in a never-ending relay race, handing the baton to colleagues on the next continent working for the same transnational clients and trading in the same assets. This global playing field operates on increasingly compressed time scales. Profits depend on instantaneous responses to fractional movements in prices. Unlike shares, there are no centralized exchanges for currencies; so prices cannot be tracked on a continuous basis as shifts in dealing show up on trading screens. This real-time monitoring is replaced by benchmark prices based on the flow of dealing complied by WM/Reuters that are then posted for 30 seconds either side of the hour prompting frenetic trading before this 'window' of opportunity closes.

The general acceleration of dealing is taken to its logical conclusion by the high-frequency traders, the 'Flash Boys' (Lewis 2014), who pay $14 million a year for access to a private cable link between New York and Chicago that cuts the time taken to send a signal from 17 milliseconds to 13. This keeps them one step ahead of investors relying on publicly accessible infrastructure so that when these 'late' entrants place an order to buy or sell, they find the market price moving against them. As the *Economist* tartly observed, '[P]erhaps the best analogy is with the people who offer you tasty titbits as you enter the supermarket to entice you to buy; [and] as soon as you show appreciation for the goods, they race through the aisles to mark up the price before you can get your trolley to the chosen counter' (*Economist* 2014: 77).

This is a particularly stark illustration of a longer-term tendency towards short-termism that observers now see as characteristic of the financial industry as a whole. As one insider noted, fund managers are judged by the immediate returns they generate for clients: 'the current quarter is what matters, perhaps the next quarter, certainly not next year's equivalent quarter' (Golding 2003: 181). As Aeron Davis points out, this emphasis fuels a continual search for the 'next big thing', which 'can aid the creation of bubbles and crashes' with their 'wider social and economic consequences'. As Alan Greenspan famously put it, with studied understatement, in a speech to the American Enterprise Institute, during the dot-com bubble of the late 1990s when the price of shares in Internet-based companies were talked up with no real basis, 'irrational exuberance has unduly escalated asset values' (Greenspan: 1996). As the opening quotation from Dr Johnson demonstrates, recognizing irrational tendencies in markets has a long history.

In 1841 the Scottish journalist Charles MacKay published his anatomy of collective behaviour, *Extraordinary Popular Delusions and the Madness of Crowds* (MacKay 2000). It was an immediate bestseller. Alongside accounts of witch hunts and religious crusades, he offered detailed analyses of three major financial speculations; the tulip bulb mania of the early seventeenth century, and the successive bubbles surrounding the South Sea Company and the Mississippi Company in the decade between 1710 and 1720. The style verged on the sensational with the frenetic nature of trading dramatized with carefully calculated anecdotes, including the story of the Parisian hunchback who reputedly rented out his hump to eager speculators looking for a handy and moveable writing desk. For investors caught up in the turbulent expansion of industrial capitalism and searching for a safe haven for their money, MacKay's inventory of 'delusions' offered a sober reminder of the tendency for financial speculation to become divorced from the 'real' economy of production. By the end of the century, however, the newly professionalized discipline of 'economics' was pushing to be recognized as the only source of reliable analysis and commentary on economic affairs. It presented itself as a new science of economic behaviour rooted in the assumption that the 'economy' was governed by rational calculation and open to precise predictions that could be codified in mathematical formulae, the universal language of 'true' sciences. There was no place in this model for Mackay's insights. As Greenspan has been forced to concede however, the belated rediscovery of 'herd behaviour' in financial markets that the 2007–2008 crisis has prompted has comprehensively undermined this 'model of the wholly rational *Homo economicus* used for so long' as the basis of neoclassical economics (Greenspan 2013: 92).

Recent events, however, have also revealed more calculated forms of collusion at the heart of the financial system with mounting evidence that institutions have systematically intervened in markets to establish a mutually advantageous operating environment. In December 2013, six financial institutions agreed to pay the European Commission 1.7 billion euros for participating in a cartel that rigged the LIBOR, the benchmark interest rate at which banks lend to each other. They included the major French and German banks, Société Générale and Deutsche Bank and the Royal Bank of Scotland (*Economist* 2013: 83). As the European Competition Commissioner, Joaquin Almunia noted, 'What is shocking … is not only the manipulation of benchmarks … but the collusion between banks that are supposed to be competing with each other' (quoted in Treanor 2013: 3). At the time of writing, investigators are pursuing claims that the key 4pm forex benchmark price posted in London has also been systematically manipulated. They are paying particular attention to the electronic chat rooms used by leading traders in the market. With names like 'The Bandits Club', 'The Cartel' and 'The Dream Team', they reaffirm and celebrate a strong sense of being a group apart that writes its own rules. Gordon Brown, who as chancellor of the exchequer throughout the New Labour administrations headed by Tony Blair in Britain had charge of steering the British economy, has candidly admitted that he, along with other leading politicians and regulators, failed to fully grasp the extent to which the financial sector had become a self-enclosed interconnected system increasingly uncoupled from national priorities. 'We didn't understand the entanglements of different institutions and we didn't understand … how global things were. That was our mistake' (BBC 2011).

As Catherine Walsh demonstrates in Chapter 3, analysing the budget speeches of successive British chancellors, throughout his time in office Brown did nothing to challenge the prevailing orthodoxy that financial services in general, and the City of London in particular, were pivotal to Britain's economic vitality and needed to be nurtured and protected from unnecessary regulation. This was in marked contrast to his Labour predecessor Denis Healey, who as chancellor in the late 1970s had seen industry as the primary driving force behind the economy and argued that any expansion in the business of banks should be 'directed to the needs of manufacturing for working capital'. The election of the first Thatcher government in 1979 saw this orthodoxy dismantled. As Walsh shows, finance quickly replaced industry as the central focus of budget statements, and a raft of measures were introduced to promote 'finance-friendly regulation, finance-friendly tax policy, and an emphasis on the City of London's power to create wealth'. As Dylan Grice has shown (again using the Google Ngram viewer database of word usage), this change of direction was a localized variant of a much more pervasive imaginative and rhetorical shift in the English-speaking world that saw the term 'financial' overtake 'industrial' from 1980 onwards, and the gap between the two widen in each successive year (Grice 2013: 4). In Britain the ascendancy of finance was anchored by two very concrete policy interventions, the 1986 'Big Bang' deregulation of financial services mentioned earlier, and increasing popular involvement in financial markets. The first gave financial institutions much more freedom of movement, the second tied increasing numbers of individuals and households into the emerging network of services through the flotation of shares in the newly privatized public utilities, the sale of council houses, and the promotion of private pensions. Financial gains became democratized. They no longer appeared as the exclusive preserve of the privileged. They became central to personal and household calculations of gains and futures. The new Labour government elected in 1997 did little to reverse these trends and embarked on their own romance with finance. As Walsh shows, from 1980, right up until the crisis of 2007, the message that successive chancellors of both major parties 'sent to financial elites and non-elites alike was unswervingly supportive'.

News talk

Although the financial crisis of 2007–2008 prompted a degree of political soul searching, with calls for a more socially responsible capitalism, the dominant impetus was to get back to 'business as usual' as quickly as possible with only minimal re-regulation of financial services or adjustments to the tax system to increase the contributions made by corporations and the most wealthy. The burden of restoration fell mainly on the public purse. In Britain, failing banks were bailed out with huge infusions of public money, and across Europe, deficits in public finances were addressed by imposing swingeing cuts in expenditure on welfare benefits and public facilities. As Justin Lewis and Richard Thomas argue in their chapter, these interventions were underpinned by a continuing political commitment to restoring the consumer-driven model of economic growth that had been instrumental in causing the crisis. This model has been under sustained attack for some time from critics pointing to its environmental limits and socially dysfunctional consequences. However, their analysis of press reporting of talk around growth in the leading 'quality' newspapers in Britain and the United States between September 2010 and July 2011 reveals that only 12 of the 591 items sampled mentioned the negative consequence and only three focused on them in detail. At the same time, very few of the items offered tangible reasons for continuing to pursue a growth model. When they did, they tended to emphasize job creation while largely ignoring alternative ways of tackling unemployment.

This analysis, conducted over two years after the advent of the 2007–2008 banking crisis, suggests that despite mounting evidence of its escalating costs to low-income households and public provision, in the two major centres of the new financial capitalism, a return to consumer-generated growth remains the taken for granted measure of successful political management.

As Lewis and Thomas point out, the rapid rise of business news constructed around corporate and consumer talk has played a major role in sustaining and cementing this orthodoxy. The expansion of multichannel television has opened space for niche business news channel such as Bloomberg and CNBC while escalating problems with the established economic models of newspaper financing have seen the number of public relations specialists overtake the number of journalists, a trend particularly evident in the United States (see McChesney and Nichols 2011: 49). With resources stretched, newsrooms are more inclined to rely on PR copy and less able to mount independent investigations.

As George DeMartino underlines, drawing on interviews with journalists working in the United States in the period leading up to the crisis, the thinning out of in-house resources left them more dependent on outside sources for commentary and analysis. Added to this, they tended to privilege economists working in the financial sector, assuming they were the best informed, and when dealing with supposedly 'independent' academics, not to probe too deeply into their ties and contracts with financial institutions and the possible conflicts of interest these might generate. As one of his interviewees conceded, with the benefit of hindsight, 'we [now] realize the people we saw before as economic gurus are more like snake oil peddlers'. This realization was driven home with particular force by Charles Ferguson's Oscar-winning documentary, *Inside Job* (2010), which both John Corner and Jostein Gripsrud discuss in their chapters. Ferguson's stark exposé of journalism's general failure to check the abuses and deceptions of financial power on behalf of the public has prompted a bout of soul searching. As the reporter just quoted put it, 'As financial journalists, we are still asking ourselves why we didn't do more to highlight the dangers of predatory lending and reckless mortgage speculation.' One practical step towards delivering on the promise of doling better next time has been the development of more extensive codes of professional ethics, but as DeMartino notes, progress on implementing them has been both patchy and slow.

The consequence, as Lewis and Thomas point out, is that most business news continues to promote a narrow view of the economy, addressing audiences either as investors (with news of stocks, shares, markets, mergers and profits) or as consumers. The bigger picture, of the social impact of finance and business, slides from view.

The general ascendency of corporate and consumerist discourse on economic affairs is confirmed by research on the coverage of economic and financial news in a cross section of Norwegian print, broadcast and online news outlets, done in one week in mid-October 2011 by Nina Kvalheim and Helle Sjøvaag in Chapter 6. News about corporate activities and market movements not only dominates the coverage of *Finansavisen,* one of the major national dailies specializing in financial news (accounting for almost 60% of the total space), it also takes the largest share of air time (37.9%) on the news channel operated by the main commercial broadcaster, TV2. Neither pays much attention to the state economy (4.1% and 2.7% respectively). This structure of attention is in marked contrast to the website of the public service broadcaster, NRK, where news relating to public enterprise accounts for almost a quarter (23.1%) of the total coverage. This suggest that as a public service organization, NRK continues to address its audiences as citizens with stakes in and responsibilities for the overall quality of public life, rather than simply as consumers making purely personal choices in the marketplace.

As Kvalheim and Sjøvaag point out, however, advising people on their consumption and personal finances is an expanding niche market, particularly online, with their results showing that it takes up almost all the available space (90.9%) in the Internet financial magazine issued by Norway's highest circulation newspaper, *VG,* and over a third of the space (35.5%) in the economic news section of the web only newspaper *Nettavisen.*

Although the study was conducted when the fall out from the global financial crisis was still reverberating, the crisis itself attracted very little coverage. The highest percentage being 7.7% on the NRK website. The escalating crisis in the Eurozone was rather closer to Norwegian national interests, however. Norway is not a member of the European Union, having voted narrowly in a referendum to stay out, but through its involvement in the European Economic Area it participates in the EU's internal market without being a member. Consequently, the state of the wider European economy has substantial implications for the national economy. Kvalheim and Sjøvaag's sample week coincided with a major escalation in the gathering crisis in the Eurozone with the German chancellor Angela Merkel and the French president Nicolas Sarkozy engaged in a series of meetings to devise a bail-out plan for Greece. However, among the news outlets sampled, only sites operated by the two national broadcasting organizations, NRK and TV2, devoted significant space to covering the Eurozone crisis, at 30.8% and 23.8% respectively. In both the major printed national daily financial newspapers attention hovered around 4%, figures that might be interpreted as supporting the argument that contemporary financial elites are increasingly likely to locate themselves within a transnational business class rather than geographically bounded spaces (see Murray and Scott 2012).

Norwegian news talk around economic crisis is explored in greater detail in Jostein Gripsrud's chapter that analyses the coverage in three national daily newspapers and the major news bulletins of the two main free-to-air television channels in the first weeks of March and September 2012. Deploying the search terms 'euro crisis', 'debt crisis' and 'financial crisis' to locate relevant items revealed a strong stratification in access to information and commentary. Whereas the business daily *Dagens Næringsliv* (DN), Norway's equivalent of the *Financial Times,* carried 22 items and the quality subscription title *Aftenposten* 19, the leading tabloid *VG* had only 4. In the absence of direct evidence on editorial judgements, any explanation of these stark contrasts has to remain conjecture, but the fact that only 15% of the readers of *VG* had more than four years of university education compared to 36% of *DN* readers and 37% of those taking *Aftenposten,* suggests a firm link between educational level and assumptions about readers' capacities and interests. Nor, as Gripsrud shows, were those with minimal formal education well served by the main broadcast channels with both the key 7pm evening bulletin on the public service broadcaster, NRK, and the main 9pm news programme on its major commercial competitor, TV2, fielding only two items each over the two sample weeks.

In an effort to promote public access to a diversity of views and debate, Norway operates a system of public subsidies to minority publications, including the broad Left-socialist daily, *Klassekampen,* which carried 20 items relating to economic crisis over the sample period. Most offered critical commentary on the EU's response to the Eurozone crisis from a Left perspective asserting that it was explicitly designed to consolidate the power of big business at the expense of workers' living standards.

This long-standing theme in Left commentary on Europe found more general expression within the EU in 2013, with the launch of the 'We are Europe!' manifesto. Arguing that the 'Europe of elites and technocrats that has prevailed up to now' is 'threatening to destroy the entire European project' by undermining its political legitimacy, it called for 're-building Europe from the bottom up' with a publicly subsidized year of volunteering as an alternative to rising rates of unemployment and underemployment. Launched jointly by the German social theorist Ulrich Beck and the European parliamentarian Daniel Cohn-Bendit, it attracted support from notable members of the European intellectual and cultural elite including the political philosopher Jürgen Habermas, the Nobel laureate for literature Imre Kertész and the leading concert pianist András Schiff (Beck and Cohn-Bendit 2013). Without further research we can only guess, but given *Klassekampen's* critical stance towards the centres of financial and corporate power, this intervention by the intelligentsia might well have resonated with a number of the 48% of the paper's readers who had enjoyed four or more years of university education.

In contrast, the coverage in the financial daily DN constructed the crisis primarily as a problem of economic management reprinting, a syndicated column by Howard Davies, a prominent British economic commentator, critiquing the argument that 'financial markets could be left to themselves' and calling for a revision of the relations between private businesses and regulatory agencies. As Jostein Gripsrud notes, this can be seen as a good illustration 'of the way media outlets aimed primarily at economic and political elites provide a platform for intra elite arguments about how best to address pressing issues that may threaten their continuing domination'. As he goes on to argue, what is missing from this 'insider' debate is any sustained engagement with the 'agonies of ordinary people affected by the crisis'. It reinforces a top-down, managerial, perspective that constructs citizens as 'faceless, collective, targets of policies or plans for intervention rather than named individuals with lives, hopes and views that deserve to be recorded and respected'.

This absence of voices grounded in grassroots experience was a more general feature of the news outlets Gripsrud sampled. As other research has shown, it leaves a discursive space open to recourse to entrenched national stereotypes, with the 'lazy', 'profligate' and 'incompetent' citizens of Greece and the nations of the southern periphery of Europe where living standards have been hardest hit by the crisis, pitched against the 'sober', 'hard working', peoples of northern Europe who are expected to bail them out. This binary construction prepares the way for blame to be shifted from financial institutions and compliant government to the victims of their actions and inactions.

As Yiannis Mylonas demonstrates in his analysis of headlines addressing the Greek crisis in Germany's bestselling daily paper, *Bild-Zietung* the language they employed systematically obscured underlying structural causes and attributed the Greeks' situations to their own character failings, cultivating a climate of indignation and spite towards the 'underserving' recipients of aid funded by German taxpayers (Mylonas 2012). As we noted earlier, however, this conservative framing of events was by no means dominant. There was still space in the German public sphere for the Left-liberal construction crystallized in the 'We are Europe!' manifesto mentioned earlier.

As Gripsrud's analysis shows, a range of discourses were also in play in the Norwegian media sphere with the quality daily *Aftenposten,* with a more broadly based readership within the professional classes than DN, explicitly presenting the economic crisis in Europe as also a crisis of political legitimacy with a major commentary piece headed 'Europe's crisis and democracy' identifying the 'lack of a common European solidarity [as] perhaps the greatest obstacle to a solution of the crisis'. The paper's own contribution to fostering solidarity took the form of a series of articles recounting the stories of immigrants from southern Europe searching for a job in Norway, exploring, in their own words, the conditions they had left behind and the hopes they had for the future.

As Gripsrud points out, however, news is not the only cultural form through which definitions of the situation circulate. Constructions of crisis, its causes and consequence, and representations of the activities of the financial institutions at its epicentre have also featured in a number of recent documentaries and feature films. There is a plausible argument that since these forms are more open and flexible than news, they are able to view situations from multiple points of view, to accommodate a diversity of voices and present more complex and nuanced analyses of the links between biographies and histories. The opportunity to tease out the connections between situated actions and the wider structures and forces that shape them is crucial to fostering public understanding but as Gripsrud argues it is largely missing from news accounts.

Screen talk

Hollywood has always had a paradoxical relation with banks and financial institutions. On the one hand they have played a major role in funding the industry (Wasko 1982). On the other, screen representations have tapped into the strong populist current in American vernacular culture to raise questions about their motives and operations.

In 1946, with the social devastation caused by the Great Depression that followed the 1929 Wall Street Crash, in which banks' speculative lending had played a major role, still active in popular memory, Frank Capra released *It's a Wonderful Life*. Although it failed to recoup its costs on its initial release, it has since been included in the American Film Institute's list as the best American films ever made and become a staple of Christmas television schedules. It opens with George Bailey, the owner of a family-run building and loan company in the archetypal small town of Bedford Falls, contemplating suicide. Depositors' money that should have been paid into the town's main bank has been mislaid by his absent-minded uncle, and he faces financial ruin and humiliation. Unknown to Bailey, the money has been found and kept by Henry Potter, the bank's proprietor, who makes his profits from renting slum properties at exorbitant rents and has long seen Bailey's commitment to providing loans for affordable housing as the major barrier to expanding his business. In a nightmarish sequence, George is shown the town as it would have been without his business and left to the unopposed ascendency of Potter's power. The main street is now a garish strip of bars and gambling joints and his mother has been reduced to running a seedy boarding house for itinerant workers. He abandons his plans for suicide and returns home to find it filled with the town's citizens donating whatever they can to save him from bankruptcy. Soon after the film's release Hollywood was caught up in the campaign, led by Senator McCarthy, to root out supposed communist influence in the entertainment industry. As a contribution to this effort, a group of right-wing industry employees submitted a report claiming that the film's negative image of Potter was a deliberate and 'common trick by communists' to undermine public trust in the banking industry (Zennie 2013). This is a wilful misreading. The film's indictment of Potter's total disregard of the negative social impacts of his single-minded pursuit of profit is pitched against Bailey's socially constructive contribution to community life. It reminds its audience of why, following the 1929 crash, legislation was introduced to separate retail banking based on carefully considered loans to households and businesses from speculative investment banking.

As Anja Peltzer recounts in her chapter, the image of financial speculation as a form of gambling on numbers, and of the stock exchange as a casino, has a history in Hollywood stretching back to the days of silent cinema. She offers the 1920 release, *The Saphead*, which consolidated Buster Keaton's career as one of the leading comic actors of his generation, as an example. Keaton's character, Bertie, the son of a Wall Street tycoon who has made his money from a gold mine, has adopted a high life of partying and gambling to impress the girl he wants to marry. Angered by his son's supposed irresponsibility his father disowns him and entrusts the running of his business to his son-in-law Mark who promptly sets about appropriating the family fortune by selling their stock. In a climatic slapstick scene on the stock exchange floor, Bertie literally wrestles the share certificates away from eager traders saving the business and regaining his father's trust. Bertie and Mark are both shown as gamblers, but where Bertie risks his own money, Mark attempts to line his pockets by using other people's assets.

As Peltzer points out, in recent years it is the figure of Gordon Gekko, the anti-hero of Oliver Stone's *Wall Street,* who has come to embody amoral speculation, appearing as an immediately recognizable image on magazine covers. Released in 1987, the same years as Tom Wolfe's *Bonfire of the Vanities*, Gekko's personal credo, 'Greed is good' updates the image of Wall Street projected in the one of the intertitles for *The Saphead* as the, 'street where money is everything and everything is money'. *Wall Street's* plot pivots on the uncoupling of financial capitalism from industrial capitalism summarized in Gekko's boast that 'I create nothing. I own'. His eager acolyte Bud Fox is the son of a mechanic and trade unionist working for the Blue Star airline company. Desperate to impress and advance his career he leaks privileged information that puts Gekko in a strong position to buy Blue Star when it runs into difficulties. But when he realizes that Gekko intends to liquidate the company and make a quick profit, he teams up with one of Gekko's main rivals to thwart the plans. The film ends with both men on their way to court to face charges of insider trading.

Despite being brought to book for his illegal actions, as Peltzer shows, Gekko's truculent disregard for ethics in the pursuit of money and advantage rapidly entered the circuits of popular culture. In her analysis of a later major Hollywood movie, *Boiler Room* (2000), she highlights how the company's financial traders are shown bonding over pizzas and beer by watching *Wall Street,* demanding absolute silence when Gekko appears and repeating each line of his dialogue. Again, the film ends with the restoration of justice with revelations by a disillusioned whistle-blowing employee leading to charges for boosting profits by selling shares in worthless fictitious companies.

When we turn to the perspectives promoted by films made after the 2007–2008 crisis, however, we find rather more ambiguity. Peltzer focuses on two releases, *Wall Street: Money Never Sleeps* (2010) and *Margin Call* (2011), which Gripsrud also discusses in his chapter.

Margin Call follows the deliberations of a long-serving trader, Sam Rogers, who is persuaded against his better judgement to organize the sale of assets held by his firm that computer projections confirm will soon be valueless. *Wall Street: Money Never Sleeps* follows Gordon Gekko as he returns to trading after serving an eight-year prison sentence for his previous illegal dealings. *Is Greed Good?,* the title of the book he has written while inside, and is promoting at the beginning of the film, suggests that he may have renounced his former credo, but true to form he uses the $100 million trust fund account he had established for his daughter to move to London and launch a new financial company having originally suggested that the money could be used to fund the alternative energy company being developed by his future son-in-law, Jacob. Having re-established himself as a player in the market, he deposits $100 million anonymously in the energy company's account and the film ends with him apologizing to his daughter and Jacob and attending his grandson's first birthday party.

As Peltzer points out, this 'excessively harmonious' resolution leaves the system that caused the crisis intact, with Gekko continuing to pursue 'business as usual' while using some of his profits to fund an ethical enterprise aimed at addressing the problem of climate change. Sustained interrogation of the systemic structures that caused the crisis, and may do so again, is displaced by an invitation to personal responsibility. Consequently, as

Gripsrud notes, because '[t]he crisis is understood as primarily rooted in the morality of individuals … its solution must be found in a kind of moral rearmament'. But as he also argues, there is another major gap. All of the films discussed 'ask the audience to sympathise or at least empathise with' the moral dilemmas and social hardships of 'upper middle and upper class people'.

Nor has the fascination exerted by ruthless individualism and its rewards, embodied in Gekko, entirely disappeared. In 2012, one of Hollywood's leading directors, Martin Scorsese, released *The Wolf of Wall Street,* based on the autobiography of Jordan Belfort who made a fortune selling worthless shares. Trading under the prestigious sounding company name Stratton Oakmont, but in reality operating out of a boiler room in a shopping mall on Long Island, his team rang investors and cold called names from the telephone directory, talking up shares in the companies he had floated, buying shares themselves to bump up the value, and then when the price reached a peak, offloading them, leaving buyers not in the know with worthless stock. Belfort, whose lavish lifestyle and legendary parties conferred celebrity status, was arrested in 1998 and convicted in 2004. On his release, like Gekko, he reinvented himself, running 'motivational training' seminars revealing the inside tricks of effective selling. At the end of the film he appears as himself, bounding onto the stage in Auckland, New Zealand, as the camera pans over packed rows of expectant faces.

Scorsese's film provoked heated debate. He and the film's star, Leonardo DiCaprio who won a Golden Globe award for best actor for his bravura performance, were adamant that it was intended as a satire and indictment of an age of excess now past. But as Alynda Wheat, the film critic of *People,* the bestselling weekly magazine in the United States, noted, the film's narrative structure reinforces an exclusively 'insider' view of the world in which action is divorced form consequence; we 'hear only his point of view … and see only his perspective. Who cares about the schnooks he's fleecing on the other end of the line? We never see them' (Wheat 2013).

This absence adds another prominent example to the list of widely circulated feature film engagements with economic crisis discussed here that have tended to reproduce the same lacunae as we noted earlier in news coverage. There is no sustained attempt to connect biographies to histories and explore how individual lives and choices are shaped by structural forces. And little attention is paid to the working and unemployed poor whose lives and life chances have borne the brunt of the lay-offs and the cut-backs in public expenditure. The question of how far documentary film is able to make good these deficiencies is discussed by both John Corner and Gripsrud. As Corner points out, documentary forms 'allow for considerable space and time to place and consider a topic, drawing on a range of contexts and generating an expositional flow less urgent and foreclosed than most news accounts, able to take side-roads and come at questions from several angles'. He investigates the way these potentials are employed in three productions that address the crisis: Michael Moore's *Capitalism: A Love Story* (2009), Charles Ferguson's *Inside Job* (2010) and the first episode of Adam Curtis's three-part series, *All Watched Over by Machines of Loving Grace* (2011), with Gripsrud adding the major Norwegian production, *When Bubbles Burst* (2012).

Curtis's account of the crisis weaves together two narrative strands; the increasing corporate and governmental reliance on computer programmes and calculations for assessing risks and taking decisions, and the role played by the novelist Ayn Rand in promoting and popularizing a militant defence of the social value and moral superiority of laissez-faire capitalism. Rand's formative experiences of growing up in Soviet Russia left her implacably opposed to state intervention. She had briefly been a student at the State Technicum for Screen Arts in Leningrad, and on moving to the United States in 1926 (initially on a tourist visa) she worked in Hollywood, as a screenwriter for Cecil B DeMille and later as the head of the costume department at RKO studios. She was concerned by what she saw as the anti-capitalist bias of some of the movies being made at the time and was a member of the group who submitted the ideological critique of *It's a Wonderful Life* mentioned earlier. She expanded on her own ideas in two bestselling novels, *The Fountainhead* (1943) and *Atlas Shrugged* (1957). At the same time, she assembled an informal seminar group ironically called 'the collective'. One of the attendees was Greenspan who, as we have already seen, was Chair of the US Federal Reserve from 1987 to 2006, presiding over a deregulated financial environment in which both regulators and traders increasingly employed computer models to predict and respond to market movements.

Although he uses Greenspan to personify the crisis, Curtis's focus on the intersection of ideological conviction and faith in technology has the effect of shifting the explanation for crisis from conscious manipulation to 'elite self-deception'. As Corner argues, the 'emphasis on the naive faith in computers works to displace direct engagement with the political and economic motives lying behind the crisis'. The result is political paralysis, a conclusion underlined in the film's commentary, in an extract quoted by Corner, which argues that 'we are now entering a very strange moment. We know that the idea of market stability has failed. But we cannot imagine any alternative'.

As Gripsrud argues in his chapter, this sense that many at the heart of the system had ceded the power to make key decisions to technologies they did not fully understand is also central to the plot of *Margin Call* where the 'toxic' nature of the asserts held by the company is only discovered, almost by accident, when a young employee looks again at the numbers on a memory stick given to him by a departing colleague. There is no place in this discourse for vigorous debate on economic alternatives or for voices from the Occupy Movement calling for those who operate and regulate the financial system to be brought to book for their actions and inactions.

In contrast, questions of blame and culpability are central to Charles Ferguson's *Inside Job*, which, as Gripsrud notes, uses a combination of factual material and assertive interviews to show how the 'crisis resulted from the reckless speculation and outright fraud' of financial institutions aided and abetted by a markedly more relaxed regulatory regime that repeatedly failed to head the warning signs of impeding collapse. In a typical interview, analysed by Corner, Frederic Mishkin, a prominent professor of economics and Republican appointee as a governor of the Federal Reserve Board, is subject to sustained questioning about the Board's refusal to follow up on evidence they were presented with on the dangerous levels of loans and his own personal failure, in a report funded by the Icelandic Chamber of Commerce, to detect the weaknesses in the Icelandic banking system, whose catastrophic collapse opens Ferguson's film. The cumulative effect is to lay responsibility for the crisis firmly at the door of the financial institutions who sought to line their pockets by selling 'toxic' products to economically venerable customers, the political class who celebrated finance as one of the pivots of the new economy, and the academic economists wedded to free market orthodoxies who furnished them with intellectual justifications. However, as Gripsrud notes, the often technical exposition leaves the lay viewer having 'to take notes or watch the film more than once' to assimilate all the information on the complex financial products and procedures.

The Norwegian production he discusses, *When Bubbles Burst,* sets out to provide a more concrete and accessible account by following two representatives from the municipality of Vik in western Norway as they journey to Wall Street to discover why local investments intended to fund a road tunnel, which they had been persuaded to make in sub-prime-based products developed by Citibank, on the recommendation of the major Norwegian financial enterprise Terra, had turned out to be worthless. In the course of their conversations with academics and specialists in finance they are offered an explanation of their situation that highlights the progressive separation of financial dealing from the 'real' economy of concrete production and infrastructural investment and outlines an alternative based on a return to the broadly Keynesian approach to investment and regulation that directed economic policy before the ascendency of neo-liberalism. The narrative device of a journey, from the periphery to the centre, and from a local economy based on industry and public investment in infrastructure to an economy organized around financial dealing, successfully dramatizes the systemic nature of the current crisis and its global reach and grounds it in concrete experience. But as Gripsrud notes, '[O]utside of a few people from Vik and home owners hit by the loan crisis in Detroit, there are few representatives of the myriad victims of the crisis who might provide opportunities for empathy and potentially for solidarity'.

Like the representatives of Vik, in *Capitalism: A Love Story,* Michael Moore, casts himself in the role of everyman, an ordinary guy trying to puzzle out what has happened. He aligns himself squarely with the working class casualties of the crisis with sequences of people being evicted from their homes and laid-off factory workers fighting to be paid the wages they are owed. He stages a morality play presenting them as victims of a gigantic corporate crime that has stolen their livelihoods, their houses, and their hopes for the future. Bertold Brecht famously asked 'what is robbing a bank to the founding of a bank'. Moore dramatizes this comparison with an opening sequence showing surveillance footage of a bank robbery in progress and pursues it with his trademark use of agitprop street theatre, taping off part of central Wall Street as a crime scene and arriving outside banks that had been bailed out by public funding with sacks to carry away the money he argues they should return.

In search of authoritative moral support for his critical construction of financial capitalism, he enlists Father Dick Preston, the Roman Catholic priest who officiated at his wedding in his hometown of Flint Michigan, the site of the Emmy award-winning documentary that launched his career, *Roger and Me* (1989) on the closure of the town's General Motors' plant. When asked 'Is capitalism a sin?', Father Preston condemns it unequivocally as 'evil [and] contrary to all that is good, to the common good, to compassion'. This is the exact moral antithesis of Gekko's credo 'Greed is Good', reasserting the primacy of mutual care and shared responsibility against the claims of possessive individualism and winner takes all.

Everyday talk

The analyses of talk and representations around finance and crisis presented in the chapters on news, documentary and feature films reveal a discursive field that is both strongly stratified and variably contested with access to visibility and voice distributed in uneven ways. While some media texts blame the crisis on the finance industry's single-minded pursuit of profit maximization and the willingness of politicians and regulators to endorse and support them, others see it as an inevitable outcome of relying on technologies that were not properly understood and could not be fully controlled. With a few notable exceptions, the consequences of crisis for ordinary people receive rather less attention than the dilemmas faced by those in the finance industries. Where the working assumption that the primary goal of policy is to restore business as usual as quickly as possible is challenged, the alternatives tend to be presented as matters of economic management (a return to tighter regulation and greater public investment as against more austerity) rather than fundamental moral choices around social justice, equity and solidarity.

As the study of popular understandings of crisis reported by Andreas Hepp and his colleagues in Chapter 10 reveals, these contests of definition and interpretation are played out on a daily basis as people struggle to identify the causes of crisis and decide on their responses. Their research is based on qualitative depth interviews with 30 citizens in each of six EU countries (Austria, Denmark, France, Germany, Poland and the United Kingdom) in the autumn of 2011, when the EU financial crisis reached its peak, with heated debate about the future of Greece within the Eurozone.

The results reveal marked differences in explanations of the Greek crisis, opinions on how it should be addressed and more general attitudes to the future of the EU. Some participants had no hesitation in blaming the situation on the inability of Greek politicians to manage the economy effectively and the willingness of the Greek people to condone this failure. This attribution of 'national delinquency' supported calls for Greece to be left to sort out its own problems, without the benefit of aid from taxpayers in richer EU countries, and with the option that continued failure might require Greece to be excluded from the Eurozone. As one young Danish respondent put it, 'Greece has made its bed, and now must lie on it' since 'there is no money to be grabbed' from other EU member states. In other comments, there were clear echoes of the ethnic stereotypes that Mylonas Yiannis uncovered in his analysis of headlines in *Bild-Zeitung*.

In marked contrast to these assertions of separation, other respondents expressed strong solidarity with the Greeks and a sense of shared European belonging. Some of this concern was rooted in a general humanitarian care for families whose living standards had been severely damaged by the crisis. But for some, like the 50-year-old Danish architect, 'The Greek crisis [could] be seen as the European time of reckoning', a litmus test of its ability to devise a common approach to emergencies that strengthened rather than weakened its integration. As a young British student put it, 'What's the point of being in [the EU] if you're not getting that [financial protection]. It's necessary to help each other out'. Opinion however was divided on how this 'help' should be organized and administered with some respondents expressing concern about the central role being played by Germany in deciding the conditions of aid. As a 50-year-old woman from London argued, 'We don't want to reach the point where one country has too much power in Europe. Because that's always been dangerous in the past … I just think this whole thing is problematic […] Ehm, I feel really sorry for Greece'.

As Hepp and his colleagues point out, in the absence of further research we cannot specify how respondents' everyday framings of finance and crisis may have been shaped by the complex interplay between their grounded experiences, their political perspectives and their media repertoires. As the preceding chapters suggest however, those relying primarily on the tabloid press, broadcast television news and mainstream Hollywood movies are likely to have access to a more restricted range of information, imagery and interpretation than readers of the quality press and audiences for documentary features that emphasize exposition rather than dramatization. These cultural forms both presuppose possession of the prior knowledge and interpretive resources conferred by education beyond the minimum age and sustained by participation in a professional occupation. These differential holdings of cultural capital are reflected in turn in audience profiles and may be reinforced by patterns of media distribution. Despite winning the 2011 Academy Award for best documentary feature, *Inside Job* did not gain a broadcast showing in Norway and its only cinema screening was at the Bergen International Film Festival.

The public sphere in crisis

As Gripsrud notes, this continuing stratification of access to the resources of information, analysis and empathetic insight needed to understand and respond to the most serious economic crisis in Europe and North American since the Great Depression produces a profound paradox in which 'those most severely affected by the crisis in their everyday lives are least likely to have access to readily intelligible accounts of its causes and possible solutions while those most involved in addressing the problems within the present system are least likely to be aware of the scale and scope of the human devastation that has followed in its wake'.

The analyses offered in the chapters that follow are necessarily selective, based on detailed explorations of particular national media systems and cultural forms. More comprehensive research is urgently needed to map the way the crisis and its aftermath have been constructed in major media forms across the full range of European countries. The evidence presented here does, however, point to an escalating crisis of the public sphere.

Accounts of economic crisis uncoupled from accessible explanations of its underlying structural causes opens space for the scapegoating of migrants and welfare claimants and increases the appeal of political movements grounded in nationalist and racist discourses. Informed analysis divorced from empathy for those at the bottom offers only the flimsiest basis on which to address the widening social separation and continuing disregard for the common good of those at the top. Acceptance of substantial cuts to welfare and public budgets transfers the costs of crisis from those whose actions and inactions caused it to those most affected by its consequences. Assumptions that continued growth requires the restoration of 'business as usual' with only minor tweaks to regulation and no extended consideration of alternatives, does little to address the underlying causes of crisis. Exhortations to continue consuming to the maximum reproduces one of the key conditions that caused the crisis in the first place and exacerbates the underlying ecological crisis.

These formations of discourse pose severe challenges to the ideal of a public sphere in which, armed with comprehensive and disinterested information and access to the full range of analysis, interpretation and argument, citizens participate in deliberation on core issues that affect them and search for equitable solutions which legislative bodies then take full account of when deciding on interventions and policies. With the aftermath of crisis continuing to widen economic and social divisions within and between European countries, the hollowing out of the public sphere places democratic ideals under increasing threat, with possible consequences that European history points up all too clearly.

References

Atwood, M. (2012), 'Our faith is fraying in the faceless god of money', *Financial Times,* 14th/15th April, p.9.

BBC (2011), 'Gordon Brown admits "big mistake" over banking crisis', www.bbc.co.uk/business-13032013.

Beck, U. and Cohn-Bendit, D. (2013), 'We are Europe! Manifesto for re-building Europe from the bottom up', http://manifest-europa.eu/allgemein/wir-sind-europa?lang+eng. Accessed 25th March, 2013.

Clopper, A. (2012), *The Craft of Economic Modelling,* 5th edn., College Park, Maryland: Interindustry Economic Research Fund Inc.

Economist, the (2013), 'The LIBOR scandal: Fixed harmony', *Economist,* 7th December, p. 83.

Economist, the (2014), 'Fast times', *Economist,* 5th April, p. 77.

Freedman, D. H. (2011), 'A formula for economic calamity', *Scientific American,* 305: 5, pp. 76–79.

Golding, T. (2003), *The City: Inside the Great Expectation Machine,* 2nd edn., London: FT Prentice Hall.

Greenfield, P. M. (2013), 'The changing psychology of culture from 1800 through 2000', *Psychological Science,* 24: 9, pp. 1722–31.

Greenspan, A. (1996), 'The challenge of central banking in a democratic society', www.federalreserve.gov/boarddocs/speeches/1996/19961205.htm.

Greenspan, A. (2013), 'Never saw it coming: Why the financial crisis took economists by surprise', *Foreign Affairs,* 92: 6, November/December, pp. 88–96.

Grice, D. (2013), 'The language of inflation', *Edelweiss Journal,* 14, 4th November, pp. 1–8.

Lewis, M. (2014), *Flash Boys: Cracking the Money Code,* New York: W. W. Norton.

McChesney, R. W. and Nichols, J. (2011), *The Death and Life of American Journalism,* New York: Nation Books.

MacKay, C. (2000 [1841]), *Extraordinary Popular Delusions and the Madness of Crowds,* West Conshohocken, PA: Templeton.

Murray, G. and Scott, J. (eds) (2012), *Financial Elites and Transnational Business: Who Rules the World?,* Cheltenham: Edward Elgar.

Mylonas, Y. (2012), 'Media and economic crisis in the EU: The "culturalization" of systemic crisis and *Bild-Zeitung's* framing of Greece', *tripleC,* 10: 2, pp. 646–71.

Piketty, T. (2014), *Capital in the Twenty-First Century,* Cambridge. Mass: The Belknap Press of Harvard University Press.

Streeck, W. (2012), 'Citizens as consumers: Considerations on the new politics of consumption', *New Left Review [Second Series],* no. 76, July/August, pp. 27–47.

Treanor, J. (2013), 'Banks take another battering', *Guardian,* 5th December, p. 3.

Twenge, J. M., Campbell, W. K. and Gentile, B. (2012), 'Changes in pronoun use of American books and the rise of individualism, 1960–2008', *Journal of Cross-Cultural Psychology,* 44: 3, pp. 406–15.

Wasko, J. (1982), *Movies and Money: Financing the American Film Industry,* Norwood, New Jersey: Ablex.

Wheat, A. (2013), 'See this/skip that: From *Wolf of Wall Street* to *Walter Mitty*', *People,* 27th December, www.people.com/people/article/0,,20769902,00.html.

Zennie, M. (2013), 'Was "It's a Wonderful Life" really communist propaganda?' *Mail Online,* 26th December, www.dailymail.co.uk/news/article-258752.

Part 1

Insider talk

Chapter 1

Financial insider talk in the city of London

Aeron Davis

Introduction

This chapter primarily focuses on private, exclusive forms of communication in London's financial networks. Its starting point is that multiple, internal forms of talk fulfil some vital communicative functions for elite participants. Such internal exchanges, which are very intense and in varied modes, produce 'City' forms of cultural cohesion and outsider exclusion. Each of these is important for sustaining the City's economic and political advantages. First amongst these, at least in the minds of participants, is the need to keep up with daily financial information flows and opinions. The communicative networks of the City are key to disseminating price-sensitive information and producing consensus trading decisions on a daily basis. It keeps insiders ahead of the investment curve (or not far behind) and leaves outsiders trailing in their wakes.

However, insider communication also serves other, less conscious and immediately instrumental functions. One of these is the generation of medium-term investment narratives and fashions. These, which include such things as the 'new economy', 'hi-tech' stocks or new trading and market philosophies, spur larger market movements over a few years. Sometimes these can aid the creation of bubbles and crashes, and with wider social and economic consequences. At a third level, comes the long-term generation of a financial market ideology that underpins beliefs, behaviours and discursive practices. This, in turn, is then exported to non-financial 'stakeholder elites', such as politicians, public company CEOs and pension funds. It is used to legitimate all market practices while delegitimizing non-market actors and institutions. It is also used to discipline states, economies and publics, remaking them, God-like, in the image of financial markets themselves. Thus, private forms of insider communication are central to the profitable workings of financial sectors, and to the maintenance of financial market power in contemporary, financialized states.

The discussion is in three parts. The first documents the communicative architecture and networks of London's financial districts. The second describes the everyday, instrumental communication that drives financial activity and pushes investment decisions. It then goes on to explain how the same exchanges and practices also create medium-term narratives and fashions that then have come to underpin new investment trends, sometimes leading to bubbles and crashes. The third, sketches the parameters of the longer-term financial market ideology that has come to dominate in recent decades and in spite of system shocks. The discussion draws on previous periods of interview-based research with fund managers, analysts, investor relations specialists and financial journalists.

Internal communication flows and financial cultures

The City, as with other financial centres, is an extremely rich and dense communication environment. Information, research and communicative exchange lies at the heart of finance as numerous decisions are made every minute of the trading day. In fact, gaining and circulating financially relevant information is a practical imperative for properly functioning financial markets. Such a goal supports financial market theory as well as attracting market participants for practical reasons.

At one level, much financial information and communication is publicly available and widely disseminated. Such information and business news coverage has expanded considerably in the post-war period (Parsons 1989; Tumber 1993; Tunstall 1996; Cassidy 2002). Standard regulations demand that companies release important financial information about themselves through the London Stock Exchange (LSE). Everyone, insider or outsider, has access to Regulatory News Service (RNS) of the LSE, either directly or via a news wire service. Everyone in the City also reads the *Financial Times* and other leading financial news publications. However, in many ways, public media are of decreasing importance in daily investment activity in the financial sector. For professional financiers publicly available information is of little use when everyone has it. To get ahead, private information and analysis is more useful. In the electronic age, public news media is far too slow to be useful to professionals. Similarly, those in the financial world rely relatively little on information they pick up from the 'amateur' observers of the media. Business and finance are highly complex topics that most journalists struggle to understand and keep up with (see Davis 2002; Doyle 2006; Tambini 2010). Public news media does serve some useful functions for insiders, as I will explain below, but its importance is longer-term, cultural and ideological.

Far more significant to financial insiders, on the day-to-day level, are the many varied forms of private communication networks and mediums. When investigating these alternatives (Davis 2002), a decade ago, I found there were over 90 exclusive financial print publications circulated in the City. On top of this, thousands of stockbroking ('sell-side') and fund management ('buy-side') analysts produced and circulated regular research reports. There are also many specialists, financial information suppliers, offering analysis at high subscription rates. In addition, there are a range of real-time electronic information feeds and database services that collate and summarize market information and trading activities in any sector.

Private, face-to-face meetings, conversations and phone calls are more intense and focused still. Analysts, brokers, public and investor relations specialists, journalists, fund managers and others are all involved in multiple dialogues every day. Many exchanges consist of formal meetings, for example, between company CEOs and fund managers (see also Holland

1997; Marston 1999). When interviewing fund managers it was not uncommon to find them involved in several hundred meetings a year with CEOs and directors: (William Claxton-Smith, fund manager) '[W]e operate as a team rather than individuals and … it's something like, for the UK equity side of the business, 700 meetings, maybe more, per year.' Rather more communication takes place in a plethora of informal conversations: (Alistair Defriez, Takeover Panel) '[E]normous communication with the brokers … They get feedback from the institutions and … the press are also talking to the analysts. The press is going to the market and asking what they think about all this'; (Graham Williams, investor relations) '[B]rokers, institutions and the press all wanted and needed more current information. A constant dialogue was created, a daily exchange of views. Some analysts used to speak to me daily.'

London's financial sector (now more geographically dispersed than before) also provides social spaces and cultural cues to support the networks. Specialist language, dress, customs and codes of practice are in evidence everywhere. There are many social and practical facilities, such as bars, clubs and exclusive gyms, that enable participants to further extend the time they spend in the City. Many participants spend far more of their waking hours within the LSE elite micro culture than they do outside it. As such, the culture, institutionalized practices, language and communications of these networks are as extensive as any other observed cultural field or profession. Such levels of communicative exchange and shared culture both distinguish City insiders and exclude outsiders.

For financial elites, this rich communicative environment is an essential requirement of their job. It serves a plethora of professional functions, from personal networking to getting up-to-the-minute investment information. At a conscious level it is fundamental that one keeps up with fast-changing events and information updates, all of which may have a bearing on decision-making. Everyone wants to keep ahead of the curve or, failing that, keep up with the pack. At a less conscious level, such information exchanges also generate more sustained sets of beliefs, norms and practices, as well as more enduring investment narratives and financial elite ideology. The narratives and ideological positions are then exported to, and imposed upon, other 'stakeholder elites', in business and politics, and indirectly to the wider public. In all of this, financial and public media does play a supportive role, as a sort of echo chamber, both reinforcing City opinions and ideologies, as well as relaying them to associated, stakeholder elites via shared financial media and lobbying (see Davis 2011).

From functional short-term information flows to medium-term investment fashions and bubbles

At the most basic level, financial talk and information flows are essential for keeping financial activity going. Everyone is engaged in buying and selling a range of items: companies (shares), commodities (e.g. oil, gold, rice), real estate and currencies, debt (bonds) and financially constructed products (derivatives, CDOs, CDSs). They have also become about selling particular market sectors (e.g. shares versus bonds, established versus emerging markets, banking versus telecommunication) and selling financial institutions (London versus Frankfurt or New York) and economies. Since the future value of most things is very uncertain, financial actors are constantly attuned to all forms of information that might influence their trading decisions.

In many ways, this is just how financial markets are meant to work. Financially relevant information circulates, 'rational' investors respond, prices go up and down. Such tendencies are most common when selling company shares. Information on corporate quarterly earnings, new acquisitions and contracts, new senior management appointments, profit warnings and dividend announcements is all regularly released, spurring market responses. Similarly, in commodities markets, from oil to orange juice, information on droughts and weather-related factors, new reserve discoveries and new global market demands is also priced in. On another plane, larger economic indicators, such as employment figures, budget deficits, new credit ratings and quarterly growth rates, push investors to switch particular market sectors or economies. Thus, investors may move from oil to gold, from banking stocks to mining company shares or from Greek government bonds to German ones.

However, such communication also works to generate wider forms of internal financial market cohesion and consensus, while also excluding outsiders. Despite being in competition, market participants also rely on larger forms of consensus. Others have to agree in order for movements to take place, and larger movements with bigger profits need larger groups to agree. This was one observation of Keynes (1936) who observed that trading was more concerned to locate the 'average' opinion than to make individual assessments. Indeed, as I found out when conducting interviews, the most important financial information for investors is knowing what everyone else is doing and what indeed the general consensus is on anything being traded: (Andy Brough, fund manager) 'To play the game you have to be aware of the psychology of the other players in the game. Because you may well need them to buy your shares, or sell you the shares at some point'; (Michael Hughes, fund manager) 'The emphasis here is that it's a score for the stock not the company. In other words he is making an assessment of what he thinks the stock price is going to do, not whether he likes the company or not.'

At another level, there is a need to generate medium-term forms of consensus that establish more stable trading patterns and environments that insiders can use to 'anchor' their everyday calculative processes. One of these is the requirement that participants have relative agreement on the means of valuation itself. What accounting measures to take note of, the significance of individual financial indicators and the basis of valuing items in each market need a minimum level of agreement. So, while, at a conscious level, investors are communicating about measures and values, at an unconscious level they are also determining what are the measures to use at any one time (see Callon 1998; Miller 1998). Another form of consensus that participants seek to establish is over what actual markets are good to invest in: stock or bond markets, new hi-tech stocks or old steady ones, established national financial markets or new emerging ones. In recent decades, before the 2008 crash, industry reports and investor guides (e.g. Siegal 1998; Glassman and Hassett 1999) argued that wise investors should always put most of their capital into company shares markets rather than other markets (e.g. bonds, property, currency). According to Shiller's research (2001: 45), in 1999, 96% of wealthy investors agreed that the stock market was the most rewarding and safest place to invest their money. Some years after the 2000 crash, my interviewees continued to affirm this pro-equities investment philosophy (Davis 2007).

In the medium term, it has also been important to generate forms of investment narrative that, in turn, drive more extended investment trends or fashions. As one anonymous investor relations consultant put it to me: 'Investment is a fashion business. There is no doubt. It's just like clothes, houses, universities – they are all fashion businesses … And certain management teams and companies are also fashionable … if you are in fashion and you have currency you can use then you use it'. Thus, in certain decades, 'balanced conglomerates' as well as certain levels of corporate 'debt' and 'leverage' have been considered 'good'. In other decades, they have not. On the larger financial narrative scale, in recent decades, we have had various versions of the 'new economy': 'the new era economy', 'the creative' or 'knowledge-based economy', the 'end of the traditional business cycle', 'the era of permanently low inflation and low interest rates', the rise of the 'Asian Tiger' economies or the 'BRIC' economies and the decline of older, welfare state economies. However, the consequences of such trends can also be quite dramatic and destabilizing. For those inside, 'greed' and 'fear' equally drive activities in rollercoaster investment periods. As an anonymous fund manager explained: 'Mr market is a moving animal, and its mood swings will change to passions.' As everyone looks to follow each other, to keep within the safety of the financial herd, so movements can become quite large and dramatic leading to financial bubbles, crashes and instability.

A common narrative of the last two decades, which has frequently pushed large investor movements, is that of 'hi-tech' stocks in the telecommunications, media and technology (TMT) sector (see Shiller 2001; Cassidy 2002). Investor narratives have been vital here as such new emerging companies usually have no trading histories, no assets and, initially, produce no profits or dividends. In other words, they cannot be valued by conventional accounting measures. Such narratives enabled stock markets to reach unparalleled heights in 2000, as accounting practices and historical norms were ignored. From 1995 to 2000, the New York Dow Jones more than tripled in value – from below 3,500 points to just under 12,000. LSE went from just over 3,000 points to almost 7,000 points. Prices, relative to company earnings, tripled in that period, and were rather more out of alignment than during the previous record set in 1929, just before the Wall Street Crash (see Smithers and Wright 2000; Shiller 2001). Individual Internet company stocks especially rose dramatically to reach valuations that could never realistically deliver. Ultimately, in the collapse that began in 2000, both the US and UK stock markets lost over half their value and many TMT companies became worthless. As many fund managers interviewed about this period admitted, values did not make sense but they felt they had to be part of it just to survive: (John Davies, fund manager) 'You then start to see real share price performance … You then start to worry because you haven't got any and you pile in. As everything keeps going up that gets worse and worse … If you think it's going to go to a 25% premium on day one you don't really care what it does is the simple answer.'

For many on the financial market inside, such developments can destroy careers and companies as well as discourage future investment. However, what has to be remembered is that the biggest costs incurred are often to outsiders such as pension funds, insurance company investments and other longer-term holdings run by arms-length committees. These operate in the long term and hence are too slow to react. Insiders have instant information, can see trends developing and have more time to protect their personal or organizational investments (see Taibbi 2011; Ferguson 2012). As one insider explained: (Tony Dye, fund manager) 'You can't be too cynical or realistic about how the system works. It's out there to make money for those businesses and money for those people … It's out there to take as much money from investors without them protesting … The outsider doesn't understand. That's why you get so many people getting so much money for relatively little … no one wants to give up on it and who can blame them if they can keep the gravy train going.' Of course, it is also the wider economy and ordinary employees who suffer from financial market crashes, losing pensions, jobs and homes.

Within a few years of the 2000 collapse, a whole new set of accounting measures and practices, as well as an accompanying set of new economy narratives, had each been created. Once again, conventional logic and historical patterns came to be ignored, covered over by creative accounting and fairy-tale stories. So, for instance, from 1995 to 2007 house prices doubled in relation to average earnings, from four-and-a-half times to nine times earnings. Banks lent out money that got more out of kilter with their actual assets. By the time Northern Rock, the first bank casualty of the credit crunch, collapsed, it had assets of £1.5 billion and loans worth over £100 billion, 80% of which was financed by the global money markets (Elliott and Atkinson 2009: 52). By 2012, new hi-tech investment fashions were again leading companies such as Facebook and Apple to reach very high and unrealistic valuation levels.

Financial market ideology

At a more enduring level, intense insider financial communication has helped sustain a powerful and distinctive financial market ideology. Earlier social studies of London's business and financial world (Poole et al. 1981; Ingham 1984; Hill 1990; Lazar 1990; Hutton 1996; Boswell and Peters 1997) certainly detected strong belief patterns. Variously, they were labelled 'entrepreneurialism', 'Thatcherism', 'liberationism' and 'neo-liberalism'. In many respects, City ideology has large overlaps with general pro-market and neo-liberal economic thinking. There are a number of common beliefs associated here (see Harvey 2007). Anything that hinders markets of all kinds, such as collectivism, strong unions and greater state intervention, through taxation, regulation or redistribution, is deemed a hindrance. In contrast, privatization, competition, deregulation and lower taxes are deemed positive for the market. Consequently, financial elites, like business elites and wealthier groups, strongly favour pro-market parties, such as the Conservatives or Republicans. In 1987, 91% of UK 'Captains of Industry' voted Conservative and just 1% voted Labour. In 1997, the year of Labour's largest landslide victory, just 7% voted Labour and 69% voted Conservative (MORI 1987, 1997).

However, financial market ideology has several additional elements (see Lazar 1990; Davis 2007). One key, long-lasting intellectual foundation stone for these additions is the Efficient Markets Hypothesis (EMH), which has dominated finance theory and practice for many decades (see Fama 1970). The EMH is all about creating ideal market conditions, where transaction costs are minimized and information is freely available to all rational participants. Rational participants agree on the significance of market information and make logical trading decisions accordingly. Irrational participants are traded out by rational ones or short-term profit-seekers. Ultimately, all relevant information will come to be reflected in market prices, market equilibrium will be maintained and irrational participants will be ejected. If markets fall out of equilibrium, it is only temporarily and often because of external incursions, such as governments, disrupting otherwise smooth internal functioning. When interviewing financial elites, several expressed some scepticism about the EMH, but all relied on it, if only for lack of an alternative: (Mark Tapley) 'That theory is something that has stood the test of time. It's a very powerful theory, a very elegant theory – the efficient market hypothesis … At the end of the day if it's down to [other factors] you can't really do much with that.'

'EMH thinking' contains many questionable assumptions. These include the following: financial elites are rational, at least more so than outsiders; 'proper' markets always find a 'true' equilibrium; and individual, self-interested actions have neutral cumulative outcomes that benefit all. Such beliefs are to be observed regularly in financial news coverage and official financial reports and documents from across the City. They were also common amongst those interviewed. So, for example, it is assumed that the City is always correct in the long-term if not always the short-term: (David Blackwell, financial journalist) 'Prices will change with announcements. But in the end the market is always right because things will settle back down – just like water'; (Andrew Kirton, financial analyst) 'Wherever a market is, whether it's priced at 15 times or 25 times earnings, it's there for a reason. There will be a justification.' Within this discourse, it becomes clear that 'the market' or 'the City' are referred to in terms similar to an all-powerful benign entity, capable of absorbing and counter-acting anything individuals might do. It both suggests that financial markets will always work out in the end and, equally significantly, that individuals can follow their own self-interests without wider repercussion (except when extreme 'rogue-traders' need to be blamed).

Another important component of financial-market ideology, directly related to City experiences and practices, is the tendency of participants to equate strong stock markets with product markets and healthy economies. Lazar (1990) observed that City participants assumed that financial markets operated the same way as real-world product markets. Similarly, Hutton (1996) noted that those in the City equated the strength or weakness of the LSE, at any one time, with that of the economy more generally. Such thinking was often relayed in remarks made by interviewees: (Chris Hopson, investor relations) 'I genuinely think that hostile takeovers are a necessary means of keeping British business strong and keeping management on their toes … I think in the long run it's good for the business and for the staff and, finally the customer. Ultimately that all feeds through and is good for the economy as a whole'; (Edward Bonham-Carter, fund manager) 'The stock market, by and large, is efficient at allocating capital … it allocates capital, takes it away from companies that aren't getting the right returns and allocates it to areas where, risk adjusted, they are making higher returns. So it is efficient every time.'

Such thinking suggests that, without question, financial markets are always good for the wider economy. Whatever financial elites determine is 'good' for them is indeed 'good' for all and that the particular interests of the City are always in alignment with wider society. It therefore follows that the LSE is essential to the health of the UK economy, regardless of how it may impact on the real economy. Similarly, it is assumed that 'financial innovation' is a necessary and productive, wealth-creating activity, similar to innovation in industry, medicine, science and other sectors. The ability to continually create new financial products, from complex derivatives to collateralized debt obligations (CDOs, which repackage different types of debt, were used to disguise the risks of sub-prime mortgages), is a means of making money, while also reducing risk and bringing stability.

There are other elements of general free-market thinking that, within financial elite networks, become amplified and skewed towards the interests of international finance. Globalization and free trade are only conceived of as positive things. This is because financial investment in national exchanges increasingly has become dominated by large international investors. They want guaranteed 'liquidity': that is to maintain their ability to move capital in and out of countries instantly and without restriction. Indeed, international flows of capital are far more 'global' than the trade of real goods, which is more regional (Hirst and Thompson 1999). Similarly, there is the notion that the world contains a finite pool of floating, talented 'entrepreneurs' who need to be attracted to nations. Such people will bring vital investment and boost economies. To attract them, countries need to reduce their rates of personal and corporation tax, to deregulate markets and free them up from the interference of states. Like top film or sports stars, they need to be remunerated with very large pay and bonus packages. Once again, this is far more important to financial elites than real economy investors (although most corporate elites are happy to reduce their tax bills). Real economies and real industry investors also require other things for business, such as good infrastructures, educated/skilled workforces and political stability. It is far easier for financial companies to move their activities abroad than to move factories, supply chains and workers.

Each of these ideological elements are generally echoed and relayed, with little question, by national and international financial news media, from the *Financial Times* and *Wall*

Street Journal, to the *Economist*, *Time*, CNN (CNNI/CNNfn) and Bloomberg. As several studies (Parsons 1989; Davis 2000; Bennett et al. 2004; Kantola 2006, 2009; Durham 2007; Corcoran and Fahy 2009; Tambini 2010) have noted, such coverage, in effect, revolves around corporate and financial elites and discourses. Thus, Doyle's study of financial reporters, in the wake of the Enron scandal (2006: 446) found that 'Several ... readily acknowledged that passivity in relation to pro-market ideologies is fairly characteristic of the sector.' Durham's (2007) and Kantola's (2006, 2009) analysis of *Financial Times* content similarly reveals its propensity to support the views of international capital, free markets and free trade, over democratically elected governments that question such views (see also Bennett et al. 2004). Since 2008, certain strands of this ideology, such as the size of banker and CEO pay, are more questioned. However, financial reporting, on the whole, continues to offer broad support for the assumptions at the heart of financial market thinking.

In fact, many of the elements of financial market ideology, at a minimum, are debatable assumptions, although you would not know that when reading financial news coverage or financial committee reports. For non-financiers, it is hard to see how financial elites may be more rational than others, or how financial markets always find some natural equilibrium, or how financial markets are always good for the economy. The scale of bank bailouts, sovereign debt levels, the extreme values reached by various financial markets and prolonged global depression suggests otherwise. There are also several studies that show that takeovers in most cases leave the companies involved worse off; large financial centres are bad for wider industry, usually increasing shareholder profits at the expense of research, investment and training; pay for top financiers and executives has steadily increased considerably above rates of inflation, and actual company profits and growth (not to mention average wages) (see detailed critiques in Hutton 1996, 2010; CRESC 2009; Elliott and Atkinson 2009; Chang 2010; Erturk et al. 2011). Despite very real concerns and studies about financial market thinking it has continued to hold real influence, both within and outside financial markets.

Each of its ideological elements played a fundamental part in allowing banks and financial markets to become so dangerously unstable by the mid-2000s. First, they worked to cohere and cut-off financial elite participants from outsiders, allowing ideas, no matter how flawed to go unchallenged. As Roger Bootle, a City insider for many years, explains in his book (2009: 21): '[T]he idea that markets know best; the idea that the markets are "efficient"; the idea that there was no good reason to be concerned about the level and structure of pay in banking; the idea that bubbles cannot exist; the idea that in economic matters, human beings are always "rational" ... if you ever questioned, never mind disputed, these ideas, you were regarded as a complete no-no.'

Second, they were exported to outsider, 'stakeholder elites', such as governments, regulators, industry bosses and pension fund managers. These associated elites, who did not understand the complexities of finance, deferred to the 'expert' consensus of those inside. Thus, legislation and regulation of the City under the Thatcher Government

(1979–1989), particularly that put into force in 1985/1986 ('Big Bang'), was strongly determined by the principles of financial market thinking. Similar things happened in financial regulation in the United States. The dismantling of financial regulatory safeguards, such as the 1933 Glass–Steagall Act, put in place following the Wall Street Crash of 1929, continued apace in the late 1990s and early 2000s (see, for example, Krugman 2008; Bootle 2009; Cable 2009; Elliott and Atkinson 2009). This enabled several extremely problematic developments to occur, allowing huge risks and imbalances to build up in the system. Investment and retail bank functions came to overlap. Little-regulated hedge funds and private equity companies flourished. A huge, barely monitored and regulatory 'shadow banking sector', developed. In the United States, by the time of the collapse, the regulated banking system accounted for some $12 trillion of funds, but the unregulated shadow banking system was worth $16 trillion (UNCTAD 2009: 13). Complex financial products were created that were inadequately monitored and risk-assessed. By 2007, the increasingly opaque derivatives market had risen in value over a decade, from $15 trillion to be valued at $600 trillion, or 10 times the total real-world output. (Cable 2009: 14, 34). Sub-prime mortgages, sold to the poorest in US society, were repackaged up with clever financial engineering and turned into investments that the leading credit rating agencies classified as Triple A, the highest possible score, awarded only to properties that were seen as having absolutely no difficulties in meeting the financial obligations.

Third, these same ideological elements were then used to absolve insiders of all real responsibility for what had happened. It could not be a financial markets problem. It had to be government budget overspending and market interference, even though these same governments have been forced into huge debts to stop the financial system from collapsing entirely (but who knows by the time this chapter comes out ...). Bankers and CEOs have continued to expect huge salaries and bonuses, regardless of whether their companies have made losses. Financial reports (see Wigley 2008; Bischoff and Darling 2009) continue to make the case for light-touch regulation and the importance of retaining the City's freedom to do business. The UK government has continued to lower personal and corporate rates of tax, in order to continue attracting these same international investors. And economic thinking is driven by the need to pay back bond markets through austerity programmes and the shrinking of all state expenditure.

Conclusion

Talk in financial markets sustains those markets and their participants in many ways. Some of those are quite obvious, instrumental and fundamental to daily investment activities. Others are less overt and conscious but equally important for developing and sustaining medium-term forms of market consensus and investment fashions, as well as long-term forms of financial market ideology. Whether conscious and instrumental or not, each of these forms of talk maintain the economic and political power of financial markets and their participants. This is often at the expense of wider industry, society, politics and publics. The more financialization comes to influence contemporary capitalist democracies, the more important it becomes to open up, reveal and deconstruct such forms of financial, insider talk, and to challenge it.

References

Bennett, W. L., Pickard, V., Lozzi, D., Shroder, C., Lagos, T. and Lasswell, C. (2004), 'Managing the public sphere: Journalistic construction of the great globalization debate', *Journal of Communication*, 54: 3, pp. 37–55.

Bischoff, W. and Darling, A. (2009), *UK International Financial Services – The Future: A Report from UK Based Financial Service Leaders to the Government*, London: HM Treasury.

Bootle, R. (2009), *The Trouble with Markets: Saving Capitalism From Itself*, London: Nicholas Brealey Publishing.

Boswell, J. and Peters, J. (1997), *Capitalism in Contention – Business Leaders and Political Economy in Modern Britain*, Cambridge: Cambridge University Press.

Cable, V. (2009), *The Storm: The World Economic Crisis and What it Means*, London: Atlantic Books.

Callon, M. (1998), 'The embeddedness of economic markets in economics', in M. Callon (ed.), *The Laws of the Markets*, Oxford: Blackwell.

Cassidy, J. (2002), *Dot.Con: The Greatest Story Ever Told*, London: Penguin/Allen Lane.

Chang, H. (2010), *23 Things They Didn't Tell You About Capitalism*, London: Penguin/Allen Lane.

Corcoran, F. and Fahy, D. (2009), 'Exploring the European elite sphere: The role of the *Financial Times*', *Journalism Studies*, 10: 1, pp. 100–113.

CRESC. (2009), *An Alternative Report on UK Banking Reform: A Public Interest Report from CRESC*, Manchester: Centre for Research on Socio-Cultural Change.

Davis, A. (2000), 'Public relations, business news and the reproduction of corporate elite power', *Journalism: Theory, Practice and Criticism*, 1: 3, pp. 282–304.

Davis, A. (2002), *Public Relations Democracy: Public Relations, Politics and the Mass Media in Britain*, Manchester: Manchester University Press.

Davis, A. (2007), *The Mediation of Power: A Critical Introduction*, London: Routledge.

Davis, A. (2011), 'Mediation, financialization and the global financial crisis: An inverted political economy perspective', in D. Winseck and D. Jin (eds), *Media Political Economies: Hierarchies, Markets and Finance in the Global Media Industries*, London: Bloomsbury.

Doyle, G. (2006), 'Financial news journalism: A post-Enron analysis of approaches towards economic and financial news production in the UK', *Journalism: Theory, Practice and Criticism*, 7: 4, pp. 433–452.

Durham, F. (2007), 'Framing the state in globalization: The *Financial Times*' coverage of the 1997 Thai currency crisis', *Critical Studies in Media Communication*, 24: 1, pp. 57–76.

Elliott, L. and Atkinson, D. (2009), *The Gods that Failed: How the Financial Elite Have Gambled Away Our Futures*, London: Vintage.

Erturk, I., Froud, J., Johal, S., Leaver, A., Moran, M. and Williams, K. (2011), '*City State against National Settlement: UK Economic Policy and Politics after the Financial Crisis*', CRESC Working Paper 101, Manchester: Centre for Research on Socio-Cultural Change.

Fama, E. (1970), 'Efficient capital markets: A review of theory and empirical work', *Journal of Finance*, 25:2, pp. 383–417.

Ferguson, C. (2012), *Inside Job: The Financiers Who Pulled Off the Heist of the Century*, London: Oneworld Publications.

Glassman, J. and Hassett, K. (1999), *Dow, 36,000: The New Strategy for Profiting from the Coming Rise in the Stock Market*, New York: Random House.

Harvey, D. (2007), *A Brief History of Neoliberalism*. Oxford: Oxford University Press.

Hill, S. (1990), 'Britain: The dominant ideology thesis after a decade', in A. Abercrombie, S. Hill and B. Turner (eds), *Dominant Ideologies*, London: Unwin Hyman Ltd.

Hirst, P. and Thompson, G. (1999), *Globalization in Question: The International Economy and the Possibilities of Governance*, 2nd edn., Cambridge: Polity Press.

Holland, J. (1997), *Corporate Communications with Institutional Shareholders: Private Disclosure and Financial Reporting*, The Institute of Chartered Accountants of Scotland, Glasgow: Bell and Bain Ltd.

Hutton, W. (1996), *The State We're In*, London: Vintage.

Hutton, W. (2010), *Them and Us: Changing Britain – Why We Need a Fair Society*, London: Little, Brown and Co.

Ingham, G. (1984), *Capitalism Divided: The City and Industry in British Society*, London: MacMillan.

Kantola, A. (2006), 'On the dark side of democracy: The global imaginary of financial journalism', in B. Cammaerts and N. Carpentier (eds), *Reclaiming the Media: Communication, Rights and Democratic Media Roles*, Bristol: Intellect.

Kantola, A. (2009), 'The disciplined imaginary: The nation rejuvenated for the global condition', in A. Roosvall and I. Salovaara-Moring (eds), *Communicating the Nation*, Stockholm: Nordicom.

Keynes, J. (1936), *The General Theory of Employment, Interest and Money*, London: Macmillan.

Krugman, P. (2008), *The Return of Depression Economics and the Crisis of 2008*, London: Penguin Books.

Lazar, D. (1990), *Markets and Ideology in the City of London*, Basingstoke: Macmillan.

Marston, C. (1999), *Investor Relations Meetings: Views of Companies, Institutional Investors and Analysts*, The Institute of Chartered Accountants of Scotland, Glasgow: Bell and Bain Ltd.

Miller, P. (1998), 'The margins of accounting', in M. Callon (ed.), *The Laws of the Markets*, Oxford: Blackwell.

MORI (now Ipsos MORI) (1987, 1997), *Captains of Industry*, London: MORI.

Parsons, W. (1989), *The Power of the Financial Press: Journalism and Economic Opinion in Britain and America*, London: Edward Elgar.

Poole, M., Mansfield, R., Blyton, P. and Frost, P. (1981), *Managers in Focus: The British Manager in the Early 1980s*, Aldershot: Gower.

Shiller, R. (2001), *Irrational Exuberance*, New Jersey: Princeton University Press.

Siegal, J. (1998), *Stocks in the Long Run*, 2nd edn, New York: McGraw Hill.

Smithers, A. and Wright, S. (2000), *Valuing Wall Street: Protecting Wealth in Turbulent Markets*, New York: McGraw Hill.

Taibbi, M. (2011), 'Why isn't Wall Street in jail?', *Rolling Stone*, 3rd March, New York.

Tambini, D. (2010), 'What are financial journalists for?', *Journalism Studies*, 11: 2, pp. 158–174.

Tumber, H. (1993), '"Selling scandal': Business and the media', *Media, Culture and Society*, 15: 3, pp. 345–361.

Tunstall, J. (1996), *Newspaper Power: The National Press in Britain*, Oxford: Oxford University Press.

UNCTAD. (2009), *The Global Economic Crisis: Systemic Failures and Multilateral Remedies, UNCTAD/GDS/2009/1*, New York/Geneva: United Nations Conference on Trade and Development.

Wigley, B. (2008), *London: Winning in a Changing World*, London: Merrill Lynch Europe Ltd.

Chapter 2

Funny in a rich man's world: The contradictory conceptions of money in forex trading

Peter A. Thompson

T̶he ubiquity of monetary forms in modern economies makes it seem a natural and inevitable feature of society. The need for money to purchase goods and services and the expectation of monetary compensation for labour-time is so taken for granted that the function of cash, cheques, debit cards and credit cards, and the expectations of interest on loans or deposits appear quite natural. Yet the vast majority of people remain oblivious to the complexity of money as a social construct and the processes of the global foreign exchange markets which underpin its value.

We receive daily reminders of the contingent status of currencies in the daily news media reports on financial markets, and periodic currency or credit markets crises remind us of the severe economic and social consequences that ensue from the failure of monetary systems. If we travel overseas or purchase goods in another currency, we recognize that the exchange rates fluctuate. These are driven not by overseas holidaymakers or consumers seeking bargains on the Internet, but by the daily US$4 trillion turnover of global foreign exchange markets (Bank of International Settlements 2010). Behind these incredible volumes of capital flows are currency traders operating around the clock and around the world in the dealing rooms of major financial institutions. Sitting in front of several screens of financial data, these traders not only monitor the lifeblood of the global markets flowing in real time, their collective trading decisions constitute its pulse.

Drawing on the author's empirical study of institutional investor's media usage in New Zealand,[1] this chapter will explore how currency traders conceive of money in their investment practices and contrast the use of money in global forex markets with those in the everyday economy. The chapter will briefly outline some of the complexities of conceptualizing money and identify some of the socio-cultural processes that constitute it. Next, some important spatial and temporal aspects of currencies will be examined from the perspective of institutional forex traders. This will lead into a brief examination of language issues that arise when reserve banks attempt to guide market expectations by issuing public statements on monetary policy. The chapter will conclude by noting emergent tensions between the high-street consumer's everyday conceptions of money and those of professional forex traders.

Money – more than just economics

As monetary sociologist Nigel Dodd (1994) has noted, despite its ubiquity and familiarity, the concept of money resists easy definition, especially given the contemporary range of immaterial, electronic forms of transaction. Monetary forms in a modern economy nevertheless exhibit some common characteristics: It needs to be portable (or transmissible), durable, divisible, homogenous in form, and recognizable. Moreover, the common functions of money include acting as a medium of exchange, a store of value, a unit of account, a means of payment and a standard of credit/deferred payment (Dodd 1994; Davies 1996; Rowbotham 1998; Smithin 2000; Ingham 2004). In banking and fiscal policy, distinctions are drawn between M0 (the base supply of 'hard' cash in circulation within the economy and held in reserve by banks), M1 (all funds that are currently available for spending excluding bank reserves), M2 (all funds currently available plus bank reserves, excepting long-term deposits unavailable for transactions) and M3 (all available funds including all reserves/deposits, institutional money market holdings and other significant liquid money-type assets) (Lawrence 2008).

Contemporary consumers have embraced an increasing variety of electronic monetary and credit systems, but relatively few people understand the mechanisms of fractional reserve banking through which private banks create money by issuing credit/debit out of proportion to their cash reserves (Davies 1996; Rowbotham 1998), even if they are acutely aware of the interest rates on their mortgages. Despite the increased availability of financial information sources and the media's promotion of finance culture to the general public (Greenfield and Williams 2007), the specialized knowledge required to engage in financial market speculation remains largely restricted to institutional investors who have privileged access to the institutional trading networks (see Thompson 2010).

It is therefore somewhat paradoxical that, even after a global financial crisis, and despite considerable criticism of the banking sector and financial system, the monetary system largely remains a 'black box'. Of course, there is a perpetual flow of news about money in regard to changing interest rates, public debt and foreign exchange. But at the same time, it is so deeply embedded into everyday social practices that its ontology typically eludes scrutiny.

One reason for this is the deep-seated fiduciary confidence of market actors in monetary forms, as noted in the seminal work of Georg Simmel (2004/1907). Modern commercial markets presuppose a network of actors who intersubjectively recognize the validity of a particular money form. Were it not for the institutionalized trust that others will continue to accept the money form as payment by others, routine transactions would break down. The fragility of the shared social meanings inscribed into money forms becomes apparent to the high street consumer only in crises or severe recessions where hyperinflation erodes buying power. In such cases, official currencies may be superseded by the adoption of a commodity-form to act as universal equivalent or community-based barter/local currency systems (such as those developed by local communities in response to the Argentinian currency crisis 1999–2002; see Pearson 2003).

In contrast, the constant fluctuation of currency values and the potential for shifts in the collective market confidence underpinning them defines the world of forex traders. The 'same' currency operates according to very different rules according to the institutional context and the economic agent. Money and (fictitious) values within the financial system dwarf the scale of the productive economy. The global crisis destroyed around US$27 trillion of financial asset values between 2007–2008, by the end of 2010 these had reached a new historical record of $212 trillion – over 350% of world GDP (McKinsey Global 2011). That recovery was assisted in no small part by huge government bailouts of the banking sector. As Oxfam (2009) pointed out, the (then) US$8.42 trillion cost of the bailout would have been sufficient to alleviate global poverty for half a century. How the former was negotiable in such a short space of time while the latter remains elusive despite decades of aid and relief efforts is not simply a moral question, however. The trillions of dollars in financial assets and indeed, in daily flows of forex trading, do not operate through channels embedded in the lifeworld, but through institutional channels that are bound up in circuits of investment and accumulation and dictate the scope of agency available to the trader.

As Viviana Zelizer (1994, 2002) has pointed out, money never exists as a neutral medium of exchange. Whether it is in the purse of a high-street consumer or the computer of a forex trader, money is always 'earmarked' in the sense that the scope of functions towards which it can be deployed are delimited either by its embedding in social convention or institutional arrangements. For example, within the private lifeworld setting, money might be earmarked for 'housekeeping' which demarcates the parameters of legitimate deployment, and often designates the family member entitled to utilize it.

In an investment bank context, traders are responsible for much larger volumes of money but they are nevertheless subject to specific 'earmarks' and codes of usage. A volume of capital will normally be allocated to an institutional investor's account, and he/she will usually work at a 'desk' specializing in trading a particular class of assets (notably currencies/forex, stocks/equities, bonds/interests, commodities and derivatives, although there are many subcategories). In addition, there will typically be a set of institutional limits on risk exposure, time-horizons, tolerance of short-term losses, volume of positions, requirements for hedging, and portfolio composition. Thus the multimillion (and sometimes multibillion) dollar transactions of investment institutions take place not only through the circuits of the computer networks wired into exchanges around the world; they are relentlessly driven by the circuits of capital accumulation.

In one respect, an institutional investor controlling a billion dollars of capital has immense wealth and power at his/her disposal. But in practice, the institutionally defined channels and modalities which demarcate or 'earmark' the range of permissible transactions are limited. The trader may be able to purchase a futures contract for a thousand tonnes of wheat, or a thousand shares in a cereals company, but the channels of investment in which the investment capital is institutionally bound up make it impossible to use such concentrated volumes of money to purchase a loaf of bread or a box of cornflakes. Although the money forms used in the high street and the financial markets have a notional equivalence (a dollar in a shopper's purse has the same notional value as a dollar in a trader's portfolio), they are embedded in quite different socio-economic networks (see Granovetter 1985) that entail different conceptions and codes of monetary practice. These are underpinned by institutional networks of information exchange that are largely inaccessible to non-professional investors (Thompson 2010a).

The decisions of financial traders directly shape the volume, value and trajectories of global capital flows. The evolving models of financial calculation, collective (and sometimes self-reinforcing) expectations and the market transactions which crystallize prices on trading screens around the globe reflexively shape the market values of financial assets, including currencies (Thompson 2003, 2010b). As a class of key financial agents, traders occupy the key financial nodes of power and have a collectively powerful influence on currency prices. But individual traders are not the masters of the monetary universe they help create. The complexity and scale of the monetary flows makes market prices notoriously difficult to predict with any consistency, and traders have to closely monitor a range of information sources to keep up to date with market activity and price fluctuations.

Forex trading may take the form of 'spot' trading, where counterparties exchange a quantity of one currency for a quantity of another either simultaneously or on a cash-payment basis within one or two business days. Spot transactions constitute approximately 37% of total forex market activity by daily volume (see BIS 2010). Another type of transaction is the 'forward' which entails an agreement to exchange currencies at an agreed price at a specific point in the future. These transactions comprise 12% of daily market activity. A further type of forex transaction is the 'swap'. These are contracts which allow currencies and their market interest rates to be traded separately over a designated period of time. In the former case the counterparties typically pay an agreed rate interest on their respective currency holdings but exchange the 'principal' on maturity; in the latter case the interest rate payments in one currency are exchanged with those of another currency held by the counterparty. Together, these represent 45% of the daily volume of forex market activity (ibid.). Finally, currency 'options' are a form of derivative contract. The basic forex option confers the right (but not the obligation) to exchange a specified volume of currency for another at an agreed exchange rate within a designated period.[2] Approximately 5% of daily forex market activity involves options.

Major financial institutions such as investment banks will have dedicated 'desks' on the trading floor, each comprising several traders who specialize in different assets and investment instruments. These may include bonds (interest rate instruments that are themselves currency-based), equities (stocks/shares), commodities (usually futures contracts) and a wide range of derivatives and other complex investment instruments (such as the collateralized debt obligations which were partly responsible for the US sub-prime crisis). In larger institutions, these desks may be divided according to the time-horizon of the investment strategy, and it is to the question of time and money that the discussion now turns.

Temporality and forex trading

Time frames are a key point of difference between the high-street's and the trading room's conceptions of money. Long-term investment strategies may be based on projections of market activity over months or years (especially in the case of long-term bonds) and ignore short-term price fluctuations as 'noise'. However, a high proportion of forex trading requires real-time responses to price fluctuations during critical events (such as official cash rate or rating agency announcements,) or periods of volatility (such as crises). A senior forex trader interviewed observed that

> Currencies move on real time. You know, that's where you're gonna make your money or lose your money, is real time news. Whereas maybe in equities that looks at more historical future data, rather than real time, [but] currencies are all based on real time.
>
> (Trader D)

The transitory nature of forex valuation and the instability of any currency's relative buying power mean that traders literally cannot afford to see money in terms of hard cash with an enduring value. The time frames of trading decisions and indeed, the temporal references points coded into the financial instruments used to trade currencies, are critical. The shared meanings that underpin the value of financial assets entail a performative inscribing of future expectations into current prices, and any factor that can alter market expectations can affect those valuations.

Although most spot-market forex traders operate on horizons of one to two days, there is always a need to keep abreast of short-term market activity. Another forex trader explained that time horizons have a significant influence on the kind of information used in trading decisions:

> If you're sitting on, say, foreign exchange desks, and you're just trading spots, so you're trading two days' time, and really you were trading minute by minute or ten minute blocs or half hour blocs. You're not really taking a long-term view on your book, because your position is being turned so often and quite quickly that you don't take a long-term view. Maybe you're there to clear the bank's risk. It all depends on what your time horizon is, and what you're looking at. So certainly filtering out the noise depends on your time horizon, so, what may be noise to some people is very relevant to others.
>
> (Trader A)

The informational symmetry that real-time financial information systems such as Thomson-Reuters or Bloomberg have made possible means that prices adjust very quickly to any salient news. Trader F noted that if he could access information even 30 seconds before the rest of the market, he would be 'thrilled to bits'. However, the time frames of different forex desks can vary:

> The Kiwi [dollar] trader in Sydney, his risk is so much more immediate, he's getting paid, he's buying, he's selling, he's trying to manage the book up, it's very much a minute by minute kind of exercise. Whereas I'm doing something that I expect to have tomorrow or the next day, so it's more of a medium term thing. He's sitting there trying to react all the

time – [to] make little bits of money here and there. [...] He's what we call a spot trader-he might do two or three hundred deals in a day, and he's very much trying to make some return for the bank. My role as a proprietary trader, who's trying to take risk, smart risk that makes money for the bank more over the medium term. So, we've all got different focuses, different time horizons, trying to do different things.

(Trader F)

The volume of currency trading varies according to the institution, with most routine transactions being in the region of US$1–5 million. By institutional investment standards, this is small change, although some of the interest rate desks using futures/options might undertake notional transactions worth hundreds of millions. As Trader B explained,

[I]n swaps it could be 20 to 50 million in a swap, in a bond an average transaction could be as low as 1 or 2, but there'd be a lot of trading goes through as 1 or 2, it could be as much as 50 to 100, futures could be anything from 10 lots which would be 10 million to 1000 lots which would be a billion. So that's in futures.

The scale of these capital transactions may also appear to be risky, but this depends on the nature of the investment strategy and the period where the trader is exposed to potential losses through a shift in values over time. Another investment bank interviewee commented that

The key thing is that $2 billion can either be a minute amount of risk or it can be a huge amount of risk, depending on the direction of it. So if you trade $2 billion of overnight, like, the risk on it is close to zero. If you trade $2 billion of two years, it's huge!

(Trader G)

Traders typically calculate the potential gains or losses on their position relative to 'basis point' movements. In forex investment a single basis points move means one hundredth of one per cent change in the official (reserve bank) inter-bank cash-rate (thus a rate of 6.00% which falls to 5.99% has moved one point).

A key reason for engaging in high-volume or highly leveraged transactions is to take advantage of marginal spreads between currency interest rates or exchange rates. Margins that would be negligible to someone changing money for an overseas trip or a mortgage loan can make the difference between significant profits or losses to a forex trader: Trader G further explained, '[I]f you trade ninety days, $2 billion is worth $48 thousand a point-so every point that the market moves, one basis point, say if it goes up from 5.25 per cent to 5.26 per cent that's $48 thousand'. Fractional differences in prices or interest rates can also be exploited by using option or swap instruments to leverage transactions and amplify the earnings (or losses) relative to the actual volume of money being exchanged. As Trader B, a specialist in interest rate instruments confirmed, '[I]f you had to physically have the cash [...] that would affect the bank's liquidity'.

The 'liquidity' of assets in the sense of ready convertibility into monetary form might seem unproblematic in forex markets, considering that both the asset and the medium of exchange are currencies. However, trading liquidity in forex forwards, swaps and options or even spot trades in a particular currency pair depends on the availability of a counterparty in the market willing to transact at a given price (indeed, some exchanges provide 'market makers' whose role is help maintain liquidity by acting as buyers and sellers on a commission basis). Although the sheer scale of the forex markets means that routine transactions are unlikely to encounter liquidity barriers, larger scale trades can require the trader to increase/decrease their ask/bid prices to motivate counterparties to transact.

As shifts in ask-bid offers or transaction prices register on trading screens, these signals feed back into the market, constituting a shift in valuation and reflexively modifying asset values across the market (Thompson 2003, 2010b). Again, these changes need not be large to be financially significant. As Trader A observed,

> I've seen instances where probably buying or selling just NZ$200 million can move the market substantially, by, you know, nearly up half a per cent. Or in other circumstances I've seen it where it hasn't moved the currency at all. It all depends on what the counter parties interests.

He went on to explain that liquidity was affected by time-zones and which of the major markets were operating at the time: '[The] London time zone coming into New York, New York coming into New Zealand, it's all [about] very different time zones and what participants are actually in the market at the time'.

Spatiality and forex trading

Another key difference in the conception of money in the high street compared with the trading room concerns the spatial imaginaries that define currencies. Most consumers experience the limits of monetary networks when they cross national boundaries and have to visit the bureau de change. In contrast, forex markets are highly globalized in terms of the extension and volume of transborder capital flows. Seamless financial information networks linking exchanges and trading rooms around the world allow the consistency of exchange rates to be maintained across national borders in real time. Nevertheless, geographic space is far from irrelevant in forex markets. Major investment institutions operate around the clock and 'pass the book' from one trading floor to another across time zones as exchanges open and close, and they derive a significant trading advantage from maintaining a global presence coupled with knowledge of regional/domestic markets (Thompson 2010a). As Trader C explained,

> The Aussie market closes after the Kiwi market – it closes around 6.30. And these Aussie bond futures trade throughout the night. And their trading in the night is dependent on

how the U.S. market's traded. So, I kind of look at what's happened overnight in the U.S. and how that's going to impact the Aussie and Kiwi markets during the day.

Forex trading entails transactions involving currency pairs (dollar-euro, dollar-yen and so forth) or, in other terms, exchanges of assets denominated in the units of account of two (or more) markets. This means that forex transactions will always be influenced by variables in multiple national markets. Trader F offered the following observations as he explained the transactions available on the trading screen of his institution's in-house forex platform:

> Now, that defaults to the nine currency pairs that I've set up. Some of them go shaded from time to time – that means you can't deal. Euro-dollar, dollar-yen, Australian dollar against the U.S. dollar, most currency pairs are quoted against the U.S. dollar as standard. NZ dollar, GBP sterling-U.S., euro-yen is traded as a cross quite heavily. There we go. Aussie against the Kiwi. Kiwi against the Aussie. In fact, you tend to find most people outside New Zealand want to trade that cross as Aussie-Kiwi whereas in New Zealand we like quoting it as .91 and customers expect to deal on that kind of basis. And Australian dollar against the yen. Now, the way that works is there's a limit as to how much you can deal on that, in that currency pair. So, if the larger limits are obviously in the most liquid currency pairs. So I can deal 15 million euro and 15 million dollar yen. That's just what's available without you having to ask anybody. Now if I wanted to deal on 40 million euros through this system, I could click on that button which is like a price request. So then […] I would go and ask for a price request on 40, that would flash as a box on the trader's desk in Sydney, and he'd see that customer.

Trading activity and currency prices nevertheless remain partially embedded in domestic economic and political activity and respond to changes both in domestic fiscal policy and reserve bank rates as well as economic conditions such as changes in GDP or the balance of trade. The US dollar's continuing status as the default international unit of account in many forms of international trading activity (notably oil) and the volume of offshore credit markets denominated in dollars[3] means it is the most heavily traded currency. The size of the US economy nevertheless means that domestic factors such as GDP, Federal Reserve policy and employment/payroll levels continue to have a significant influence on dollar's value, and indeed on the financial markets as a whole. In contrast, the European Union has no nationally defined domestic economy underpinning it, and is subject to a range of influences that extend beyond the respective economic conditions in its member states, including European Central Bank policy and the complex politics of the Eurozone (which at time of writing is enduring a period of severe uncertainty because of the negotiations over bailouts for Greece and other indebted economies).

The national currencies of smaller economies, such as the New Zealand dollar or 'Kiwi' are subject to significant influences from offshore markets. Although not used as an international unit of account, the Kiwi dollar's exchange rate often fluctuates in response to forex markets. The relatively low volumes in circulation mean that large volume trades can easily exceed current liquidity and move the price.[4] As several forex traders confirmed, it is often traded by major investment forms as part of a hedging strategy to offset risks incurred in deals involving other currencies. This means that the Kiwi dollar's value can periodically move independently of conditions in the domestic economy (see IMF 2007; RBNZ 2007).

The influence of offshore trading activity is shaped in part by the way national economies are represented in the financial media. Although professional traders rely more on specialist financial media and expert networks than publicly-available news media, international investment firms are less likely to have full-time financial analysts devoted to covering smaller economies. This increases the potential for media representations to shape investor/ analyst perceptions of domestic market conditions, especially where the firm has no locally based analyst (see Rothkopf 1999; Kunczik 2002; also Bryan 2001). As Trader K observed, the way in which domestic conditions in New Zealand are monitored and framed by offshore investors can influence their trading decisions:

> People who are sitting here in New Zealand who can see what's been going on – you can see prices creeping up, you see house prices creeping up and have an actual feel for how the economy's going on a day by day basis – have tended to be the hawkish people. They're the ones who think that rates are going high or staying high. The offshore people, who really only look at the New Zealand probably for, maybe an hour a week, that's a small part of their portfolio – they just look at New Zealand in very simple terms. They look at the high interest rates, they look at a high currency, and they say, 'well this can't be sustained'. […] Therefore they're looking at New Zealand relative to other markets and on that basis our cash rate looks very high by global standards, our exchange rate looks overstretched – and therefore they assume that can't be sustained – that these things are out of equilibrium and at some stage they'll come back.
>
> (Trader K)

Another interesting spatial-modelling influence on forex trading can be seen in the strategy of bundling together multiple currencies and trading them in 'blocs'. For example, some institutions trade forex blocs based on region (e.g. Australasian) or dollar denominations (e.g. United States, Canadian, Australian, New Zealand and Singapore). As several interviewees noted, offshore investors with an interest in New Zealand financial assets tended to trade off variables that could be calculated and readily compared with indicators from other countries, whereas local investors focused more on contextual domestic factors. The models/trading schemata adopted by international investors may reflexively generate correlated price movements across several currencies even when their respective domestic economic conditions are quite different. However, as Trader E explained, this is neither predictable nor sustainable:

> The trouble is, those correlations keep breaking down, periodically. One day it's in, next week it's out, you know. And it's hard to explain why, you know, why was [the Kiwi

dollar] tracking the Euro for no apparent reason […] Next week the New Zealand dollar is trading in line with the US dollar. A very strange correlation, just to add to that, is it seems to be fairly highly correlated with gold movements […] So that's bizarre – and it's hard to explain. And again, it will break down. So it's almost fads, trends – people look for things to trade off. You could almost argue some will use [correlations] as a selling point to others to generate trade.

The interplay between domestic economic fundamentals and the global trends of international money markets becomes particularly evident in the way forex traders prepare for and respond to reserve bank announcements of revisions to the base inter-bank interest rate. The base rates set by reserve banks are the principal lever of monetarist policy. In simple terms, a 'dovish' reduction in the interest rate will promote an expansion of the money supply through the issuance of cheaper bank credit. Conversely, a 'hawkish' increase in the interest rate will slow the expansion of the money supply by making it more expensive to borrow. Although the base interest rate serves as a benchmark for expected returns (and hence the values) of other financial securities, its effect on the value of the currency in question is complicated. On the one hand, a reduced interest rate makes holding the currency (and bonds) less attractive, but on the other hand, cheaper borrowing can help stimulate the economy.

Commenting on an anticipated reserve bank announcement on the official interest rate for the Kiwi dollar, Trader F observed that the effect of any change on the exchange rate was difficult to predict:

> Again, we don't know which way. You know, 'cause there's the two arguments as to which way it can go on the back of that. […] That's why currency trading is so difficult. It's hard to know. Rates are high, it should be going up – or God, he's strangling the economy, sell it! You know, it's quite difficult to tell.

This is revealing because it shows that even basic market 'fundamentals' can be interpreted in different ways.

Reserve bank language games and market expectations

In New Zealand, the Official Cash Rate (OCR) is set every six weeks by the Reserve Bank (RBNZ). Because this is a core fundamental, it has market-moving potential. Consequently, a series of strict protocols govern the announcement ritual,[5] partly to ensure that any planned revision to the rate is not leaked in advance and partly to ensure that the markets are not unduly surprised by any change. Even an adjustment of a few basic points is significant because it provides the basic benchmark for calculating the relative value of all other financial securities denominated in the Kiwi dollar, including bonds and currency/bond futures. Moreover, because it affects the retail level of interest on mortgages and borrowing, it has an indirect long-term impact on economic growth and inflation.

Although the RBNZ operates several forex funds which can be used to intervene in the market, its strategic aim is not returns, but monetary policy objectives. These include the provision of liquidity, stability of currency prices and control of inflation. RBNZ Official 1 likened its role to a sheepdog, trying to move the financial 'flock' in the desired direction. However, this requires the management of market expectations, including those concerning investor's perceptions of the RBNZ's intentions concerning the OCR.

As Official 2 noted, the intention here was to avoid surprising the market and triggering price fluctuations. By communicating RBNZ's views in advance of the OCR announcement, investors would adjust their positions gradually, and volatility would be minimized. Official 1 pointed out that even though the market understood RBNZ wanted to avoid shocks, ambivalence was nevertheless necessary where the bank itself was uncertain about changing market conditions and the need to alter the OCR: Making concrete statements about cutting or hiking rates in advance was risky lest changing market conditions force a revision/reversal which would confuse or panic investors.

Consequently, a very nuanced set of discourses reflecting degrees of certainty and relative strength of the bank's 'dovish' or 'hawkish' predilections had developed. Key financial actors were also routinely consulted to check that the market was decoding RBNZ statements as intended and to identify the terminology likely to influence interpretations in a particular direction. However, as several officials confirmed, this meant that the market would routinely second-guess RBNZ's intentions based on how recent statements compared with previous statements and actions:

> It's an intriguing dynamism between us and the market, and how much the market reads the same data we're reading […] because they know us and how we operated in the past, they'll anticipate what our reactions are. And how much the market correctly anticipates […] is quite an interesting exercise in itself. […] because we're all in the same challenging environment – you know, is inflation about to head up or down or whatever – it's not so clear at certain times.
>
> (Official 3)

In crafting RBNZ statements, there is even consideration of how particular words and phrases influence market interpretation. As Official 3 explained, 'no prospect of a cut' may not mean the same as 'no prospect of an easing', while 'in the future' is different from 'in the foreseeable future', and 'OCR' may seem more specific than 'monetary policy'. He went on to explain that RBNZ recognized that investors examined the structure and content of the statements and attached meaning to small points of structural difference (i.e. paradigmatic and syntagmatic variation) in the selection of words, the use or non-use of familiar adjectives, or the sequence of points. Although there was RBNZ interest in using more 'plain English', officials readily confirmed that, ironically, suddenly changing the language of statements to reduce literal ambiguity would probably increase market misunderstandings.

> If [the Monetary Policy Statement] were to be changed to something else, it would be picked up immediately and [investors] would be looking to see what we mean by that. Now we know they look at the words that way, so we're very careful if we do change words. […] We do a lot of thinking beforehand, in terms of the set of words – particularly in that [OCR] Chapter – how will they be interpreted. […] It has become so ritualised and standard as to how we will do things – and if you're not aware of that, you're missing something, I think […] People have learned to expect a certain set of phrases, a certain way of talking, a certain timing […] To make those changes [to plainer English] people will pick over it, over the entrails and say 'what do they mean by this?'.
>
> (Official 3)

Official 4 further explained that

> [t]he information that the market analysis people glean from this doves-and-hawks type questioning enables the advisory group to tweak the language in the statement, to reinforce or de-emphasise. Of course, sometimes it doesn't work very well. It gets lost in translation. […] So in the statement, you can use greater or less conditionality – so for example we could say if economic indicators do not follow as we expected then we 'may' or 'could' tighten them – that's putting in the conditionality. You could otherwise say it is 'likely' that economic indicators will confirm our thinking. So it's just the nuancing of the conditionality […] Sometimes you get compound sentences which are quite long and convoluted and the market misreads those. So there's a lot of work goes into drafting what's called Chapter One of the Monetary Policy Statement.

It is nevertheless apparent that RBNZ and the financial markets are not always on the same wavelength. Official 1 pointed out that other investment institutions sometimes ignored central bank statements or challenged the official interest rates in their trading activity:

> Sometimes the market will turn round and say, 'No – as a central bank, you're wrong.' And they've done it before. There were probably two statements last year [where] the market delivered price action that was completely at odds with what we would have expected. And the [RBNZ] statement after that was designed to bring them back into line. The market then turned round and said 'you guys are flip-flop – you don't know what you're doing!'.

One interesting example of misinterpretation that unfolded during the course of the researcher's visits to RBNZ was the atypical decision to reissue a previous statement[6] from the Governor. As Official 1 confirmed, RBNZ had felt the market reaction was not pricing in the possibility of a rate hike and so repeating the statement was intended to make sure that investors did not rule out the possibility: 'It was repeating what we'd said before. But the real

information content for the market is the fact that we repeated what we were saying before –
And that's not something we would do very often. So there is a message in that.' Official 3
further explained,

> That was done because, a few days after the Monetary Policy Statement, we felt that one of
> the messages in there had not really been taken on board by the market […] We thought
> there was no room for our message not to get through, so we reinforced it. Now apparently,
> that was the first time a statement like that had gone out without an accompanying press
> conference – without a warning that we were going to put something up – since about
> 1999. […] You don't want a market surprised by what we're doing later on if they've
> missed the first signal either – and that's a judgement you have to make.

However, some of the forex traders interviewed were displeased with RBNZ's tactic.
Although they knew there was no intention to mislead, as Trader E pointed out, the unusual
reissuance of the statement had led forex traders to believe a rate hike was imminent:

> The market wasn't really pricing much chance of a rate-hike […] I think that the bank
> was very keen to make sure that the market was pricing a reasonable possibility – so that
> the market wouldn't be surprised on the day if that rate hike actually happened. Now as
> it turned out, that communication was pretty widely criticised amongst the traders in
> our room. […] A lot of people read the Reserve Bank's comments as being almost a cast
> iron guarantee that they were going to hike rates in June. And that subsequently didn't
> happen. So some people would have said that the bank misled the market.

RBNZ officials were aware that some NZ-based traders found the repeat statement confusing,
but they also pointed out that the message was aimed at two investment audiences:

> I don't think [the confusion] was to do with the language we used. We used fairly tough
> language by our own terms. There was just so much else going on at the time […] The
> domestic market might read it one way, but the weight of investments is coming from
> offshore, and they had taken a particular view. It may be, for instance, that they were
> thinking, looking at our economy, looking at the cycles, that sort of thing, 'You guys are in
> for an easing – come on!' And all their pricing in futures was gearing that way – whereas
> the domestics were starting to say, 'Hmmm – I'm not sure of that, now we know what's
> going on in New Zealand a bit more. And we're getting that dichotomy of expectations.
> And so I guess part of our judgements has [sic] to be have we used the right words, the
> right tone, the right strength to hit both of those markets?'
>
> (Official 3)

However, other traders evidently thought RBNZ may not have fully anticipated the
impact of the repeat statement and suggested that there was sometimes a problematic

discrepancy between RBNZ statements, OCR decisions and the comments from the Governor:

> They're probably not careful enough, actually. I think there's a misunderstanding there over how markets work. What they think they're trying to say, versus how it's interpreted are frequently two different things. [In] some of their monetary policy and OCR statements, there have been dichotomies between what the Governor says and what the document says – which leaves the market in a bit of a bind [...] The monetary policy statement I've not read now for a couple of quarters, 'cause I don't think it's that much value. Because the Governor – all he says is what's important. So I know the Governor writes his own statement and the monetary policy statement is written by other people in the RBNZ [...] If you're looking at the messages emanating from the two, in terms of what the Governor actually says versus the document, you can sometimes get a bit of a biased or a different view – I think that's a dangerous place to be.
>
> (Trader L)

Given such comments, it is clear the semantic nuance of RBNZ's statements cannot eliminate ambiguity or misinterpretation, especially when the aim to communicate degrees of uncertainty about the likelihood of a change in the OCR. Officials confirmed an interest in moving to a plainer mode of communication, but any sudden shift in the language would require breaking down the intersubjective codes that, by and large, do allow expectations to be coordinated. Statements by key officials, policy makers or top analysts can influence market expectations and thus financial values. Phil Graham has suggested that language has a direct and performative role here and that financial values can be literally talked up or down by key actors, although it is important to bear in mind that changes in investors' collective perceptions still have to be crystallized as price changes through financial transactions. Nevertheless, such examples confirm that language and discourse play a constitutive, not merely descriptive role in the functioning of monetary systems.

Conclusions – funny in a rich man's world

Professional investors evidently recognize the transitory nature of the variables driving forex trading and the potential for investment models/schemata to reflexively influence currency values. The calculative epistemologies of currency valuation help to constitute and reproduce exchange rates. Indeed, forex trading can be regarded as a constant negotiation of intersubjective codes and meanings which sustain (or erode) the collective trust that Simmel recognized as essential to monetary functions. Professional investors' immersion in the complex calculative processes that drive the constant flux in monetary values therefore contrasts with consumers' more conventional engagement with money on the high street. Used in everyday retail/consumption, money appears to be a concrete object with (inflation permitting) a relatively persistent value over time for which (perhaps with the exception of the euro) overseas markets are only remotely salient.

Of course, many consumers will have sufficient education and experience to understand some of the underlying complexities – even professional investors inhabit a lifeworld and need money to buy the weekly groceries. But the temporality and spatiality of monetary transactions on the high street entails an entirely different set of earmarks and institutional codings from forex transactions in the trading room. Money's functionality as a routine medium of exchange arguably depends precisely on the 'black boxing' of the complex epistemologies that underpin it (including the process of fractional reserve banking and the shaping of exchange rates by global money markets). Its very utility as a medium of commodity exchange would be compromised were it necessary to bring the contingencies, time-horizons and global market influences of forex trading to bear on high street consumption.

Indeed, the difference between the use of money in the lifeworld, to purchase and consume commodities with a use-value stands in stark contrast to the forex markets, where one money form is exchanged for other money forms as both the means and the end of accumulating ever-increasing quantities of money. Asked about the nature of money, one interviewee candidly surmised that is was simply an 'an object of relative price' (Trader F), in other words, a medium defining relationships of value rather than something with its own intrinsic value. It is perhaps ironic that the market actors who are most aware of money's artifice also have the greatest incentive to accumulate it.

References

Bank of International Settlements (BIS) (2010), *Triennial Central Bank Survey: Report on Global Foreign Exchange Market Activity in 2010*, http://www.bis.org/publ/rpfxf10t.pdf. Accessed 20th December, 2011.

Bryan, D. (2001), 'Reporting the "Asian financial crisis": Australian financial journalists; construction of a national threat', *Southern Review: Communication, Politics & Culture*, 34: 2, pp. 14–25.

Bryan, D. and Rafferty, M. (2007), 'Financial derivatives and the theory of money', *Economy and Society*, 36: 1, pp. 134–58.

Davies, G. (1996), *The History of Money*, Cardiff: University of Wales Press.

Dodd, N. (1994), *The Sociology of Money: Economics, Reason and Contemporary Society*, New York: Continuum.

Dodd, N. (2005), 'Reinventing monies in Europe', *Economy and Society*, 34: 4, pp. 558–83.

Granovetter, M. (1985), 'Economic action and social structure – the problem of embeddedness', *American Journal of Sociology*, 91: 3, pp. 481–510.

Greenfield, C. and Williams, P. (2007), 'Financialization, finance rationality and the role of the media in Australia', *Media Culture & Society*, 34: 2, pp. 415–33.

Ingham, G. (2004), *The Nature of Money*, Cambridge: Polity Press.

International Monetary Fund (IMF) (2007), New Zealand: Selected issues, IMF Country Report No. 07/151, May, Washington, DC: IMF.

Kunczik, M. (2002), 'Globalisation – news media, images of nations and the flow of international capital with special reference to the role of the rating agencies', *Journal of International Communication*, 8: 1, pp. 39–79.

Lawrence, G. (2008), 'The reserve bank, private sector banks, and the creation of money and credit', *Reserve Bank of New Zealand Bulletin*, http://www.rbnz.govt.nz/research/bulletin/2007_2011/2008mar71_1lawrence.pdf. Accessed 11th November, 2011.

McKinsey Global Institute (2011), 'Mapping global capital markets'. August 2011 Report, http://www.mckinsey.com/Insights/MGI/Research/Financial_Markets/Mapping_global_capital_markets_2011. Accessed 19th December, 2011.

Oxfam (2009), 'Bank bailout could end poverty for 50 years – Oxfam tells G20', 1st April, 2009, http://www.oxfam.org/en/pressroom/pressrelease/2009-04-01/bank-bailout-could-end-poverty. Accessed 12th January, 2012.

Pearson, R. (2003), 'Argentina's barter network: New currency for new times?', *Bulletin of Latin American Research*, 22: 2, pp. 214–30.

Reserve Bank of New Zealand (RBNZ) (2007), 'Foreign exchange and derivatives turnover survey', RBNZ report, 26th September, 2007, from www.rbnz.govt.nz/news/2007/3112486.html. Accessed 31st October, 2011.

Rothkopf, D. (1999), 'The disinformation age', *Foreign Policy*, 114, pp. 83–97.

Rowbotham, M. (1998), *The Grip of Death – A Study of Modern Money, Debt Slavery and Destructive Economics*, Charlbury: Jon Carpenter.

Simmel, G. (2004/1907), *The Philosophy of Money,* 3rd edn (edited by D. Frisby, Trans. T. Bottomore and D. Frisby with K. Mengelberg), London: Routledge.

Smithin, J. (2000) (ed.), *What is Money?*, London: Routledge.

Thompson, P. A. (2003), 'Making the world go round? Communication, information and global trajectories of finance capital', *Southern Review – Communication, Politics & Culture*, 36: 3, pp. 20–43.

Thompson, P. A. (2010a), 'Sold short: New communication technologies and the "democratization" of financial markets', in G. Murdock and P. Golding (eds), *Digital Dynamics: Engagements and Connections,* New York: Hampton Press.

Thompson, P. A. (2010b), 'Worlds apart? The political economy of communication, information and institutional investor media usage in global financial markets'. PhD thesis, RMIT University, Melbourne, http://researchbank.rmit.edu.au/view/rmit:10303. Accessed 2nd February, 2012.

Zelizer, V. (1994), *The Social Meaning of Money*, New York: Basic Books.

Zelizer, V. (2002), 'Fine tuning the Zelizer view', *Economy and Society*, 29: 3, pp. 383–89.

Notes

1   The author's doctoral work (Thompson 2010b) addresses informational reflexivity in regard to institutional investor media usage. The material here draws on one component of the study comprising 39 semi-structured interviews of analysts and traders and reserve bank officials,

including several periods of non-participant observation in the trading rooms at Deutsche bank, ANZ and the Reserve Bank of New Zealand between May 2004 and September 2005. Because of varying degrees of consent to personal identification, all respondents are referred to anonymously. The contribution of all the participants and their respective institutions is gratefully acknowledged.

2   The cost of a derivative contract is usually a few per cent of the notional value of the denoted asset being exchanged. The value of the option depends on the price movement of the underlying asset, with the holder having the option to execute the transaction depending on whether the agreed price is favourable. Thus the option can be used to either hedge particular risks between counterparties or leverage a trading position to amplify potential profits. There are numerous other forms of derivatives, including bespoke 'over-the-counter' forms (see Bryan and Rafferty 2007).

3   It was the growing size of the 'Eurodollar' markets in the 1960s, driven in part by the reluctance of Soviet-aligned nations to maintain the dollar holdings they required for international commodities (such as oil) within the US banking system that eventually undermined the Bretton Woods system pegging the US dollar to gold. The removal of this peg helped usher in 'floating' international currency markets and expedite the shift from the Keynesian to the Monetarist macroeconomic paradigm.

4   Trader D explained that even relatively liquid currencies such as the Australian dollar can be subject to price movement in response to large volume transactions which exceed the current volume available for exchange at the current market price. As Trader D explained, 'You're talking hundreds of millions – I mean, the market parcel size on a [normal-size] trade is $5 million, so, you're talking a transaction of $200 or $300 million may cause some sort of move'.

5   These include strict controls on access to the OCR documents and decision within RBNZ itself and also sequestering investment analysts and financial reporters who attend the pre-announcement briefing. At 9.00 am the announcement is then transmitted simultaneously to all the financial media, at which point the analysts present at the briefing then call their institutions to explain the context and any important details in the report as quickly as possible to enable the traders to respond.

6   The reissued RBNZ statement is below (3rd May, 2005: The previous statement came as part of the OCR commentary on 28th April).

> *Reserve Bank Governor Alan Bollard today reinforced his statement of 28 April 2005 that economic data suggests that underlying demand and inflation pressures remain strong and that, in this environment, further policy tightening cannot be ruled out. Dr Bollard was speaking to a Masterton District Council Business Community Breakfast Meeting. 'Last week I announced that the Official Cash rate (OCR) would remain at 6.75 per cent,' Dr Bollard said. 'But I reiterated our concerns about the persistence of inflation pressures in the economy, which are severely limiting our inflation headroom.' Dr Bollard said that over the coming weeks the Bank would be reviewing its forecasts in more detail, in particular to assess the strength of pipeline interest and exchange rate effects, household demand and on-going labour market pressures. 'This assessment will be used to confirm whether further policy tightening is warranted at the June 2005 Monetary Policy Statement. Certainly, the current outlook offers no scope for an easing of policy in the foreseeable future.'*

Chapter 3

Stating support for the city: Thirty years of budget talk

Catherine Walsh

Introduction

In the aftermath of the 2008 Financial Crisis, we are all asking the question: how did this happen? The drama in the banking sector was a climactic moment that caught our attention, an earthquake arriving after decades of quieter, steadier socio-economic shifts emanating from financial centres like London. But neither the worldwide rise of finance nor the dominance of the City within the UK's economy is a natural phenomenon; both are social changes brought about by agents at work in their own time, a time that is now our history. In this chapter I describe a set of public statements made by a set of key agents in this history: the budget speeches delivered to the House of Commons by successive chancellors of the exchequer between 1976 and 2007. From these primary documents, I show that since Thatcher came to power in 1979, chancellors have been assertively pro-finance, and have repeatedly adapted their messages to economic change within the financial sector. These chancellors have also enthusiastically recommended the so-called 'democratization of finance' (Erturk et al. 2007), a new breadth of financial participation for the general public through investment in share- and home-ownership (Langley 2008; Martin 2002). My findings show that between 1979 and 2007 chancellors signalled via their budget statements how the financial sector would be nurtured and protected, and contributed to a larger discourse about the growth of finance being good for Britain. I argue that the interests of financial elites have been served by state rhetoric about the democratization of finance, both directly in terms of sales, and indirectly in terms of a public justification of finance as, again, good for Britain. In this chapter, then, I ask what we can learn from budget statements about the state's role in making investing and trading in the City more profitable, and how official and public state communication publicized the idea of finance as an individual and public good.

As an institution, the sovereign state has been already implicated in the historical rise of finance (for examples, see Arrighi 1994; Seabrooke 2006; Konings 2009; Krippner 2011), and institutional frameworks of analysis have done a great deal to illuminate this historical and social phenomenon beyond the obvious arenas of economics and business studies. But with analyses based on institutional power there always lurks a danger that individual agency will become obscured, that we will lose sight of the historical persons who took decisions that proved consequential, even pivotal. As data, budget statements straddle this divide between agents and institutions, being both a reflection of *a priori* institutional arrangements of the state, yet still deliberate discursive constructions of the chancellor himself, an illustration of the choices that his office empowered him to make, and the way he chose to announce them. The budget statements of the chancellors are official expressions of this coordinating institution, and thereby the words of these men have added to public, normative discourses about economic life, which in turn have assisted both financial elites and ordinary citizens in assessing their respective social places. My analysis of budget statements shows some of the explicit steps that chancellors took to make particular economic activities more profitable, illustrates the economic arguments that they hoped to make and win, and provides a survey of the official intentions of the state across parliaments and across parties.

Empirically, budget statements offer a wealth of advantages: they are public-record texts that are consistently delivered by the same office-holder to the same audience on the same subject, year in and year out, creeping across time, socio-economic change, and political party. The chancellor speaks for the government of the day, and thus for the state in his time, on economic matters, creating a composite text: part idealized narrative, part technical manual. Both the ideals and the details illuminate the history. Because the budget statements provide such a concise snapshot of changing regulations, laws, tax policies, and idealized economic narratives, they lend themselves handily to *longue durée* enquiry. In this chapter I take a long view by sampling the budget statements of Labour chancellor Denis Healey (1976–1979), Conservative chancellors Geoffrey Howe (1979–1983) and Nigel Lawson (1984–1999), and (New) Labour chancellor Gordon Brown (1997–2007). I have chosen not to include the budget statements of the intervening Conservative chancellors of the 1990s, Major, Lamont and Clarke, both for the sake of concision, and because after studying their budget statements, I judge that they add only marginally to my arguments and do not run contrary to them.

In the next section I shall briefly describe how Chancellor Denis Healey talked about the industrial sector, not finance, as the driving force behind the UK economy in the late 1970s. I do this in order to provide a 'baseline' against which I can compare later chancellors. In the third section I illustrate just how abruptly Thatcher's first chancellor, Geoffrey Howe, switched from talking about industrial strategy to signalling that the new regime would actively protect and promote financial interests instead. I then describe how Thatcher's next chancellor, Nigel Lawson, and Blair's only chancellor, Gordon Brown, expanded upon and adapted Howe's pro-finance messages in ways that benefited elite participants in City finance. In the fourth section I explore a related kind of budget talk, the state's encouragement of widespread participation in financial markets, through share-and home-ownership. Absent in Healey's budgets, these messages are very much of the neo-liberal era, illustrating the state's direct support for the sale of financial products, and also the indirect, public-relations side of state support for finance, in which the state insists that the financial sector is good for everyone's needs and desires. In the final section I summarize my argument, that whether technically specific or more broad and idealized, budget speech rhetoric illustrates how chancellors have chosen to use their institutional position to support elite financial interests.

Healey's budget statements: Establishing a basis for comparison

In order to establish a basis for meaningful comparison, I want to begin first by describing budget statements in which there was very little talk of finance, but a great deal of talk about industry, during the chancellorship of Denis Healey. Healey faced very serious economic problems in the 1970s, a time of high inflation, high interest rates and erratic currency values. He addressed these issues in his budget statements with insistent talk of industrial strategy and physical export, scant mentions of finance, and no mention at all of mass-participation in financial markets. Even if his industrial strategy proved largely ineffective in solving his many problems, the very fact that he kept manufacturing, employment, and export at the centre of the economic argument makes him the last of the industrial chancellors. In stark contrast, Thatcher's chancellors Howe and Lawson all but abandoned talk of industry in their budgets, and although industry did see a modified revival under Gordon Brown, it was limited in terms of high-value, technologically advanced industry.

Decades earlier, Healey consistently described manufacturing, industrial strategy and physical exports as the keys to economic prosperity. He insisted that the UK must 'create new jobs particularly in profitable firms in manufacturing industry and so strengthen the industrial base on which our whole economy depends' (Healey 1978, col. 1187). His budget statements cast finance as a servant to industry as he urged that banks 'ensure that any expansion of their business was directed to the needs of manufacturing industry for working capital, expansion of exports, import saving and industrial investment at home' (Healey 1976, col. 236). Healey did very occasionally talk about finance, but it was as a necessity for the real economy, not an engine of growth, or a road to fulfilment for the UK and its citizens. He showed no special consideration towards the City, saying he was unmoved by financial sector representations made to the Treasury. He was sufficiently unmotivated to aid the City that in his April 1976 budget statement he explicitly refused to insulate capital gains from inflation for tax purposes, saying that this would be unfair to people who held cash instead of shares. This is a stark contrast to the pro-finance nature of future chancellors, and to Geoffrey Howe in particular, who would acquiesce to this request from the City in his 1982 budget statement. Healey's most acute financial crisis was brought about by the weakness of sterling on world currency markets, and is acceptance of an emergency IMF loan facility in 1976 in order to support the pound was politically divisive for the minority Labour government, as well as humiliating (Burk and Cairncross 1992; Harmon 1997). Unsurprisingly, Healey's 1977 budget statement casts currency markets as a problematic site, the source of Britain's woes and yet a powerful external force that needed to be appeased. He described the loans from the IMF and central banks as a necessary but temporary solution, a stop-gap measure until Britain could regain her industrial strength and return to glory as a trading nation.

Against all this, Healey did not praise the domestic financial sector, he did not ask it for help or suggest it might hold the answer to Britain's economic problems. He did not indicate that the state would protect or promote it, and he did not recommend that the masses participate in it. As the next two sections will make clear, these sorts of attitudes towards finance are a world away from the attitudes of Thatcher's chancellors. The changes in chancellor rhetoric over the last few decades have followed global patterns of the displacement of manufacturing to the developing World, movements in exchange rates, interest rates and inflation, advances in technology, and the rise of finance as a First World phenomenon. But Healey's budget rhetoric shows how a politician makes deliberate choices about the worth and use of particular kinds of economic activity. Recognizing this casts a bright light on the future choices of subsequent chancellors. Healey's economic narrative was centred around industry, the interests of the City of London were of no interest to him, and not once did he suggest that the man of the street should invest directly in any financial market. Throughout the rest of this chapter I will demonstrate how pro-finance chancellors became in their budget statements after Healey's departure, after Thatcher's 1979 election.

The rise of finance talk

I have now arrived at the heart of the matter, how budget statement rhetoric concerning the financial sector evolved as that sector came to dominate the economy. As Healey was replaced by Howe, the budget statements underwent a radical break: Howe abandoned industry as a topic in favour of finance, specifically finance-friendly regulation, finance-friendly tax policy and an emphasis on the City of London's power to create wealth. Following Howe, Lawson promised to protect and promote the City, and demonstrated his resolve by depriving the Treasury itself of substantial revenues in order to do so. And as the new century drew near and finance became even more global, and yet more concentrated in the hands of institutional investors, Brown moved to protect and promote the City in terms of global and institutional investment. More importantly, Brown's talk about finance reassured investors that New Labour could be trusted to protect the City's position and the interests of the financial elite. The pattern that I describe is one of an early and sudden shift to finance, followed by a stepwise strengthening of this position, flexible and responsive to changes in the City regardless of which political party was in power.

With Howe's assumption of the chancellorship comes a radical shift in the state's official position towards financial regulation and the role of the City in creating 'invisible earnings':

> We have removed many unnecessary controls to enterprise and individual effort. We have removed controls on pay, prices, dividends and foreign exchange which can now be used freely to acquire productive assets overseas to the benefit of our exports and invisible earnings alike.
>
> (Howe 1980, col. 1441)

Contrary to Healey, Howe adjusted inflation-adjusted assets for the purposes of capital gains tax, which he called a matter of 'simple justice' meant to significantly increase the attraction of equities to United Kingdom taxpayers. One result should be that companies can raise more equity at lower cost than would previously have been possible.

(Howe 1982, col. 755)

Capital gains tax (CGT) is payable by individuals rather than corporations, yet Howe understood very well the connection between lower real CGT rates and the ability of City traders to sell shares. Howe was not only far more interested in talking about banks than Healey, he was eager to help them and loathe to penalize them. For example, he admitted in his 1980 budget that the banks were enjoying high interest rates while paying no interest on current accounts, and while he agreed that this was a matter of good fortune for banks and not a matter of enterprise or efficiency:

> [I]t is equally irrational to attribute these profits to some wickedness on the part of the banks. They need the major part to strengthen their capital base, which would otherwise have been eroded by inflation. There could, of course, be a case in principle for a special tax related to the windfall element in these profits, and I shall be considering that further. However, it has not yet been established that such a tax is either practical or entirely desirable in today's conditions.

(Howe 1980, col. 1466)

Similarly, Howe said that although tax havens might be offensive, 'we must be very careful not to prejudice legitimate business, particularly because of the importance of London as a financial centre' (1982, col. 748). Thus began with Howe a tradition of protecting banking and the City, one which was faithfully followed by Lawson and Brown.

Lawson made clear in his budget statements that the government would continue to protect and promote the City's trade in equities so long as he was chancellor, and that this favour extending to depriving the Treasury itself of substantial revenues. Not only did Lawson announce in his first budget that he would slash the main corporate tax rate, progressing from 52% that in 1984 to 35% by 1988, but he explicitly said he was doing so in order to make the purchase of equities more attractive:

> Our imputation system allows a company to offset in full all interest paid. But only a partial offset of dividends is allowed. Companies thus have a clear incentive to finance themselves through borrowing and in particular bank borrowing rather than by raising equity capital. The closer the corporation tax rate comes to the basic rate of income tax, the smaller this undesirable distortion becomes.

(Lawson 1984, col. 297)

In other words, Lawson said that he expected this change in tax policy would to allow companies (which were deterred from bank borrowing by historically high interest rates), to raise money more cheaply through share issue. Similarly, in 1986, the year of massive UK financial deregulation now known as the Big Bang, Lawson spoke at length in his budget speech on of the importance of the City, then promptly halved the stamp duty on shares. Not even the stock market crash of October 1987 pierced the confidence of a true believer. In his next budget statement Lawson only briefly mentioned the 'dramatic collapse in the world's equities markets last October … essentially an overdue market correction which did little more than reverse the rapid rise in share prices of the previous year' (Lawson 1988, col. 994). Lawson's enthusiasm for financial markets cemented Howe's changes, and together they provided a foundation for the New Labour position of Gordon Brown.

Brown's disposition towards the City was as supportive as Lawson's and Howe's, and in the same ways, but Brown also adapted his messages to twenty-first-century trends in finance. Building on Lawson's legacy of improving trading conditions for shares, Brown cut the main corporation tax rate, part of 'a long-term commitment that will increase both inward investment and domestic investment to the benefit of the whole country' (Brown 1997, col. 305). Building on Howe's legacy, Brown made capital gains on assets more profitable for individuals by greatly reducing the tax on these capital transactions. When Brown began delivering budgets in 1997 the rate of capital gains tax was 40%, but by 2002 he had lowered the CGT to 20% for assets held for 1 year, and 10% for assets owned for 2 years. Brown referred to this aggressive reduction as 'rewarding entrepreneurship and giving Britain overall a capital gains tax regime that is more favourable to enterprise than that of the United States' (Brown 2002, col. 581). Indeed, international competitiveness in the world of finance was a theme in Brown's finance talk; when he liberalized City trade further he said it was to keep it internationally competitive:

> The international competitiveness of the bond market in the City of London depends upon a level playing field. This is why today I am announcing that from April 2001 we will abolish the withholding tax on the interest paid on international bonds. We will legislate so that we can proceed on the basis of exchange of information nationally and internationally This change should be welcomed in all parts of the House. There is no clearer indication of our determination to stand up for what is right for Britain.
>
> (Brown 2000, col. 861)

As the City had seen the growth of large-scale institutions investing on behalf of millions of small, passive investors, Brown made it known that their interests were especially important to him:

> Institutional investors are today responsible for assets of £1.5 trillion. To promote long-term investment in our country, and to protect investors, I have accepted the recommendations of the Myners report. We will abolish the minimum funding requirement; through tax and regulatory reform we will make it easier for life-insurers and pension funds to invest in venture capital; and we will ensure both a strengthened role

for pension fund trustees and a clearer duty on fund managers to promote beneficiaries' interests.

(Brown 2001, col. 298)

Brown described his support for the City in terms of the new realities of globalization and the dominance of institutional shareholders, but most importantly he asserted his support for the financial sector.

Across several decades and across political parties, budget statement rhetoric since Thatcher has remained strongly supportive of the City, and chancellors have been able to flexibly adapt to new financial regimes over time in order to keep their pro-finance message effective. Howe was the man with the radical plan, the man who broke with the past and set the tone for the future. Lawson's stepwise strengthening of Howe's positions made the commitment even more clear, as did his willingness to put the Treasury's money where his mouth was. Brown's modification of Lawson's message, still enthusiastic for the City but with a new focus on international competitiveness, shows that this pro-finance message from the chancellor was not only stable across the major political parties, but also that a chancellor could be flexible and responsive to changes in the City. A first and obvious implication of these conclusions is that with each budget statement these chancellors have communicated to economic elites that City investment would be privileged, promoted, and protected by the state, making it appear to be a profitable and secure place for returns, which for very many years it was. Second, the long-view of this trend suggests that the state has been persistently active in creating a cultural input: consistently broadcasting the idea that a larger and larger financial sector is good for Britain. I shall explore this idea further in the next section, in which I illustrate how these same chancellors have all come to recommend participation in finance for all.

The democratization of finance talk

Post-1979 chancellors have preached about the edifying potential of ownership for all, that widespread financial participation was a private good and a public one. Like his embrace of the City as a key ingredient in Britain's economic life, Howe's ideas about widespread ownership of housing and shares were a radical new development in budget statements that proved to be enduring. Lawson preached share ownership especially throughout the City's equity boom, and would not be dissuaded from doing so by its 1987 Crash. Brown did not make a habit of encouraging the public to invest in homes or shares (although on occasion he did so), but instead he talked often about ensuring that the financial participation to which people had already committed themselves was a safe practice. In each case, the comparison to be made with Healey's budget statements is incredibly straightforward: there is no mention of finance for the masses in Healey's budgets. As with finance talk, democratization-of-finance talk has been remarkably persistent since Thatcher came to power, and has proven flexible and adaptive.

Each year Howe would take a few minutes to champion Thatcher's ownership society, an idea completely foreign to the chancellor who preceded him and yet a key idea that set the pattern for all chancellors who have followed him. In 1980 he lessened stamp duty on house purchases, stating that promoting private home ownership was a way of promoting private endeavour. In 1981 he declared that, for anyone buying his or her council-flat, only the discounted price was to be considered for stamp duty, not the market value. In 1982 he gave all employees the option of buying the shares of their own companies without paying tax, explicitly saying this was meant to encourage ownership. In 1983 he doubled the tax exemptions for investors in new businesses, calling this measure 'a further move towards removing the bias in the tax system against the personal shareholder, and a further measure to encourage wider share ownership' (col. 154). Howe was enthusiastic about encouraging personal investment, and spoke of it like an education or self-improvement programme: 'I believe that share ownership can also spread a wider understanding of the role for risk taking and initiative in the economic system' (Howe 1980, col. 1481).

Lawson's budget-speech enthusiasm for private shareholding was even greater than Howe's, and he made even greater fiscal concessions to it through the tax system. In 1984, to encourage more property-owning and share-owning, Lawson halved stamp-duty on both shares and homes to 1% in order to 'contribute further to the creation of a property-owning and share-owning democracy in which more decisions are made by individuals rather than by institutions' (col. 292). In that first budget Lawson argued that democratized finance served multiple purposes:

> At its present level [the stamp duty] is an impediment to mobility and incompatible with the forces of competition now at work in the City … Reducing the rate of duty on share transfers will remove an important disincentive to investment in equities and increase the international competitiveness of our stock market. It should also help British Companies to raise equity finance.
>
> (Lawson 1984, col. 293)

In other words, Lawson said he was halving the stamp duty on homes and shares because it would encourage more people to own them, and because it would simply sell more shares. Where Howe had presented the democratization of finance in terms of self-improvement for the masses, Lawson made the twin aims explicit. By the end of his tenure, Lawson found himself having to confront the fact that shares do not always appreciate in value, and that not all ownership is stable and committed. By 1988 the London stock market had fallen sharply, and many of the people who had bought undervalued shares in newly privatized industries had now sold them for instant premiums. Lawson's response to this, to these challenges to the wisdom and appeal of popular share-ownership, was to defend his position even more vigorously:

> Despite all the stories of people taking quick profits on privatisation shares, and despite the stock-market collapse, the results show that the number of individual shareholders

has risen further over the past 12 months, to very nearly 9 million, This illustrates in a quite remarkable fashion how wider share ownership is now taking root.

(Lawson 1988, col. 1004)

Gordon Brown talked about share-ownership less often than his predecessors. It is true that Brown sounded for all the world like Lawson or Howe when he announced that he would 'remove the old barriers to a share-owning democracy', with an all-employee shareholding scheme, which he modestly called 'the biggest boost to employee shareholding that our country has ever seen' (Brown 2000, col. 861). But as this example is a rare occasion for Brown, I interpret it as indicating that he was not opposed to Lawson's and Howe's earlier thinking, rather than indicating the same passion. Rather than an explicit call to wider participation, Brown's democratization-of-finance talk took the form of reassurances about consumer protection, an acknowledgement from Brown that the wider public was now already exposed to an array of financial products. Brown's innovation was to make the financial participation that was already widespread appear safe, rather than to convince people to buy shares or purchase a home.

The Financial Services Authority will now publish league tables of costs and charges in savings, insurance and pension products, to guarantee a better deal for consumers and to avoid the mis-selling of the past. To help all home-owners, all building societies and banks will, for the first time, be obliged to publish reliable price information on mortgages.

(1999, col. 178)

Where the democratization of finance rhetoric of Howe and Lawson was blatant and constant, Brown was less insistent that ordinary people should buy shares or homes. Rather he attempted to reassure his audience that financial products were safe.

The message of democratization for financial participation started suddenly with Howe, who began to create a new state discourse about ownership and an ownership society, as if it were a matter of civic education. From the very beginning, this rhetoric of ownership was intended for societal change. When Lawson boasted of the ownership culture he was creating in Britain, he made its connection to the City's trade more explicit, and he continued to deprive the treasury of immediate revenues in order to support it. Both Howe and especially Lawson publicized the ownership of shares, a rather ethereal investment vehicle which few people owned directly and which were the basis of the City's expansion in the mid-1980s. In contrast, Brown's budget speeches do not promote the democratization of finance as keenly as Howe's and Lawson's did. Brown's budget speeches talk about protecting those people, which is both an acknowledgement of threat and an attempt to reassure. My interpretation of this data is that Howe and Lawson were more keen to encourage ordinary people into markets, especially equity markets, whereas by 1997 Brown assumed for his budgets that such participation was already widespread enough, and he chose to focus instead on assurances that such investment was safe. Throughout the 1980s ordinary investors were initially challenged to accept ownership and risk, and to keep investing even in the face of adverse signals from the markets themselves. At the turn of the century Brown assumed widespread financial participation in his budget speeches, and so instead reassured his audience that the state would mitigate risk for ordinary investors who were so committed.

Conclusions

In this chapter I have described how successive chancellors of the exchequer have talked about the financial sector as it has risen in prominence within the UK economy, with a view to understanding how the UK state publicly supported the rise of finance between 1976 and 2007. Each budget statement broadcasts the chancellor's intentions for tax policy and legislation, giving its contemporary audience a very explicit steer towards the state's preferred economic sectors and activities, often with direct incentives and recommendations. More subtle, and more interesting in retrospect, is the way that the chancellor's ideal of economic life is described in budget statements, and how it both reflects and makes a contribution to public discourses. Between Thatcher's first parliament and the Financial Crisis of 2008, chancellors of each main party remained strongly supportive of the City and actively adapted it to new financial regimes as the financial sector has changed. Chancellors Howe and Lawson turned the narrative about prosperity from industry to finance, promoted and protected finance, and sought to popularize finance as part of this narrative in which finance was good for all, a public good. Chancellor Brown continued to privilege City interests and boost City prospects, and he reassured his audience that the state would mitigate the risks to which financial products exposed ordinary people.

The message that the chancellors sent to financial elites and non-elites alike about finance and its popular reach was unswervingly supportive between 1980 and 2007. Where the pro-finance message has altered from chancellor to chancellor, it has been to respond to changes in the financial sector itself, such as globalization, or the rise of the institutional investment, or the degree to which ordinary people are exposed to financial products. When financial markets floundered, or the dependability of financial products appeared uncertain, the chancellor took it upon himself to reassure his audience to have faith that all would be well. For financial elites, chancellors explicitly communicated that the state stood ready to protect and promote the profitable operation of the City. For ordinary people, too, the state's official narrative was one of reassurance, I argue that this reassurance for them was also further reassurance for the financial elites who could expect more assets to enter financial markets through wider financial participation, thus boosting the profitability of the City. Furthermore, the state's insistence that financial participation through ownership was good for everyone regardless of personal wealth, that it was good for Britain, made a contribution to public discourses about the place of the financial sector in British society as a whole. If widespread participation in financial markets is an individual good for everyone, then financial markets must be a public good. Through this narrative the state helped to create a public justification of the ascendant financial order.

In light of this long-standing and robust tradition of protecting finance, it is not surprising that two successive UK governments (first Labour and now a Conservative-Liberal Democrat Coalition) have rushed to the aid of the sector since 2008, and been slow to penalize or regulate City operations or elites. History shows that this is merely a new and exaggerated example of a pattern which until 2008 moved more slowly, steadily, and stealthily, in which state elites privileged the City. When the chancellor stands up in the House of Commons and delivers his budget statement, he personifies the state, and reminds us that the rise of finance was not a natural phenomenon that grew organically of its own accord, but the consequences of a series of choices made by people empowered by prior institutional arrangements. My history of chancellors talking illustrates how, as a coordinating institution for economic life, the state has made and remade its normative principles, and broadcast its intentions so that financial elites might better devise their strategies. It also illustrates how men in power made choices. History illuminates agency, and when confronted with the enormity of regulating bodies that set the rules and socio-economic changes that appear overwhelming, we should not lose sight of actors who choose. As the economic leaders of states create, or fail to create, new rules of governance and new stories about the route from austerity to prosperity now, we must not let either the institutions or the people who hold institutional power escape scrutiny.

References

Arrighi, G. (1994), *The Long Twentieth Century*, London: Verso.

Brown, G. (1997), Speech to the House of Commons, 2nd July, *Parliamentary Debates*, Commons, 6th Series, vol. 297 (1996–1997), cols. 303–16.

Brown, G. (1999), Speech to the House of Commons, 9th March, *Parliamentary Debates*, Commons, 6th Series, vol. 327 (1998–1999), cols. 173–90.

Brown, G. (2000), Speech to the House of Commons, 21st March, *Parliamentary Debates*, Commons, 6th Series, vol. 346 (1999–2000), cols. 858–72.

Brown, G. (2001), Speech to the House of Commons, 7th March, *Parliamentary Debates*, Commons, 6th Series, vol. 364 (2000–2001), cols. 295–308.

Brown, G. (2002), Speech to the House of Commons, 17th April, *Parliamentary Debates*, Commons, 6th Series, vol. 383 (2001–2002), cols. 577–92.

Brown, G. (2005), Speech to the House of Commons, 16th March, *Parliamentary Debates*, Commons, 6th Series, vol. 424 (2004–2005), cols. 257–69.

Burk, K. and Cairncross, A. (1992), *Goodbye, Great Britain: The 1976 IMF Crisis*, New Haven: Yale University Press.

Erturk, I., Froud, J., Johal, S., Lever, A. and Williams, K. (2007), 'The democratization of finance? Promises, outcomes and conditions', *Review of International Political Economy*, 14: 4, pp. 553–75.

Harmon, M. D. (1997), *The British Labour Government and the 1976 IMF Crisis*, London: MacMillan.

Healey, D. (1976), Speech to the House of Commons, 6th April, *Parliamentary Debates*, Commons, 5th Series, vol. 909 (1975–1976), cols. 232–81.

Healey, D. (1977), Speech to the House of Commons, 29th March, *Parliamentary Debates*, Commons, 5th Series, vol. 929 (1976–1977), cols. 256–86.

Healey, D. (1978), Speech to the House of Commons, 11th April, *Parliamentary Debates*, Commons, 5th Series, vol. 947 (1977–1978), cols. 1183–208.

Howe, G. (1980), Speech to the House of Commons, 26th March, *Parliamentary Debates*, Commons, 5th Series, vol. 981 (1979–1980), cols. 1439–90.

Howe, G. (1981), Speech to the House of Commons, 10th March, *Parliamentary Debates*, Commons, 5th Series, vol. 1000 (1980–1981), cols. 757–83.

Howe, G. (1982), Speech to the House of Commons, 9th March, *Parliamentary Debates*, Commons, 6th Series, vol. 19 (1981–1982), cols. 726–57.

Howe, G. (1983), Speech to the House of Commons, 15th March, *Parliamentary Debates*, Commons, 6th Series, vol. 39 (1982–83), cols. 134–57.

Konings, M. (2009), 'The construction of US financial power', *Review of International Studies*, 35, pp. 69–94.

Krippner, G. (2011), *Capitalizing on Crisis: The Political Origins of the Rise of Finance*, Cambridge, MA: Harvard University Press.

Langley, P. (2008), *The Everyday Life of Global Finance*, Oxford: Oxford University Press.

Lawson, N. (1984), Speech to the House of Commons, 15th March, *Parliamentary Debates*, Commons, 6th Series, vol. 56 (1983–1984), cols. 286–304.

Lawson, N. (1986), Speech to the House of Commons, 18th March, *Parliamentary Debates*, Commons, 6th Series, vol. 94 (1985–1986), cols. 166–84.

Lawson, N. (1988), Speech to the House of Commons, 15th March, *Parliamentary Debates*, Commons, 6th Series, vol. 129 (1987–1988), cols. 993–1013.

Martin, R. (2002), *The Financialization of Daily Life*, Philadelphia, PA: Temple University Press.

Seabrooke, L. (2006), *The Social Sources of Financial Power: Domestic Legitimacy and International Financial Orders*, Ithaca, NY: Cornell University Press.

Part 2

News talk

Chapter 4

More of the same: News, economic growth and the recycling of conventional wisdom

Justin Lewis and Richard Thomas

W̶e begin this chapter with a review of critiques of the traditional model of economic growth that have emerged in recent years. Together these critiques make a powerful case that for developed nations in the twenty-first century, a consumerist growth model is becoming increasingly dysfunctional. The banking crisis in 2007/2008 sent shock waves through the media commentariat, undermining faith in the dominant economic model. The familiar coterie of experts – who had offered bland reassurance rather than warnings – no longer sounded authoritative or prescient. But to what extent did this financial crisis precipitate a more critical, questioning attitude? We look at press coverage of economic growth in the United States and Britain in 2010 and 2011, to see how far the landscape has shifted.

Questioning the 'growth is good' orthodoxy

Throughout the twentieth century, there were many challenges to consumer capitalism as a model for human progress. If the consumer capitalist model ultimately triumphed, it was not without the growth of a significant public sector and a wide variety of regulatory instruments installed to deal with consumer capitalism's many shortcomings. Public bodies controlled its excesses, compensated for market failures, subsidized research and development, and provided a degree of equity (in areas like health and education).

Twentieth-century critiques of consumer capitalism were generally moral in character, focusing on issues of exploitation and inequality. Proponents of consumer capitalism conceded on many of these points, but their trump card was the system's flair for wealth creation. The system that could best deliver economic growth was, almost by definition, the best system. And as the century progressed, a political consensus emerged that the central purpose of government was to encourage and guarantee increases in material wealth.

This consensus remains firmly intact. Indeed, the recession that began a little less than a decade into the twenty-first century appears to have amplified the clamour for growth. There is, however, a growing body of evidence from across the social sciences that economic growth – and the consumer capitalist model that drives it – is becoming increasingly dysfunctional. This evidence is quite different in character from the moral critiques of the past: it suggests that for developed countries in the twenty-first century, a system designed to deliver growth is failing even on its own terms and that, as a model of human progress, it is becoming tired and irrelevant.

Before we briefly review this evidence, it is worth noting that our obsession with wealth accumulation and economic growth in an age of plenty is, anthropologically speaking, a fairly recent phenomenon. The American social critic Vance Packard (best known for his analysis of the advertising industry) identified a new 'clamour for growth' in the late 1950s (Packard 1960: 20). The emergence of what he called 'growthmanship' at this particular time and place was, in many ways, a curiosity.

This was, after all, a period of unprecedented affluence. Markets were becoming saturated, forcing advertisers to go to new lengths 'to try and stimulate markets to pay for over-produced goods' (Brierley 2002: 7). Economists like John Kenneth Galbraith (1987) and political philosophers like Herbert Marcuse (1964) were charting the possibilities of a new era, an affluent society in which most material needs had been met, and where we might turn, instead, towards less materialistic ambitions.

What transpired instead – as Galbraith, Marcuse and Packard, in different ways, feared it might – was a new era of rampant consumerism, what Colin Campbell (1989) has called the 'insatiable age'. This drive towards a permanent state of abstract material desire – one where, as Steve Jobs famously remarked, 'people don't know what they want until you show it to them'[1] – has no clear historical precedent. A permanent, constantly changing desire for accumulation, writes Campbell, is a quite new and remarkable phenomenon: '[R]arely can an inhabitant of modern society, no matter how privileged or wealthy, declare that there is nothing new that they want. That this should be so is a matter of wonder' (Campbell 1989: 37).

By the twenty-first century, the wealth of developed nations makes the 'affluent society' of the 1950s look positively austere. And yet we have become so accustomed to a consumerist lifestyle based on decades of economic growth that this seems a natural way of being, the end-point of human progress and development (a notion most famously advanced by Francis Fukuyama 1992 book, *The End of History and the Last Man*). Such complacency is being unravelled by three increasingly robust critiques of consumer capitalist based on permanent economic growth.

The first of these is economic. We caught a glimpse of this in the recent economic meltdown, when the increasing debt-dependence of consumer economies (in which the goal was to ensure that regardless of need, we kept on consuming) over-reached itself. As Tim Jackson puts it:

Allegiance to growth was the single most dominant feature of an economic and political system that led the world to the brink of disaster. The growth imperative has shaped the architecture of the modern economy. It motivated the freedoms granted to the financial sector. It stood at least partly responsible for the loosening of regulations, the over-extension of credit and the proliferation of unmanageable (and unstable) financial derivatives.

(Jackson 2010: 22)

Behind this over-extension is a more profound moment of reckoning, when an economic model based on never-ending expansion comes up against the finite nature of human experience.

The average American supermarket stocks five times as many goods as it did in 1975,[2] while the stagnation in the growth of leisure time (Schor 1991) means people have no more time available to shop. In 1992 US food companies launched, between them, 11,500 products (Giles 1993), a level of proliferation far beyond our capacity to make informed judgements about the superfluity on offer.

The economic historian Avner Offer (2006) describes how, under these very contemporary circumstances, choice becomes difficult to manage. The proliferation of commodities, he suggests, has become a source of stress rather than pleasure, pushing us towards over-consumption and a loss of self-control. Our choices keep expanding while the time available to make them does not, limiting our ability to act independently. The idea of the rational consumer choosing the best product at the best price has become an anachronism: we simply do not have the time (see also Iyengar and Lepper 2000).

The clash between infinite growth and the finite nature of human experience has an even more basic manifestation. Put simply, the more we have, the less we need. While the law of diminishing returns refers to production, it might equally apply to consumption. The relative value of each new object depends, in part, upon its scarcity. The more objects we possess, the less value each new object will have – a phenomenon economists refer to as declining marginal utility. In the twenty-first century, citizens of the developed world have reached a point where promise of each new commodity becomes increasingly difficult to fulfil.

The fixation with growth is, in this sense, a kind of pretence. It imagines a world in which need remains constant and the time available to make choices expands in proportion to the growing abundance of commodities. Observers saw this world unravelling in the 1960s, but, more than 50 years on, it looks increasingly out of kilter.

The second challenge to the growth orthodoxy follows from this. Social scientists have been measuring quality of life since the 1950s, but it is only in recent years that this research has blossomed into a sub-discipline of its own. Perhaps the most conspicuous branch of this work focuses on happiness (Bok 2010; Layard 2011), regarded by some as a 'soft' social science because of its reliance on people's self-perceptions. But research on quality of life embraces a range of indicators, incorporating surveys of reported well-being as well 'harder' data on areas like crime and mental and physical health (see, for example, Wilkinson and Pickett 2009; or Ruut Veenhoven's 'World Happiness Database').

The economic critique of the growth model would predict that the capacity of economic growth to deliver quality of life steadily diminishes as we become more prosperous and superabundance pushes up against time constraints. Research on quality of life confirms this. So while GDP growth does appear to improve quality of life up to a certain point – a point most developed countries exceeded well before the turn of the century (Jackson 2010; Wilkinson and Pickett 2009) – beyond that it appears to have *no impact at all*.

So, for example, Wilkinson and Pickett's remarkable book, *The Spirit Level*, found no correlation between the GDP income of developed countries and their quality of life, by any measure. How income is distributed, on the other hand, does appear to be linked to a range of quality of life indicators – for both rich and poor. Thus it is that wealthier countries with high levels of inequality appear to be worse off than less wealthy countries with more equal patterns of distribution. For the old economic model, this is a paradox. For approaches that go beyond purely material measures of well-being, it is entirely plausible.

Indeed, the growth of materialist lifestyles – a necessary response to maintain demand in wealthy societies – appears to *decrease* levels of well-being (Kasser 2002; Schor 2004; James 2007). This is, in part, because consumerism pushes us away from those non-material social, recreational and civic activities that *do* appear to be linked to well-being, towards what Sut Jhally refers to as the less fulfilling 'dead world of objects' (Jhally 2006).

Again, the economic critique we have outlined would predict this outcome, which completely undermines the direction of travel embarked by Left-leaning political parties like 'New Labour' at the turn of the century. Their focus – to increase wealth across the board rather than concentrating on its distribution – would appear to be based on a series of flawed assumptions. It turns out that an evidence-led policy (an idea New Labour publicly embraced, in theory at least) would suggest going in the opposite direction, focusing on distribution rather than GDP.

The third challenge to the growth model is, perhaps, the best known. Environmental science has grown increasingly concerned about the impact of the last 50 years of economic growth. Even an optimistic view of the resources left available to us – notably oil, gas, and water – will not withstand the increasing level of demand for much longer (Owen, Inderwildi and King 2010). Even apparently 'clean' industries like media and telecommunications produce ever an increasing volume of toxic waste, contaminating the soil, the air and the sea (Kuehr and Williams 2003; Gabrys 2007; Maxwell and Miller 2012). We have, in expanding these industries, wiped out species (McKibben 2006) and degraded 60% of the world's ecosystems (Jackson 2010).

Many economists would argue that a growth-based market system can adapt to these changes. The finite nature of resources, they would suggest, will prompt technological advances in areas like renewable energy. But the most serious environmental problem we face – climate change – works on a time scale that is entirely at odds with a growth-based consumer economy. On a planetary time-scale, the delay between increasing the level of greenhouse gases in the atmosphere (as we have been doing for the last 50 years) and its impact on the climate is a mere blink of an eye – measurable in decades rather than millennia (IPCC 2007). In the context of the balance sheets that govern most forms of production, on the other hand, a threat that is 50 years hence is always going to be low down on a list of priorities.

Because business models rarely plan more than 10 years ahead, they are only suited to dealing with more immediate problems. The time scale of climate change means that when the more catastrophic effects begin to take hold, it will be too late to do anything about it. Thus it is that the Inter-governmental Panel on Climate Change (IPCC) has been warning about the impact of anthropogenic global warming since their first report in 1990 and yet we have continued to pump an ever increasing volume of greenhouse gases into the air. Between 1990 (when the IPCC issued its first report) and 2010, global carbon emissions rose by 40% (Jackson 2010).

We have already reached a critical stage. In November 2011, the International Energy Agency (IEA) released a report that suggested that current plans for industrial growth and energy provision will mean that we will have passed the point of maintaining climate change within manageable levels by 2016. 'If we don't change direction now on how we use energy', the IEA's chief economist suggested, 'we will end up beyond what scientists tell us is the minimum [for safety]. The door will be closed forever' (Harvey 2011).

Existing emissions targets based on current levels of output are already regarded as politically untenable. But for every percentage increase in economic growth, we exacerbate the problem, necessitating ever more drastic decreases in greenhouse gas emissions (Jackson 2010). In short, the growth model, without drastic alteration, is becoming a significant threat to life on earth. Economists refer to such problems as 'externalities' – an unintended consequence of an economic system that is beyond that systems purview. For our current model based on economic growth, climate change is the mother of all externalities.

The rise of business news

Our aim, in this chapter, is to consider the extent to which these serious challenges to the 'growth is good' orthodoxy have begun to permeate the public sphere through news coverage. Before we present out findings, we shall briefly consider the context of news coverage of economic and business issues.

Over three decades ago, a corpus of research by the Glasgow Media Group suggested that the views of business leaders tended to receive more favourable news coverage than the unions representing the people that worked for them. Their series of books – *Bad News*, *More Bad News* and *Really Bad News* – reported a systematic bias toward a pro-business view (Glasgow Media Group 1976, 1980, 1982). The world they describe – in which there was at least *some* attempt at balancing a union and management perspectives – seems a far more dynamic public sphere than the one we are offered today. The genre of 'business news' is now a significant part of everyday news reporting, while unions have almost disappeared from view, displaced, almost entirely, by the voice of the 'consumer'.

This growth of business news began most conspicuously in the United States, with the emergence of business news channels – such as Bloomberg, CNBC and CNNfn – and a three-fold increase in the number of business journalists in the United States between 1988 and 2000 (Roush 2006). The increased prominence of business news subsequently spread to most parts of the developed world with, for example, more than 10% of BBC news devoted specifically to business (Svennevig 2007).

This is, in theory, something to be welcomed. The growing power of an increasingly global corporate world requires robust journalistic monitoring. Most business news, however, takes a narrow view, divided between the interests of business owners and investors – with news of stocks, shares, markets, profits and losses, regulation, takeovers and mergers, appointments and announcements – and consumers – new products, consumer protection etc. (Svennevig 2007). The bigger picture – examining the role of business in society – is obscured by details of who is up and who is down. The rise of business news is reflection of the growing power of the corporate world, but how much does it do to challenge it?

A comprehensive review of UK Business Reporting for the BBC Trust in 2007 avoided some of the ideological questions raised by the growth of business news, generally hailing it as a positive development. The review sidestepped the broader question of whether a focus on business creates a slant toward a particular view of the world and focused on the narrower question of whether business was viewed from a consumer or a company perspective:

> We note that many of the BBC's business stories are framed through the perspective of the consumer. We believe the BBC's intention in adopting the consumer's viewpoint is to try to engage its audiences by approaching issues in a way that it thinks affects them and about which they care ... However, such an approach can create a prism through which much business coverage is seen as a battle between 'unscrupulous' company bosses and their 'exploited' customers.
>
> (BBC Trust 2007: 15–16)

The report's desire for a more consensual approach glosses over the different interests of producers and consumers. While consumers may have an interest in businesses remaining profitable, they have little interest in making business owners (and/or shareholders) rich. Consumers want the best product at the cheapest possible price, while businesses want to spend as little on the product as they can and sell it for as much they can. One wants margins low, the other wants them high.

More importantly, the citizen – who might take a broader view of the role of business in society – has no place in this framework. The BBC Trust review did not explore this point, but they did acknowledge it, observing that

> [a]round 29 million people work for a living in the UK and spend a large proportion of their waking hours in the workplace. However, little of this important part of UK life is reflected in the BBC's business coverage ... the audiences are served in their identity as consumers. But they are not that well served in their role as workers.
>
> (BBC Trust 2007: 9)

As workers, we have distinct interests – we want well-paid, secure jobs with profits shared amongst the workforce, rather than passed to owners, shareholders or consumers. For many workers in the developed world, outsourcing jobs to low-wage economies depresses wages – in what Jeremy Brecher and Tim Costello have called a race to the bottom as countries compete to offer businesses cheap labour (Brecher and Costello 1994). For both businesses and consumers cheap labour is a good thing, for workers it is not.

There are, however, examples of reporting that considers the wider social or environmental role of businesses – so, for example, around 6% of broadcast business news in the United Kingdom touches on environmental issues (Svennevig 2007). To what extent, however, does news tend to assume that what is good for business is good for society? More broadly, has the growth in business news provided a framework for thinking critically about the growth model that has such a profound impact on our economics, our politics and the culture of everyday life?

The purpose of our study was to establish, first of all, the extent to which newspaper coverage of economic growth is dispassionate or even-handed. More specifically, we wanted to see whether coverage is now inflected by the various economic, social and environmental critiques of the growth model to emerge in recent years.

We looked at 591 newspaper articles in 2010 and 2011[3] that referred to economic growth in developed countries in the British and US press. Our sample was based on articles about (or which made substantive references to) economic growth in eight newspapers (four in both countries) generally acknowledged to be at the 'top end' of journalism.[4] We picked broadsheet style, well-resourced newspapers that were most likely to exhibit a degree of critical reflection.

Quite apart from the growing body of evidence questioning the growth orthodoxy, there were, during this period, a number of clear opportunities to question the assumptions behind the growth model: in the United Kingdom, in particular, the government launched its plan to use surveys about well-being to measure quality of life (in November 2010) while in February 2011, Prince Charles made a speech in which he tackled the growth model head on, urging us to move away from the model of economic growth based on increasing consumption.

Growth is good

Table 4.1 shows that while a high proportion of articles about economic growth were found in Business/Economy/Finance sections, half (49.9%) were outside these specialist sections in the main body of the newspaper. Most of these were conventional news articles, although we also found economic growth discussed in a wide range of opinion, editorial and review articles – places where there is ample space to question conventional wisdom.

These proportions are similar on both sides of the Atlantic, although there are variations between newspapers (most articles about growth in the *New York Times* and the *Telegraph* were in their Business/Economy/Finance sections, for example, while most in the *Washington Post*, the *Chicago Tribune* and the *Times* were in the main body of the paper).

Table 4.1: Where do we find news about economic growth?

Business/Economy/Finance sections	50.1%
News article in main body of newspaper	38.7%
Comment/Opinion/Editorial in main body of newspaper	11.2%

Table 4.2: How is economic growth presented?

	Clearly positive	Assumed as positive	Just the facts	Negative	Positive and negative	Total
US News	20%	77%	1%	0.5%	1.5%	100%
UK News	12%	81%	4%	0.5%	2.5%	100%
Total	**15%**	**79.5%**	**3%**	**0.5%**	**2%**	**100%**

Critiques of the growth model take place at a broad societal or economic level. Articles written from the perspective of a particular business sector – such as housing, retail or manufacturing – are likely to see growth as positive because, from this purely sectional set of interests, growth *is* likely to be good for business. However, we found that most articles – 80% in our sample – address 'the economy' on a broader, macro-economic level, either dealing with the economy as a whole or broad economic and political issues (such as regulation, taxation or employment). A majority were, in this sense, dealing with broad questions of national concern, rather than narrower, sectional interests.

Despite this, our headline finding, outlined in Table 4.2, suggests that the idea that growth is good remains deeply embedded, and that the economic, social (quality of life) and environmental critiques are generally ignored. While all the newspapers in our sample claim to separate fact from opinion, we found only a small proportion of articles (5%) that adopted a neutral position on the subject of economic growth – either by referring to both positive and negative aspects of growth (in 2% cases) or by avoiding any value laden language (in 3% cases). The overwhelming majority (94.5%) stated or assumed economic growth was unambiguously positive – either by their use of language or by overt statements – while only 0.5% (just 3 out of 591 articles) gave voice to more critical positions.

Although UK newspapers were more than twice as likely to offer value-free or balanced assessments of growth (6.5% as opposed to 2.5%), and a little less inclined to be overtly pro-growth, the 'pro-growth' slant is clearly present on both sides of the Atlantic.

Table 4.3 suggests that this slant is present in all sections of the newspaper. If there are references to negative aspects of growth these are more likely to be found *outside* the Business/Economy/Finance sections. While this is not entirely surprising, it does provide an

Table 4.3: How is economic growth presented in different newspaper sections?

	Clearly positive	Assumed as positive	Just the facts	Negative	Positive and negative	Total
Business/Economic	15%	81%	3%	0.5%	0.5%	100%
News articles	14%	78.5%	2.5%	1%	4%	100%
Comment/Opinion	16.5%	76%	4.5%	0.5%	3%	100%

indication that the growth of business news, as a genre, is not politically innocent, and that it tends to narrow the range of discourses available in discussions of the broader economy.

Table 4.2 shows that, overall, 15% of articles substantiated their pro-growth stance with evidence. In most cases, however, the benefits of growth were assumed rather than explained, assumptions conveyed by the use of positive or pejorative language. This example from the *Guardian* is typical of the language used – a no growth economy is portrayed as a 'bleak' and 'stagnant' place:

> The Office for National Statistics confirmed the economy grew by 0.5% in the first three months of the year after contracting 0.5% in the last three months of 2010. Analysis showing the economy stagnated for much of last summer reveals *an even bleaker picture* of zero growth for eight months.
>
> (The *Guardian* 29th June, 2011, our emphasis)

The dominant metaphor is one of movement (as in 'we need to get the economy moving again') where growth is associating with progress and moving forward. This article from the *New York Times* is a typical example of the 'moving forward' metaphor:

> The reports suggested growth was being hampered by a combination of bad weather at home and supply disruptions caused by the March earthquake in Japan, and analysts said the economy should regain momentum by the second half of the year.
>
> (The *New York Times* 20th May, 2011)

The fact that the positive nature of growth is much more likely to be assumed than explicitly stated is, in many ways, indicative of the degree to which it is embedded in conventional wisdom – an idea so well established that it no longer needs asserting.

We explored this further by looking for instances in which articles indicated what some of the benefits of growth might be (whether or not the article itself adopted a positive stance). As we have indicated, most articles (94.5%) suggest that economic growth is positive. Table 4.4 shows that while many articles either provided reasons for or alluded to the benefits of growth (by, for example, associating it with lower unemployment), most (52.5%) do not. The absence of discussion about the benefits of growth is striking – particularly in the British press, where, despite a general sense of enthusiasm, 59% of articles offered no tangible reasons for pursuing the growth model.

Table 4.4: Were reasons given for asserting growth good?

	UK press	US press	Total
Yes, reasons given	14%	23%	**18%**
Reasons alluded to	27%	34%	**29.5%**
No	59%	43%	**52.5%**

Because the benefits of growth tend to be assumed, many articles concern themselves with the best way to encourage growth – a source of considerable discussion and debate amongst economists. One such article in the *Daily Telegraph* concludes:

> Still, slow growth is better than none. With growth of less than 1 per cent this year, Britain is increasing exports, particularly in manufacturing. A total of 286,000 new jobs have been created. Helped by the weak pound, we are staggering back to our feet. Progress is likely to remain painfully slow.
>
> (The *Daily Telegraph* 24th November, 2010)

While the article pays little attention to the benefits of economic growth (the mention of jobs is ambiguous here, since new jobs have been created despite low growth) the metaphorical flow – a nation 'staggering' forward at a 'painfully slow' pace – leaves the reader in no doubt that growth is, for whatever reason, key to the nation's health.

A *Guardian* article under the headline 'Economy: Holidays hit growth' was based on similar assumptions, suggesting that an extra days holiday for the royal wedding – creating a 4-day weekend – was problematic because it impeded growth:

> One problem is the paucity of working days this month. How can the economy grow in the second quarter when there are only 18 working days? The royal wedding bank holiday tomorrow and the mass exodus of workers linking Easter with May Day, usually a quiet time for long foreign holidays, could depress the figures. A similar extra day for the Queen's golden jubilee in 2002 affected growth.
>
> (The *Guardian* 28th April, 2011)

The pleasure afforded by an extra day off, in other words, is offset by the negative impact on economic growth. This begs a larger question. The quality of life data suggests we benefit more, collectively, from having more free time than more money (Coote, Simms and Franklin 2010; Layard 2011) evidence that is over-ridden in this article by the conventional wisdom that priorities growth in one area (income) over another (growth in free time).

Table 4.5: Economic growth is good because it …[5]

	UK press	US press	UK and US
Creates employment	59%	72%	65%
Creates collective/corporate/individual well-being	41.5%	35%	38%
Reduces the national debt	23%	15%	19%
Has a positive political impact	15%	12%	13%
Is good for the public sector	4%	2%	3%
Has a positive effect on the environment	0.5%	0.5%	0.5%

Those articles that did offer details on the benefits of growth offered various reasons, listed in Table 4.5. The most commonly referenced benefit, in both Britain and the United States, is that economic growth creates employment.

The link between growth and employment is particularly strong in US newspapers: this example from the *Washington Post* was particularly explicit:

> The U.S. economy needs to grow about 2.5 percent annually to keep unemployment steady given continual growth in the labor force and in worker efficiency; even stronger GDP growth is needed to bring unemployment down.
>
> (The *Washington Post* 29th April, 2011)

There is, of course, a verifiable connection between growth and employment. What tends to be ignored is consideration of other ways of tackling unemployment – notably, a reduction in the working week (see Coote, Simms and Franklin 2010; Jackson 2010).

The second most commonly acclaimed benefit of economic growth – the idea that growth improves our well-being – is far more speculative. A leader article from the *Times*, for example, opened with the premise that we needed growth to cheer us up:

> *First job is to restore the nation's spirit of optimism.* Growth is good, whatever some environmentalists might say. Increasing the rate of economic growth, even by a little over a long period, makes a big difference to a country's prosperity.
>
> (The *Times* 21st June 2011)

This implication here is firmly tied to conventional wisdom about the nature of prosperity, and yet, as we have suggested, the idea that growth has a positive effects on our collective prosperity and well-being is questionable at best. The growing body of evidence on this topic suggests that there is *no* link between economic growth and well-being – or indeed, most other positive social indicators (from health to crime).

The third most common reason for promoting economic growth was to provide revenues to reduce levels of national debt. As the *Times* put it:

> The deterioration in the Government's finances is partly the result of much weaker growth, which will drag down tax revenues.
>
> (The *Times* 24th March, 2011)

This point is widely accepted – even by critics of a growth model – but it offers only a partial view. So for example, both the United Kingdom and the United States devote a significant proportion of government spending to defence, and a reduction to more moderate military spending levels could make major inroads into deficit reduction without damaging public services. None of the 591 articles we looked at raised this or any other alternatives to growth-related solutions (such as the possibility of reducing working hours to maintain employment levels). The overwhelming picture, in sum, was of a relentless need to maintain – or regain – the momentum of economic growth and to ignore other ways of tackling problems like debt and unemployment.

When royalty is on the margins: Questioning the growth model

Only a handful of articles – 3 out of 591 – focused on the negative aspects of economic growth, while 12 (2% or the sample) made references to negative aspects alongside more positive assessments (we found one other reference to negative aspects of growth in an article that otherwise took a positive view). The numbers in Table 4.6 are so small that it would be unwise to draw any conclusions from them beyond their paucity. It is worth noting, nonetheless, that in the British press the most conspicuous downside of growth is its environmental impact – an idea entirely absent in US coverage.

Interestingly, most of these more critical references did not appear in the more left-leaning newspaper titles. On the contrary, we found 9 of the 11 references in the United Kingdom in the right-leaning *Telegraph* and *Times* and only one in the left-leaning *Guardian* (the 5 US references were spread across the 4 US titles). We should, however, note that these more right-leaning titles were *also* more likely to report calls for scrapping environmental regulation and green taxes. This article from the *Telegraph* is fairly typical:

> HIGH tax rates, red tape and 'green' regulations are choking off the economic recovery, a number of leading economists declare today. George Osborne should lighten the burden on companies to help the economy return to growth, the experts say in a letter to *The Daily Telegraph* … The real threat to growth, they claim, is tax and regulation, including environmental levies such as fuel duty, taxes on North Sea oil and European Union emissions limits 'Tax, regulation and expensive, ill designed "green" measures will not cure our problems', the experts write. 'Indeed, the economic evidence suggests that they are strangling our recovery'.
>
> (The *Telegraph* 8th June, 2011)

In the same spirit, most of these references to negative aspects of growth fell well short of any serious questioning of the growth model. The environmental consequences of growth, for

Table 4.6: Number of references to negative consequences of growth (*n=591*).

	Quality of life	Economic issues	Environment	Total
US	3	2	0	5
UK	2	2	7	11
Total	5	4	7	16

example, were usually overridden by an appeal to 'green growth', with investment in clean technologies. So, for example, an article in the *Times* about the growth of car usage dwells briefly on the clash between economic growth and the environment, before suggesting that technology will provide the answer for the maintenance of both:

> In the long run the improvement of our roads will increase road usage, and while this advances the economy it is potentially bad news for the environment. But the answer is to reduce the pollution and noise caused by cars, not to constrain the traffic.
>
> (The *Times* 17th May, 2011)

In other words, we should protect the environment as long as we do not constrain the traffic – a metaphor, in many ways, for the way in which critical views are absorbed by the growth model. An article in the *Telegraph* ('Proof that green means growth') while more sympathetic to the importance of the environment, also attempted to align environmentalism with the politics of growth, arguing that

> Investing just 2 per cent of GDP a year into such projects as energy efficiency and renewable sources … would quickly produce greater growth, while saving an average of £467 billion a year in energy costs over the next 40 years and bringing global warming under control.
>
> (The *Telegraph* 5th March, 2011)

Research on the news coverage of climate change suggests that this focus on 'techno-solutions' to environmental problems is fairly typical of environmental coverage more generally, which tends to avoid dealing with solutions that involve reducing consumption (Lewis and Boyce 2009).

As we have suggested, while these techno-solutions provide a discursive solution to the problem of the environment, they conceal an increasing tension between the two. Any simple economic/environmental modelling shows that every percentage point we add to economic growth makes the targets for reducing greenhouse gas emissions (suggested by the IPCC, amongst others) considerably more difficult to achieve (Jackson 2010).

Similarly, the few references to quality of life as a marker of progress tended to portray these measures as existing *alongside* GDP growth as an indicator of human development. Only two articles dealt with the most dramatic finding of quality of life research – namely the failure of growth to improve quality of life in developed countries. These were a book review (in which the reviewer adopted a faintly mocking, sceptical attitude) and a single report of a speech by Prince Charles (in the *Times*[6]).

The speech by Prince Charles is notable because it offered a more thorough-going critique of growth (referring to evidence that growth fails to promote well-being while damaging the environment) than anything else in our sample. We did find two other reports of the speech, both of which missed what might appear to be a radical – and newsworthy – challenge to the dominant consumer capitalist consensus by the world's most famous heir to the throne.

Both focused on his comments on the environment rather than his broader questioning of the economic growth orthodoxy.

The fact that the most critical voice in our sample was a member of the British Royal family is, in many ways, bizarre. It highlights the notable absence of many other people – notably critical economists, environmental and social scientists – who might have offered a very different view of the merits of growth. Nearly all the sources quoted in our sample came from the political, financial and business sectors, all of who were tied to the growth orthodoxy – the same people, one might add, who failed to see the looming financial crisis created by weak financial regulation and the credit crunch. No one from groups like the New Economics Foundation – whose research offers a trenchant critique of the growth model – was quoted in our entire sample.[7]

This is not to say that there is no debate about economic growth, but the terms of the debate are emphatically *not* about its desirability as our central economic and political goal. Nearly half the article in both countries (47% of articles in the United States, 48% in the United Kingdom) referred to the need for government action to encourage growth, and another quarter (24% of articles in both countries) reported or debated the way in which their respective governments were tackling the need for growth. Voices on the right tended to converge on the need to cut taxes and regulation, while voices on the left tended to promote a more Keynesian approach.

Our role, as citizens, is highly constrained by this debate. We are urged by both sides to keep on consuming in order to put momentum back into a sluggish economy (even if this means increasing our personal debt), while the benefits of so doing are assumed rather than examined. Our failure to do so is seen only as a problem, as this article from the *New York Times* puts it:

> For now, it is clear that the traditional drivers of recovery – consumer spending and residential real estate – have failed to rebound, with the latest report showing consumers extremely cautious about spending on anything and the housing market stuck at its post-bubble lows.
>
> (*The New York Times* 31st July, 2011)

The crisis, here, is not the sense of malaise that manifests itself in advanced consumerist economies or the environmental problems ahead, but a *lack* of consumerism:

> Weak demand leads to slow growth, and slow growth leads to high and rising unemployment, which then reinforces weak demand and slow growth, and so on, in a vicious cycle from which the economy, obviously, has found no escape.
>
> (*The New York Times* 31st July, 2011)

This view of the world is widely held yet narrow. It could be argued, alternatively, that the 'vicious cycle' is built into the consumer capitalist model itself, with the constant need to accumulate goods to sustain a never-ending need for economic growth. Despite the mounting body of evidence to support this alternative view, in the US and British press it appears that you won't be able – yet – to read all about it.

Concluding remarks

The economic, social and environmental critiques of consumer capitalism based on economic growth have emerged in response to its increasing failure to promote human progress. And the more we commit to economic growth, the more compelling these critiques become. They do not propose an immediate abandonment of growth-based consumer capitalism: there are too many structural features of modern life – notably, the need to create employment – that depend upon it. But they make a strong case for rethinking our commitment to a growth model, and for creating the conditions for what Tim Jackson calls 'prosperity without growth'.

On a more profound level, we need the critical space to re-examine our understanding of human progress, to question the increasingly lazy assumption that conflates progress with quantitative – more money, more things – rather than more qualitative measures (such as the pursuit of meaning, fulfilment and a good society). But to do this we need to open public debate beyond the narrow confines in which it is so patently trapped.

It would be unfair to blame the news media for its failure to question the growth orthodoxy – they are, after all, very much in line with the dominant political consensus. But they are, nonetheless, in a pivotal position to begin to question this conventional wisdom and open up a more productive debate – one that might allow us to imagine new forms of human progress outside the confines of consumerism.

This requires a journalism that genuinely embraces the new rather than the current obsession with the more ersatz 'newness' of being up to date (Lewis 2010). There are, of course, many impediments to this – not least the growth of the fairly uncritical genre of business news. But if we take an optimistic view, we can see how such a paradigm shift might be incorporated within the routines of news reporting.

Journalism finds it difficult to deal with probabilities: it tends to assume some contested ideas (such as the 'growth is good' orthodoxy) as objective fact and others (like, for example, climate change) as controversial, requiring two sides to be balanced against one another. It is time, we would suggest, to shift the reporting of economic growth towards that more contested terrain.

References

BBC Trust (2007), *Report of the Independent Panel for the BBC Trust on Impartiality of BBC Business Coverage*, London: BBC Trust, pp. 15–16.

Bok, D. (2010), *The Politics of Happiness: What Government Can Learn from the New Research on Well-Being*, Princeton: Princeton University Press.

Brecher, J and Costello, T. (1994), *Global Village or Global Pillage: Economic Reconstruction From the Bottom Up*, Cambridge, MA: South End Press.

Brierley, S. (2002), *The Advertising Handbook,* 2nd edn, London: Routledge.

Campbell. C. (1989), *The Romantic Ethic and the Spirit of Modern Consumerism*, Oxford: Blackwell.

Coote, A. Simms, A. and Franklin, J. (2010), '21 hours: Why a shorter working week can help us all to flourish in the 21st century', http://www.neweconomics.org/publications/21-hours.

Cushion, S. (2012), *The Democratic Value of News: Why Public Service Media Matters*, Basingstoke: Palgrave Macmillan.

Fukuyama, F. (1992), *The End of History and the Last Man*, London. Hamish Hamilton.

Gabrys, J. (2007), 'Media in the dump', in J. Knechtel (ed.), *Alphabet City: Trash*, Cambridge: MIT Press, pp. 156–65.

Galbraith, J. K. (1987), *The Affluent Society*, Harmondsworth: Penguin, p. 127.

Giles, M. (1993), 'Indigestion: A survey of the food industry', *Economist,* 4th December, pp. 1–18.

Glasgow Media Group (1976), *Bad News*, London: Routledge.

Glasgow Media Group (1980), *More Bad News*, London: Routledge.

Glasgow Media Group (1982), *Really Bad News*, London: Routledge.

Harvey, F. (2011), 'World headed for irreversible climate change in five years, IEA warns', *Guardian,* 9th November at http://www.guardian.co.uk/environment/2011/nov/09/fossil-fuel-infrastructure-climate-change.

Inter-governmental Panel on Climate Change (IPCC) (2007), *Climate Change 2007 – Synthesis Report*, Cambridge University Press, p. 44.

Iyengar, S. and Lepper, M. (2000), 'When choice is demotivating: Can one desire too much of a good thing?', *Journal of Personality and Social Psychology*, 79: 6, pp. 995–1006.

Jackson, T. (2010), *Prosperity without Growth? The Transition to a Sustainable Economy,* London: Sustainable Development Commission.

James. O. (2007), *Affluenza*, London: Vermilion.

Jhally, S. (2006), *The Spectacle of Accumulation*, New York: Peter Lang, pp. 99–112.

Kasser, T. (2002), *The High Price of Materialism,* Cambridge, MA: MIT Press.

Kuehr, R. and Williams, E. (2003) (eds), *Computers and the Environment: Understanding and Managing their Impacts,* London: Springer-Verlag.

Layard, R. (2011), *Happiness, Lessons from a New Science*, London: Penguin.

Lewis, J. and Boyce, T. (2009), 'Climate change and the media: The scale of the challenge', in T. Boyce and J. Lewis (eds), *Climate Change and the Media,* New York: Peter Lang.

Lewis, J. (2010), 'Democratic or disposable? 24-hour news, consumer culture and built-in obsolescence', in S. Cushion and J. Lewis (eds), *The Rise of 24-Hour News Television,* New York: Peter Lang.

Marcuse, H. (1964), *One-Dimensional Man: Studies in the Ideology of Advanced Industrial Society,* Boston: Beacon Press.

McKibben, W. (2006), *The End of Nature*, New York: Random House.

Offer, A. (2006), *The Challenge of Affluence: Self-Control and Well-Being in the United States and Britain since 1950*, Oxford: Oxford University Press.

Owen, N., Inderwildi, O. and King, D. (2010), 'The status of conventional world oil reserves – Hype or cause for concern?', *Energy Policy,* 38: 8, pp. 4743–49.

Packard, V. (1960), *The Waste Makers*, Harmondsworth: Penguin.

Rantanen, T. (2009), *When News Was New,* Oxford: Wiley-Blackwell.

Roush, C. (2006), 'The need for more business education in mass communication schools', *Journalism and Mass Communication Educator,* 61: 2, pp. 196–204.

Schor, J. (1991), *The Overworked American: The Unexpected Decline of Leisure*, New York: Basic.

Schor, J. (2004), *Born to Buy*, New York: Scribner.

Svennevig, M. (2007), *BBC Coverage of Business in the UK: A Content Analysis of Business News Coverage,* London: BBC Trust.

Veenhoven, R. 'World Happiness Database', available at www2. eur.nl/fsw/research/happiness.

Wilkinson, R. and Pickett, K. (2009), *The Spirit Level: Why Equality is Better for Everyone,* London: Penguin.

Notes

1   BusinessWeek, 1998.

2   'The Tyranny of Choice', *Economist*, 16th December, 2010. http://www.economist.com/node/17723028.

3   From 29th September, 2010 to 20th July, 2011.

4   These were the *Chicago Tribune*, the *LA Times*, the *New York Times* and the *Washington Post* in the United States and the *Guardian*, the *Independent*, the *Telegraph* and the *Times* in the United Kingdom.

5   Because a number of articles contained more than one reason, percentages add up to more than 100%.

6   On 9th February, 2011.

7   We did find a series of three article in the *Independent* that featured NEF sources just outside our sample period (in September 2010), but no other newspapers picked up the story.

Chapter 5

Conflict of interest disclosure in economics: Will journalists aid the cause?

George DeMartino

Introduction

The film *Inside Job* provoked serious concerns amongst business and economic journalists and policy-makers about the independence and reliability of the policy-relevant work of academic economists. In particular, the film raised awareness in regard to two features of contemporary economic practice. First, many leading academic economists routinely secure very substantial income from outside interests, and then produce research and take positions on pressing policy matters of concern to those interests. Second, these economists do not always provide a full disclosure of their apparent conflicts of interest (COIs). While the film identified just a few instances of high profile and influential economists who appear to have failed to provide adequate disclosure of their conflicts of interest, subsequent research by economists Carrick-Hagenbarth and Epstein (2012, published digitally in 2010), and by journalists Emily Flitter, Kristina Cooke and Pedro da Costa (2010) documented many more instances of failures to disclose. These studies leave the clear impression that the norm in economics, unlike in medicine and many other professions, is not to disclose conflicts. Indeed, prior to late 2010 (when the film appeared) many economists failed to recognize the existence of apparent or real conflicts of interest in which they were implicated, let alone their duty to disclose them.

Under scrutiny from the outside – especially from business and economic journalists – leading economic associations began to explore the need for COI disclosure rules in late 2010; and by the end of 2012 several had come to adopt guidelines or codes. In the United States, the American Economic Association (AEA) strengthened its pre-existing disclosure rules in January 2012. The new rules mandate disclosure of various conflicts whenever authors publish in its journals. Notably, the AEA also adopted a guideline that urges economists to make full disclosure whenever publishing anywhere, or otherwise providing their expertise. In January 2012 the Toulouse School of Economics (2012) adopted a 'Scientific Integrity Statement', which involves inter alia the creation of an Ethics Committee. In July 2012 the main German economic association, Verein für Socialpolitik (2012), adopted a new (substantially weaker) ethical COI code. In August 2012 the National Bureau of Economic Research (NBER) in the US implemented very strong disclosure rules, and in September 2012 the Paris School of Economics (2012) adopted a set of 'Transparency Principles'.

To date, however, the uptake in COI rules has been very slow. Of the 47 economic associations that belong to the Allied Social Sciences Association (ASSA) in the United States, for instance, only 7 make mention of ethics on their websites, and only a few of these impose COI disclosure rules for their journals. By and large, then, economists today are on their own to decide whether to report COIs when publishing their research.

On the limitations of the codes

The new attention to COI disclosure is important – it is in the interest of individual economists and the economics profession to have clear, strong COI disclosure rules (Carrick-Hagenbarth and Epstein 2012). Clear rules provide guidance to virtuous economists who want to behave properly on just what are conflicts, when they should be reported, and how. At the same time, individual economists and the profession as a whole benefit from the trust-building function of disclosure rules (Thompson forthcoming). And on the presumption that the rules are adequate and widely followed by economists, the public benefits by being provided with information that is vital to their judgments about the policy or other advice of individual economists – just as they do from the disclosure by physicians of their associations with pharmaceutical companies.

That said, the new codes by themselves are not apt to provide sufficient protection against COI in economics, at least in the US context. First, only that portion of the new AEA guidelines that relates to publishing in its own journals are enforceable by the Association. There is no licensing for economists, of course, and no mechanisms by which the AEA or other economic associations can sanction economists who simply ignore the duty to disclose COIs except when publishing in their own journals. While economic associations can adopt rules that allow them to cancel the membership of any economist who violates their disclosure guidelines, this is a fairly mild form of sanction since professional association membership in economics is often endured as a mild burden rather than a consequential privilege.

Second, even in those professions where COI disclosure has a long history and is mandated by code or statute, there are generally inadequate mechanisms for policing disclosure obligations (DeMartino 2011a). Institutions that employ professionals often do not have sufficient incentive to police COI aggressively. A 2009 report by the Inspector General of the Department of Health and Human Services of the US government found that

> 90 percent of universities relied solely on [medical] researchers themselves to decide whether the money they made in consulting and other relationships with drug and device makers was relevant to their government-financed research, while half of universities do not ask their faculty members to disclose the amount of money or stock they make from drug and device makers.
>
> (Harris 9th November, 2009: A17)

Moreover, Eric Campbell of Harvard Medical School claims that universities often fail to police federal conflict of interest rules out of fear of losing their 'star researchers' (Harris 9th November, 2009: A17).

Help from beyond?

These considerations suggest that resolving the COI problem in economics might require the participation of those outside the profession and, especially, consumers in the market for economic expertise. One type of consumer with the interest in and ability to police COI disclosure in economics comes to mind: business and economic journalists. In the aftermath of *Inside Job* it seemed that these users were both embarrassed by their ignorance of potential conflicts of interest amongst the economists they routinely engaged for economic analysis, and angered by the failure of these economists to disclose their financial entanglements. It also seemed that they would henceforth demand full disclosure from academic economists when relying on their expertise. At the time I expected that the demand from consumers of economic expertise for full disclosure would overwhelm any resistance on the part of the profession itself to introduce or police new disclosure rules. One exchange that I had with an economic columnist at a leading publication in January 2011 is worth sharing. The interview concerned how the AEA might solve the problem of inadequate disclosure amongst its members (and other economists). In the context of our discussion I asked whether the columnist routinely asked academic physicians if they had any conflict of interest when interviewing them about the virtues of new drugs. He said, 'Yes, of course.' I then asked whether he and his colleagues also routinely asked academic economists for full disclosure when interviewing them about matters pertaining to public policy. Here is his reply: '(Expletive!) We don't! We should!'

Have the consumers of economic expertise altered their behaviour vis-à-vis economic disclosure since the appearance of *Inside Job*? To begin to explore this issue we contacted 20 business and economic journalists, asking amongst other things whether the media outlet for which they worked had adopted new policies that required its journalists to demand full disclosure when interviewing economists; or whether the respondents themselves had amended their practices even in the absence of new rules. We targeted a subset of the many journalists who had written about the lessons of *Inside Job* or the problem of inadequate disclosure in economics between the fall of 2010 and the fall of 2012. Not only are these journalists aware of the problem of inadequate disclosure in economics, they are also apt to know of changes in institutional policies, and they are most likely to alter their own behaviour even in the absence of new policy.

The results or the informal survey are mixed but on the whole, disappointing. On the one hand, not one of the respondents identified any policy changes by their employing institutions regarding the need to extract full disclosure from economists of potential COI when interviewing them on matters of public policy. One respondent expressed frustration at his own publisher's unwillingness to implement reform. Paraphrasing, he had this to say:[1]

Mainstream economists are angry. The confidence in the profession has been eroded by 'cowboys' who know nothing; they are offended by what some of their members are doing. The economic associations are now implementing new codes of conduct. So the economics profession says we have to change. But journalism? Here we see no changes at all. Our publication doesn't question its own practices.

But did journalists alter their own behaviour, despite the absence of new rules? The interviews reveal a range of responses. One prominent business journalist, David Cay Johnston, argued that journalists' practices have not changed at all. He went on to say:

> My guess is that hardly anyone even knows about this issue. I know my editors at the time AEA brought up [the new COI disclosure policy] … were about as interested in it as they are in how the creation of capacity markets for electricity undermines the whole idea of electricity generation as a competitive business. If your eyes are glazing over right now I am not surprised.

A second kind of response, provided by several journalists, indicated that they had always been vigilant when interviewing economists. It is difficult to know how to square this response with the surprise expressed by many journalists in the wake of *Inside Job* though it is likely that some business journalists had always searched for potential conflicts when interviewing academic economists. As one respondent put it,

> If we do not know that one of our academic sources has a historical relationship with a particular industry or interest group, we have not done a thorough job on one of the first steps of writing a news story. This kind of skepticism is built into the news writing process.

Other respondents claimed that they had in fact altered their own behaviour when interviewing or reporting the research of academic economists. As one journalist put it:

> Personally, I have been more careful about who I interview and about trying to determine what agenda might be behind research, especially on items that land in my e-mail box.

And another:

> I am more sensitive to the issue these days but I can't say I make it a formal part of my due diligence. A lot depends on the nature of the research – if it is potentially commercially sensitive one is more cautious about the background of the researchers.

Johnston expressed the view that the emphasis on disclosure was somewhat misplaced. In his view, the real problems concerning the objectivity of one's economic sources ran deeper. In his words:

[The] problem is not just with disclosure. It also goes to actual relationships, which are often far more important than disclosure. Journalists often use disclosure as an easy proxy for conduct. And we are, of course, limited to what we can document. I generally ask people I interview if they have any sources, jobs, investments or relationships I should know about. I typically take people at their word, which is an important point.

One theme emerged in the interviews was surprising since it was only tangentially related to the questions that we put to the journalists. At least some business journalists believe that they are now more astute and sophisticated consumers of economic research owing to what they view as the extraordinary failures of the economics profession over the past two decades. Rather than accept at face value economic analysis, these journalists now believe themselves to be more sceptical about the capacities of leading economists. In the words of one respondent,

I have become more careful and skeptical because of what has happened, starting back in the late 90s, but especially after 08, rather than because of the AEA and NBER rules.

In the words of another:

The response of the journalistic community has been to conduct a tremendous cultural post-mortem in the wake of the financial crisis, similar to the one carried out after the Iraq invasion. As financial journalists, we are still asking ourselves how we could have called farce on the bubbles in credit and real estate and why we didn't do more to highlight the dangers of predatory lending and reckless mortgage securitization. We realize the people we saw before as economic gurus are more like snake oil peddlers, and we promise to do a better job next time.

Accounting for the failures

I see now that my own expectations in early 2011 regarding the reform of rules and practices amongst journalists and media outlets were naïve. What factors might account for this? Here, the interviews shed some light as well. Indeed, respondents cited several factors that might weigh against adequate due diligence surrounding economists' disclosure of COIs.

First, one journalist argued that substantial budget and staffing cuts along with shifting priorities at his publication has led to the elimination of in-house economic expertise:

Thirty years ago, there would have been in-house independent economic experts; now, though, that's not the case; and so the journalists have to rely on outside expertise.

In his view, journalists are now in a position of dependence vis- à-vis outside economists, and so the preservation of good relationships with them is more important today than in the past.

Second, in the view of one respondent only certain kinds of economists are accepted as legitimate providers of that outside expertise, and these are necessarily conflicted by virtue of their affiliations. In his words:

[T]he only kind of economic expertise this is sanctioned is financial sector economists … It is now accepted that you can call on only banking institution economists … what the media wants to be said will be more easily said by this kind of economist; the media routinely turns most to economists who will say just what the media wants to hear.

This reporter emphasized the herd mentality amongst the leading financial economists, and the difficulty of introducing economic pluralism into business news reporting. He claimed that some business journalists today are attempting to push back against demands to limit the range of economic experts who can be consulted, but that his institution at least has proven to be unreceptive to dissenting voices in economics.

A third problem concerns complications associated with the changing forms of news reporting and commentary that leave many journalists little time or opportunity to undertake intensive due diligence when citing economists (or other experts). As Johnston put it, 'Many online outfits these days expect their staff to crank out piece after piece so there is little time to ask such questions.' Another identified a change in the nature of reporting, away from investigation to 'curation', which places the burden for due diligence onto the reader or audience. Regarding online and social media reporting he said

That type of journalism favors volume and speed, getting information out, rather than vetting it or coming up with original research and analysis. A tweet, for example, will include a link to the original source, where the reader is allowed to come to his or her own conclusion. Even in our longer stories, we are including links to the original sources of our data. So I would say you have these two conflicting currents in journalism, which for a lack of better term I would refer to as objectivism and subjectivism. Objectivism would seek to vet information more thoroughly and to be more skeptical given the fallout from the crisis. The other argues we are less gatekeepers than curators and should point readers towards the stream of information, leaving them to come to their own conclusions and allowing them to contribute to the conversation. Expertise and authority carries a different importance in this approach, and the assumption is that everyone has a bias.

A final problem bears mention (though it did not arise in the interviews). It relates to the concern expressed by one respondent about the culpability of the business press in the events that spawned the crisis of 2008 (summarized above). In particular, the 'cultural post-mortem' to which he refers also involves an investigation of business journalists' own COI issues. Could it be that some of the leading journalists who are entrusted with independent oversight of financial institutions and markets are themselves conflicted by virtue of their financial entanglements – or by personal relationships that must be preserved so that they can sustain important sources within the industry?

A recent article that appeared in the *Columbia Journalism Review* by Paul Starobin (2012) sheds some light on this matter. Starobin reports that leading business journalists frequently accept invitations to give talks to business audiences, and that some of them are rewarded handsomely for their troubles.

The list of business writers who actively seek speaking engagements for hire at Wall Street events 'is star-studded'.

> The list includes Michael Lewis, a best-selling author and contributing editor to *Vanity Fair*; Niall Ferguson, the author, Harvard professor, and a featured contributor to *Newsweek* and *The Daily Beast*; James Surowiecki, who writes 'The Financial Page' column for *The New Yorker*; and James B. Stewart, the author and Pulitzer Prize-winning journalist who has written widely for newspapers and magazines.

Fees can be considerable. Starobin reports that Niall Ferguson's 'booking fee range is $50,001 and up', while Fareed Zakaria ('host of the weekly CNN show *Fareed Zakaria GPS*') receives $75,000 per speaking engagement. His recent client list includes 'Baker Capital, Catterton Partners, Driehaus Capital Management, ING, Merrill Lynch, Oak Investment Partners, Charles Schwab, and T. Rowe Price'.

If financial entanglements of economists are problematic, so must they be for those professionals upon whom society depends for independent investigative reporting. At a minimum, accepting fees from a firm or industry may alter what the journalist believes he can do, ethically, in subsequent work. According to Starobin,

> A financial journalist who has been paid for speeches by Wall Street firms told me that he would never write a story about any company that has paid him a fee. Great, except that the more speaking he does, the more he will be restricting his range of coverage.

Equally troubling, of course, is the effect of the financial entanglements on the reporting that the journalist subsequently undertakes.

> Unconscious self-censorship could be a factor, too, as journalists who enjoy Wall Street's money might come to feel more simpatico toward their benefactors' perspectives on various issues. It's a pretty typical human reaction, after all. *The New York Times* reported recently that doctors who take money from drug makers often are more willing than doctors who don't to prescribe drugs in 'risky' ways. Why should journalists be any more immune to this than physicians are?

Starobin reports on recent efforts by leading media institutions to tighten rules pertaining to COI amongst its staff. The *Wall Street Journal* now bans all paid speeches by staff, as well as reimbursement by outside interests for travel or other expenses. Other institutions have rules of varying strength. But, as Starobin explains, these rules generally apply only to those on the institution's staff. Hence:

> The bad news is that these institutional ethical standards are likely to become less meaningful as the number of salaried journalists continues to shrink and the ranks of independent journalists, without a permanent staff affiliation, continue to grow. These reporters are free to effectively draft their own ethics policies. In such a media universe, the ethical trajectory is apt to be downward, as experience suggests that it is corporate management that provides the hard push for strict standards.

Conclusion

There is certainly much greater awareness today than there was before *Inside Job,* within economics and beyond, about the problem of COI amongst academic economists, and about their failure to disclose these conflicts. Moreover, there have been important gestures within economics to promote COI disclosure, especially in the form of new rules and guidelines. But I think it is reasonable to conclude that the changes to date in rules and norms are inadequate. On the one hand, the economics profession has done far too little – especially in its insistence that the only problem that needs fixing is the failure of economists to disclose conflicts. So far, the profession has demonstrated no interest in promoting a careful investigation into whether and when academic economists should refuse extra-curricular opportunities that could compromise the integrity of their scholarship and teaching, or seriously undermine public trust. On the other hand, there appears to be much less pressure on economists from the business press than we might have expected in early 2011 to ensure adequate disclosure (let alone to dissuade economists from placing themselves in conflicted positions in the first place).

These insights compel the conclusion that the economic profession needs to do far better in constructing mechanisms that ensure appropriate COI disclosure, on the one hand, and awareness about the complexity of the matter of COI, on the other. The former might involve coordinated efforts with universities and research organizations, as Carrick-Hagenbarth and Epstein (forthcoming) suggest, the establishment by the AEA of an online clearinghouse for information about economists' conflicts, as economist Peter Dorman suggests, or other mechanisms (see DeMartino 2011b). Raising awareness about the complexity of COI in economics requires something more ambitious. The time has come for the economics profession to launch professional economic ethics as a new field of inquiry into what it means to be an ethical economist, and what it would mean for economics to be an ethical profession (DeMartino 2011a). Managing COIs in economics requires much deeper understanding of the problem than economists typically display (Thompson forthcoming). And yet, COI is amongst the simpler of the ethical challenges facing economists. If we cannot make substantial headway on that problem, absent a tradition of careful inquiry, then it should be clear that we cannot and will not begin to resolve the more intractable ethical problems until we marshal the energy and commitment to inaugurate and sustain the field of professional economic ethics.

Acknowledgement

Thanks to Patrick Sutherland and Noelle Frampton for research assistance on this project, and to participants at the ASE session where the paper was presented.

References

Carrick-Hagenbarth, J. and Epstein, G. (2012), 'Dangerous interconnectedness: Economists' conflicts of interest, ideology and financial crisis', *Cambridge Journal of Economics,* 36: 1, pp. 43–63.

Carrick-Hagenbarth, J. and Epstein, G. (Forthcoming), 'Considerations on Conflicts of Interest in Academic Economics', in G. DeMartino and D. McCloskey (eds), *The Oxford University Press Handbook of Professional Economic Ethics*, New York: Oxford University Press.

DeMartino, G. (2011a), *The Economist's Oath: On the Need for and Content of Professional Economic Ethics*, New York: Oxford University Press.

DeMartino, G. (2011b), 'Full disclosure in economics – the role of the economic associations', *TripleCrisis*, 14th January. Available at http://triplecrisis.com/full-disclosure-in-economics/.

Flitter, E., Cooke, K. and da Costa, P. (2010), 'Special report: For some professors, disclosure is academic', *Reuters*, 20th December.

Katz, D., Caplan, A. L. and Merz, J. F. (2003, Summer), 'All gifts large and small: Toward an understanding of the ethics of pharmaceutical industry gift-giving', *American Journal of Bioethics*, 3: 3, pp. 39–46.

Paris School of Economics, 9th September, 2012, *Principes de transparence et d'integrite professionnelle a PSE-Ecole d'économie de Paris*. Available at http://www.parisschoolofeconomics. eu/en/outline/transparency-principles/.

Starkman, D. (May/June 2009), 'Power problem', *Columbia Journalism Review*. Available at http:// www.cjr.org/cover_story/power_problem.php?page=all.

Starobin, P. (March/April 2012), 'Money talks', *Columbia Journalism Review*. Available at http:// www.cjr.org/feature/money_talks_marchapril2012.php?page=all.

Thompson, D. F. (Forthcoming), 'Professional disequilibrium: Conflict of interest in economics', in G. DeMartino and D. McCloskey (eds), *The Oxford University Press Handbook of Professional Economic Ethics*, Oxford: Oxford University Press.

Toulouse School of Economics (2012). *Statement on Scientific Integrity*, 1st January. Available at http://www.tsefr.eu/index.php?option=com_content&task=view&id=755&Itemid=633.

Verein für Socialpolitik. (2012), *A Code of Ethics for the Verein für Socialpolitik*. Available at http://www.socialpolitik.org/vfs.php?mode=ethik&lang=2.

Paper prepared for the session 'Ethics and Professional Economic Practice – Has Anything Changed?' at the annual meetings of the Association for Social Economics and the Society of Government Economists, January 2013, San Diego, CA.

Note

1   Respondents were of both genders, but for the sake of preserving anonymity I refer to all respondents with the male pronoun. I refer by name to just one journalist who authorized me to do so.

Chapter 6

Trouble in the markets: Differentiation in the Norwegian financial news landscape

Nina Kvalheim and Helle Sjøvaag

Introduction

This chapter presents a case study of content diversification strategies of the Norwegian financial media. The premise behind this investigation is the observation that financial news seems to represent a favoured content for which mainstream media may erect digital paywalls. It is thus hypothesized that economy sector news represents an attempt at securing added income through content diversification targeted at valuable audience groups. The question in this regard is what kind of market strategy financial news represents in the Norwegian news landscape. We approach this question by way of a quantitative content analysis mapping the differences in content profile along nine Norwegian financial media outlets. As the selection of publications ranges from printed newspapers, television, online and tablet technologies, the differentiation thesis is further investigated along the issue of publication platform. The content analysis reveals that the financial news sector in Norway can be said to reflect the presumed cost-effective nature of the product as high in value and low in production cost. Moreover, we find that the platform expansion strategies of these media outlets can be characterized as strategies of differentiation and diversification, however with a distinct mid-market crowding effect.

This chapter presents a comprehensive picture of Norwegian economic and financial news across nine news media outlets during the week of 10th–16th October, 2011. We primarily address two questions in this regard. The first relates to financial news content and the representation of economic issues – including the Eurozone crises – in the various media outlets. We ask this question on the basic presumption that news in a competitive media landscape needs to cater to the specific needs of audiences and hence to be made relevant to their needs and interests. Financial news is particularly suited for such an investigation, as it represents highly specified content that conveys potentially valuable information to particular segmented audience groups working within the financial sectors, as well as to the general public. In this respect financial news represents one of the few areas of daily news production where media companies have been able to produce income-generating services on the online and mobile platforms (e.g. *Financial Times* and the *Wall Street Journal*). As such, the other central issue addressed here is the question of differentiation strategies and platform divergence, and consequently how financial news services are adapted to suit different publication cultures and audiences. In this chapter we therefore discuss financial journalism in Norway in light of the potential of economic news in the development of new business models for mainstream media.

New business models

Economic scholars have yet to agree on what a business model is, although consensus seems settled on a wide application of the term to explain value capture and value creation, particularly in relation to information technology, the emergence of the Internet, and competitive advantage in this regard (Zott et al. 2011: 1020–23). For our purposes, a business model is a strategy for obtaining revenue. What business model a media company chooses depends on the competitive landscape and the strategic interaction of players within the market (Kind et al. 2008). As the economist Michael E. Porter observes, market competition is determined by the degree of differentiation between products on offer and the distribution of cost (Porter 1985: 11). Important for the success of any business strategy, then, is the differentiation strategy that separates a company from its closest rivals (Porter 1998: 38, 43). Commercially run media such as the newspaper have traditionally found themselves in a dual market serving two customer groups – audiences who finance newspapers via direct payment or subscription, and advertisers who pay for advertising space based on the audience reach of the paper (Picard 2009: 75). With the advertising market predicted to move online,[1] the dual revenue model is presented with a challenge. The business model that has traditionally split revenue between audience and advertising sales is steadily losing its viability. As a result, news media are working to establish new revenue generating features, particularly as part of their online services.

However, there are conflicting views on how to achieve this. Whereas Bob Franklin claims that, 'The business model for newspapers simply does not translate to online news' (Franklin 2008: 25), Donica Mensing identifies advertising as the primary online revenue model (Mensing 2007: 24). There are findings that support Mensing's claim. For instance, Thurman and Herbert find that advertising remains the primary source of revenue for UK national and regional newspapers, but that most also charge for unique content to generate extra revenue (Thurman and Herbert 2007). This would imply a transfer of the traditional business model online, rather than any development of new business models specifically suited to digital media services. This is perhaps due to the low willingness amongst audiences to pay for news online (c.f. Anderson et al. 2010; Chyi 2005; Thurman and Herbert 2007; Mensing 2007). Norwegian economist Hans Jarle Kind and his colleagues have found that access to direct payment from customers decrease with increased substitutability between products (Kind et al. 2008). Because audiences are less willing to pay for products that serve similar purposes, this also affects the advertising market and the advertising revenue model. Here, Richard van der Wurff remarks, prices in the market are determined by the distance between products. 'Differentiation is therefore an attractive strategy for firms in competitive markets' (van der Wurff 2005b: 145).

Whereas printed newspapers have traditionally found themselves in a situation where their profiles are sufficiently differentiated to warrant either steady advertising income based on a loyal readership, or state support (in the case of the Nordic countries), online newspapers lose some of the differentiation that exists in the printed market as geographical audience ties become weaker. Internet and print markets consist of many of the same suppliers and consumers, and thus affect each other. The online channel is therefore considered either to be cannibalistic or complementary to existing products. Cannibalization effects do not seem to deter newspapers from employing an online strategy, despite the fact that free online content tend to remove paying customers from the brand all together. However, an online presence can also promote print sales by practices of differentiation that drive users to the print edition through marketing and branding efforts (Thurman and Herbert 2007). Stahl and colleagues have here found that revenues for paid online news are higher when the content is rebundled rather than when it is sold separately or in versions identical to the print version. Hence, there is a problem of cannibalization with digital information goods that have low levels of differentiation from offline versions. As such, they argue that the traditional newspaper business model cannot be transferred to the online world without product differentiation (Stahl et al. 2005: 65). The financial news sector provides a good case for analysing how such differentiation strategies function, primarily because the market for business news is expanding due to the needs of managers to keep informed in the current market (van der Wurff 2005b: 144).

Data and methodology

We have collected data from the financial news coverage across media platforms in the Norwegian media landscape for the week of 10–16 October 2011. The sample consists of 1,477 items in total. This includes $n=536$ news articles published in the two printed national daily financial newspapers *Dagens Næringsliv* and *Finansavisen*; $n=261$ news reports from TV 2 News Channel – a subsidiary of the commercial public service broadcaster TV 2 (with 4 business news updates daily); and $n=680$ news items taken from six financial online news services, including the website of the Norwegian Broadcasting Corporation at www.nrk.no/okonomi, the website of the leading financial newspaper *Dagens Næringsliv* at www.dn.no, the largest online business news site E24 at www.e24.no, the online financial news portal www.hegnar.no, the online-only newspaper Nettavisen's economy news section NA24 at www.na24.no, and Norway's largest newspaper VG's online financial magazine Dine Penger at www.vg.no/dinepenger. In addition, we have collected and compared the online financial news sites with their iPad and iPhone editions.

The codebook[2] is designed to register cases according to news angle and contains 4 primary variables. The content variable (v1) consists of 10 categories specifying content along the following topics: markets (stock markets, currencies and oil price); personal finance (housing market, banking and loans, tax issues, consumption and lifestyle); companies (their productivity and management, mergers and acquisitions); state economy (budget issues and economic policy); financial crime (white collar crime, organized crime and fraud); the job market (employment issues); cultural economy (the media, cultural and tourism sectors); the financial crisis; the Eurozone crisis; and other issues. Subsequent variables include location (v2), sources (v3) and type of story (v3) (whether commentary, report or interview).[3] Inter-coder reliability was established using Cohen's kappa ($\varkappa$) and found to be acceptable at .74/77%[4]

The unit of analysis for online news is an emerging topic of discussion amongst media researchers. In traditional, linear forms of media, such as newspapers and television broadcasts, the boundaries of messages, such as a news article, are clearly defined. However, as Weare and Lin noted already in 2000, the size and chaotic structure of the Internet complicates efforts to select representative samples for analysis (Weare and Lin 2000: 273). A particular challenge in this regard is how to match the units of analysis when comparing online and print content (c.f. Keith et al. 2010: 93), particularly when comes to the issue of versionality of online news (Kautsky and Widholm 2008: 85). Our unit of analysis is the single news report, logged in the form of a headline. The section principle has been based on headline uniqueness. This means we have only registered new and unique stories as part of the sample.[5] Measurements are in news items only, not column inches or minutes. Although this might present a problem in terms of representation of actual time and space devoted to the various economic issues measured within these publications, the headline emerged as the preferred unit of analysis because this better facilitates comparison and generalization across platforms. Moreover, we have not logged every item on every page. Instead we have collected the items considered news stories or news articles about financial and economic issues.[6] As demonstrated by the overview of results in Table 1, this has led to some variety in items per outlet. These numbers do however reflect accurately the variation in publication frequencies.

Findings

The news in brief
Amongst the major stories making headlines in the financial news sections the week between 10 and 16 October, 2011, was the emerging Eurozone crisis in which the German chancellor Angela Merkel and the French president Nicolas Sarkozy were engaged in a number of

Table 6.1: Overview of findings (%) (*n*=1,477).

	TV 2 News Channel	Dagens Næringsliv	DN. no	Finans- avisen	Hegnar. no	E24. no	Dine Penger. no	NA24. no	Nrk. no
Markets	27.2	15.2	12.3	28.2	39.6	17.9	0.0	3.2	18.4
Personal finance	9.6	2.5	10.9	8.6	9.0	3.8	90.9	35.5	7.7
Companies	10.7	25.4	19.6	31.2	25.1	23.1	0.0	9.7	0.0
State economy	2.7	10.2	9.8	4.1	2.6	7.7	0.0	12.9	23.1
Financial crime	4.2	9.0	6.5	3.4	2.9	5.1	9.1	4.8	0.0
Job market	5.0	9.0	7.6	2.1	3.8	5.8	0.0	3.2	0.0
Cultural economy	1.1	16.0	1.1	5.8	1.7	8.3	0.0	11.3	0.0
Financial crisis	5.7	2.0	1.1	2.4	0.6	6.4	0.0	0.0	7.7
Eurozone crisis	23.8	4.0	21.7	4.1	8.1	10.3	0.0	6.5	30.8
Other	10.0	4.6	6.5	5.5	6.6	11.5	0.0	12.9	15.4
Total	*100*	*100*	*100*	*100*	*100*	*100*	*100*	*100*	*100*
N=	*261*	*244*	*92*	*292*	*346*	*156*	*11*	*62*	*13*

meetings intent on saving the Greek nation from bankruptcy. Another major story within the same category concerned the Slovakian vote on the Eurozone bailout expansion plans. This week also saw the surrender of the Belgian bank Dexia to bankruptcy, as well as an increasing danger of the same happening to Swedish and Danish banks. At the top of the national agenda was the discovery of the Aldous/Avaldsnes oil fields in the Northern Sea, one of the largest finds ever made. Amongst other oil related news was the British government's approval of British Petroleum's application for drilling in the Norwegian Sea. Other heavily repeated stories across media outlets were a few financial crimes stories – one concerning a possible tax evasion by the merchant Odd Reitan and one concerning corruption in the Oslo-based bus company Unibus. A curiosity that also engendered some discussion during the week was the launch of journalist Mimir Kristjnasson's book De superrike ('The Super Rich') in which he accuses Norway's wealthiest of being tight-fisted whiners. In terms of the distribution of stories across media, we would characterize this as a fairly average week and more or less representative for the second half of 2011.

Newspaper competition

Evidence from the field of research has established that the main competitive advantage behind financial news concerns the concept of differentiation. The logic behind the differentiation tactic lies with targeting an audience that is willing to pay for specialized content. *Finansavisen* and *Dagens Næringsliv* are the two main financial newspapers in Norway. This means they address a specific segment of readers, consisting mainly of high-income, well-educated males working within the financial sectors (Sjøvaag 2012). With all the attention given to new media ventures lately, we should remember that intra-platform competition still takes place. There is evidence of such a competitive relationship between the two main financial newspapers in the data presented here, particularly in regards to how they position themselves in relation to each other. Table 6.1 shows how the largest content category in both newspapers concerns 'companies' (registering news concerning the performance, productivity and management of companies), with 31.2% and 25.4% respectively. Both newspapers also display little concern for the ongoing financial crisis, with only 2.4% (*Finansavisen*) and 2% (*Dagens Næringsliv*) specifically concerning the crisis. The two printed newspapers hence display certain similarities in their editorial considerations. Differences primarily amount to the degree of market information (stocks, currencies and oil price) found in the two papers, where *Finansavisen* is more concerned with reporting on the markets than *Dagens Næringsliv*. There is also a notable difference in the 'cultural economy' category (news and commentary from the media, cultural and tourism sectors) – a common segment found in *Dagens Næringsliv* that clearly serves to differentiate it from its closest rival.

This comparison suggests that the theory of differentiation is insufficient in explaining what is going on in this market. To understand the similarities between the two papers it is perhaps more fruitful to refer to the Hotelling location model as applied to fixed duopoly markets. The economist Harold Hotelling developed a location model that explains how and why in duopolistic markets two competitors tend to converge in the middle – concentrating their efforts towards the same mid-market customer group rather than diversifying at each end of the market – thus creating similar content profiles. This is because the middle customer group is potentially larger than marginal groups, even if the competition is stronger within this customer segment. Hotelling uses ice cream vendors as his example, demonstrating why it is that ice cream stands, coffee shops and fast food restaurants tend to set up shop next to each other (Hotelling 1929, see also Hamilton 2004). In a market with two financial newspapers seeking to maximize their audience potential, content convergence is an inevitable result of attempts to capture a competitor's audience. A closer look at *Finansavisen* and *Dagens Næringsliv* displays evidence of the presence of a Hotelling model in the financial newspaper market in Norway. We could assume from this competitive situation that the two newspapers are of equal size with similar economic prospects. The latest circulation figures reveal, however, that this is not the case. *Dagens Næringsliv* appears as the strong market leader, with a circulation of 80.559. In comparison, *Finansavisen's* circulation of 25.556 newspapers keeps it firmly in second place (Opplag.no 2010). Nevertheless, the high level of substitution between the two newspapers suggests there is a market for financial news. Moreover, it seems likely that value and audience potential within the financial news sector lies with exclusive content.

In the age of ubiquitous and instantaneous news services, it remains a curiosity to see financial newspapers still printing stock market sections. This type of financial information is only valuable in its updated form. What remains of differentiation potential within the financial news sector can therefore be reduced primarily to the level of unique content offered in the form of analysis, and the level of trust enjoyed by the brand. Both aspects provide valuable audiences that in turn can render advertising income. This seems to be the strategy behind TV 2 News Channel's constant expansion of its financial content platform. The analysis of the financial news sections of TV 2 News Channel reveals two things primarily – the exclusivity of its content and what we presume to be signs of low production costs. Each bulletin opens with cheap-to-produce information about how the various markets are acting at the moment – information that is valuable to its audiences. Our October data also shows that the television channel has a predominance of news of the Eurozone crisis – on which point it stands out amongst the other outlets surveyed. The high attention paid to the Eurozone crisis reflects the extent to which this was the dominant story on the general news agenda for this particular week. This also reflects the high level of commentary present on the channel, as it was the favoured topic of discussion during analysis segments. These two factors – the low production cost and the simultaneous differentiation offered by having experts from the financial and policy sectors in the studio analysing recent developments – in fact comprise the two textbook means of competitive advantage as described by Porter (Porter 1985: 11).

Such product differentiation not only creates a viable business model, but also ensures the added branding effect that can inspire audience loyalty (c.f. Hamilton 2007: 10). Differentiation strategies become increasingly important with growing competition, and have proved to be a viable means of encountering new competitors throughout the history of the mass media – creating new genres and increased content variety with each new segmented audience group (for instance popular journalism or female readership expansion) (Conboy and Steel 2009: 24). The strategic decision to launch or expand financial news services can therefore be considered part of the branding of the institutional news product, referred to as 'a process of continually perfecting the alignment between public perceptions and organizational performance' (Lowe 2011: 24). Branding effects hence amount to intangible assets that can create competitive advantage (Varadarajan et al. 2008: 302). Brands can reduce the so-called 'search costs' associated with choosing media products – primarily by presenting consumers with a readily understood approach to the news (Hamilton 2004: 13). Branding has emerged as a media strategy because it creates and preserves competitive advantages through a process of differentiation that Lowe says, 'depends in part on crafting symbolic representations' (Lowe 2011: 24). As Philip Meyer explains, the media operate in a market of attention scarcity where trust remains an equally scarce good that also has high switching costs, meaning it usually takes a lot for loyal readers to change their preferred news sources (Meyer 2009: 26; see also van der Wurff 2005a: 10). In the competition for such attention, brand identity functions as a tool for capturing trust (Meyer 2009: 46). Established relationships with audiences thus become increasingly valuable to a news organization facing commercial pressures. Not only because audience loyalty represents a clear market value for any news provider, but also because this trust represents a crucial lever for capturing advertisers (Meyer 2009: 11).

Print versus online

On a general level, content analyses of online news usually tend to either compare online news outlets across the market (c.f. Barnhurst 2010; Boczkowski and de Santos 2007; Chadwick 2011; Greer and Mensing 2006; Messner and DiStaso 2008;) or between the print and online editions of newspapers (e.g. Engebretsen 2006; Keith et al. 2010; Neuberger et al. 1998; Oblak 2005; Song 2007; van der Wurff 2008). These studies primarily conclude that there is considerable overlap between two outlets that share an editorial parent. Thorsten Quandt has shown in his analysis of online news publishing across Europe that online journalism is fairly conventional. Quandt thus concludes that there is little to suggest there has been a revolution in journalism as it moved online (Quandt 2008: 735). Findings from the work of van der Wurff and Lauf (2005; see also van der Wurff 2008) indicate that online publishing primarily entails more content rather than new content. In fact, argues An Nguyen, online news development is driven partly by fear of becoming obsolete or falling behind the competition (Nguyen 2008: 92). As such, we are witnessing not only an increase in overlap, shovelware and versionality in the news industry (Bozckowzki and de Santos 2007; Kautsky and Widholm 2008; Quandt 2008), but research also shows that there is increasing convergence in print, broadcast and online publication formats (Deuze 2007; Quinn 2005; Singer 2004).

Research within the field is fairly concurrent in findings regarding newspapers' online strategies. More often than not, this strategy consists of moving the content produced for the paper copy on to the new platform, known as 'shovelling'. This is a cheap process that ensures an online or tablet presence, but the shovelling strategy can also result in cannibalization (c.f. Franklin 2008). This is particularly the case in the relationship between online and print. The online version, carrying practically the same content as the printed version, steals audiences from the hard copy paper where audiences are significantly more valuable to advertisers than online readers. We initially assumed financial news to represent a viable strategy for obtaining additional profit for news organizations, based on the high value of the content in terms of audiences' willingness to pay. There is some evidence to support this assumption; however, most newspapers that have erected paywalls for this type of exclusive content have also quickly removed them – the *Wall Street Journal* remaining the only one gated. Its paywall success has been attributed to its unique brand value in the specific niche market, with a business strategy resting on differentiation (Mensing 2007: 24). The *Financial Times* remains another example of a newspaper that is able to charge customers on the basis of unique content; however, it only charges for its business and finance news (Franklin 2008; Thurman and Herbert 2007). None of the online news sites examined in this study had put their content behind paywalls at the time of sampling. As the news provided by these sites is free, the interesting question is if and how they differ from their parent outlets.

The overall distribution of coverage in our sample by topic is shown in Figure 6.2, while Figure 6.1 shows the variations in attention across the different news outlets. The most

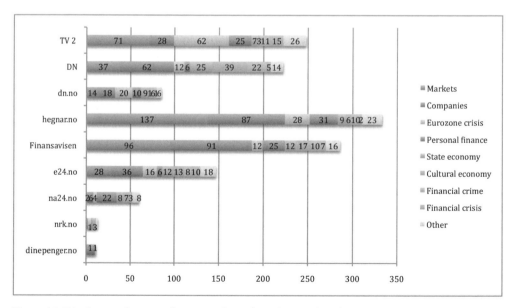

Figure 6.1: Distribution of content, all categories by media outlet. Number of articles (n=1,477). Categories read from left to right in the same order as they are listed from top to bottom on the right hand side of the chart.

striking difference between *Dagens Næringsliv* and its online channel dn.no is the number of items published. During our week dn.no published 129 articles, while the printed version published 303 articles. This strategy of restricting the content overlap between the printed and online platform indicates audiences interested in more detailed information should also buy the printed copy. This suggests financial news can serve as a strategy in attracting readers to paid premium content. Second, our findings show that while the largest content category in the newspaper edition concerns news about companies, at 25.4%, the online edition is most focused on the Eurozone crisis, at 21.7%. Moreover, the lowest ratio of content found online – news about cultural economy (1.1%) – is the third largest content group in the paper edition (12.9). These findings suggesting that the two versions can be viewed as complementary rather than as substitutes. That being said, a closer look at the articles reveals that the online stories are primarily print stories adapted to the online version. Hence the headline might be updated to suit the online medium, but the content is the same on both platforms. This implies that the news organization might regard the paper copy as their main product, while the online version functions as a way to attract new readers.

We find the opposite to be case in the online–offline relationship between *Finansavisen* and hegnar.no. These outlets enjoy the same relationship as *Dagens Næringsliv* and dn.no, where hegnar.no is considered the online version of *Finansavisen*. Again, the number of published items constitutes the most striking difference between the two; however, in this case, the online version carries more stories (346 stories) than the printed edition (292 stories). This could be explained by referring to hegnar.no's identity as a site primarily catered to stock market information – its largest content category at 39.6% – a category in need of constant updating throughout the day. These types of news items are not necessarily suited to publication in the printed edition. Nevertheless, both versions are more geared towards market reports and news about the performance of companies than other types of content (see Table 6.1). Similarities continue in the less prioritized categories, in this case the financial crisis, with 2.4% of the coverage in *Finansavisen* and 0.6% on hegnar.no. Hence the two outlets seem to have many editorial similarities. Comparing *Dagens Næringsliv*/dn.no and *Finansavisen*/hegnar.no, we find similar content profiles along the light and heavy content categories. It seems differentiation efforts lie with the mid-level content categories such as job market issues, state economy and the cultural sector. Differentiation efforts between the two editorial offices can also be said to reside with the level of focus on financial news, where *Finansavisen*/hegnar.no moves more towards the markets, while *Dagens Næringsliv*/dn.no has a wider focus that to some extent also includes the general news agenda.

Omnibus news services

So far we have looked at platforms that exclusively publish financial news. We have seen that these tend to focus their attention on news about companies, market information and commentary and analysis. Curiously, the Eurozone crisis does not feature heavily as part of the printed news output. It features more in the online environment, but most of the Eurozone news is to be found in the television format. This discrepancy could perhaps be explained with reference to differences in news agenda cultures in television and newspaper newsrooms. Continuous coverage on the online and news channel formats requires more attention to the topics currently on the agenda, while newspapers are settling in as slow mediums carrying analysis and background that is more focused on the long-term agendas. That being said, the news of a financial crisis amongst the Euro countries entails a complex set of events difficult to form into breaking news. As such, it remains rather curious that such 'thick' news developments could engender such broad televised coverage. This is perhaps the reason why TV 2 News Channel devotes most of its attention to the Eurozone coverage through commentary and analysis by experts in the studio, and not in the form of location packages. This is in line with the differentiation thesis for news market strategy that we find evidence of also amongst the remaining outlets. What, then, of news outlets that publish financial news as a part of an omnibus news service?

Three outlets in the sample belong to such an omnibus news provider – NA24, E24 and dinepenger.no. E24 and dinepenger.no are both owned by the national tabloid VG. This relationship means the publications sometimes share online content. *Dine penger,* meaning 'Your Money', is a news site providing tips and expert advice regarding personal economy.[7] 90.9% of articles collected from this site belong to the content category registering cases about personal finance (concerning the housing market, banking and loans, tax issues, consumption, goods and services and lifestyle issues). It should be noted here that the sample consists of only 11 original articles. It is difficult to draw statistically significant results from this sample; however, the figure provides an indication of the main characteristics of the content on this site. The fact that VG, as the leading national tabloid, focuses on personal economy directed at regular readers, and not market information directed at business workers, is in line with the newspaper's identity as an omnibus newspaper. On the other hand, personalizing financial news also amounts to a differentiation strategy that could serve to differentiate VG from the leading financial news outlets such as *Dagens Næringsliv* and *Finansavisen,* who cater to this segment only to a very limited extent. At the same time, VG also owns E24, a site that focuses more broadly on financial issues and politics, something that is reflected in the variation in its content. Differentiation from dinepenger.no can here be observed in the site's limited focus on personal finances. E24 is hence more similar to its rival outlets dn.no and hegnar.no – another indication of the Hotelling model at work within the financial news sector.

The only outlet in our sample that does not seem to assume a strong model of differentiation is NA24, with a personal finance ratio of 35.5%, the highest in the sample aside from dinepenger. no. It seems to be competing with the other outlets in all of its major categories. That being said, however, NA24 overall has a differentiated identity, with a focus on state economy and the cultural sector that could be seen as an attempt to cater to audiences interested in finance and economics, but not necessarily from an investment angle. In the case of our last medium included in the survey – the economy section of the public service broadcaster NRK's online services – the limited number of unique cases published throughout the week largely deters attempts at comparisons with other outlets. However, stories on nrk.no/economy seem concerned with the macro-level of economic developments, with a predominance of stories concerning the Eurozone crisis and state economy. Perhaps the most curious finding here is how little attention is paid to economic news by the PSB channel – otherwise number one in the television market and amongst the leading online news sites.

Platform differentiation

With the rapid developments within tablet technology, and the industry buzz surrounding the issue of platform expansion strategies towards these technologies, we were looking to include the iPhone and iPad editions of the news outlets analysed in this survey. The two newspapers *Dagens Næringsliv* and *Finansavisen* had both made available their publication in the tablet format at the time of sampling. However, as the tablet content was the same as the printed content for both newspapers, we decided to refrain from conducting a duplicate content analysis. In late 2011, iPhone versions existed of TV 2 Economy, E24, NA24 and Dine Penger. Again, the mobile content is identical to the online content. We suspect our findings reflect a tendency amongst many news media outlets seeking to capture new audiences on these novel publication platforms. Mobile publication – even to some extent online publication, represents duplication at best, shovelware at worst. The reason for such double publication, we presume, is the need to be perceived as innovative, experimental and at the forefront of developments. Online and mobile ventures should therefore be seen as part of the branding effort of mainstream media attempting to capture and retain migrating audiences. Moreover, trying to erect paywalls without offering either premium or original content does not seem to represent a viable business model based on differentiation along publication technologies.

Conclusions

This content analysis reveals certain characteristics of the competitive landscape of financial news in Norway. Overall, the type of stories that most concerned Norwegian financial media during the second week of October 2011 was news about markets and companies – overall 26% for markets and 22% for companies. News about companies was the top category for three outlets (*Dagens Næringsliv, Finansavisen* and E24.no), while news about markets was primary content for TV 2 News Channel and hegnar.no. The Eurozone crisis was the top category for dn.no and nrk.no, while issues concerning personal finance dominated dinepenger.no and na24.no.

The various outlets measured in this analysis differ in profile to the extent that we can recognize a differentiation strategy at work – here within a news market segment that carries certain Hotelling characteristics of convergence towards the middle. Such mid-market crowding is evident in outlets operating on the same publication platform – a curious finding as technological convergence is said to erase the significance of original platform on audience reach. It seems we cannot yet dismiss the identity provided by original

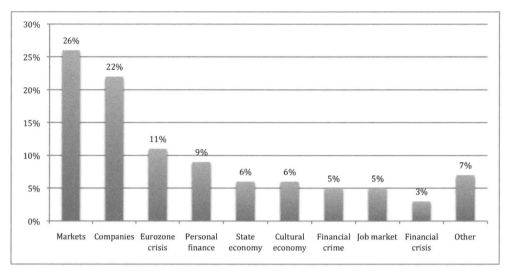

Figure 6.2: Distribution of content, all categories. Per cent (n=1,477).

publication technology on the strategic and competitive thinking of editorial organizations. At the same time, we find that the main criteria of competitive advantage – the low cost and differentiation factors described by Porter (Porter 1985: 11), are evident indicators of market positioning. We see this primarily in the cost and differentiation strategies of *Dagens Næringsliv, Finansavisen* and TV 2 News Channel. Findings also indicate that financial news represents a cheap production cost for omnibus news services that has potential for value creation. Because financial data can easily be made relevant to Norwegian conditions and hence to Norwegian audiences, it remains valuable as content for most mainstream media, as well as the more specialized financial media. Adding to this, however, is the insight that financial news in 2011 was not yet able to sustain paywalls to the extent that economic news content entailed a viable business model on its own.

References

Anderson, S. P., Foros, Ø. and Kind, H. J. (2010), 'Hotelling competition with multi-purchasing: Time magazine, *Newsweek*, or both?', Working Paper No 21/10, SNF, Norwegian School of Economics.

Barnhurst, Kevin (2010), 'The form of reports on US newspaper internet sites: An update', *Journalism Studies,* 11: 4, pp. 555–66.

Boczkowski, P. J. and og de Santos, M. (2007), 'When more media equals less news: Patterns of content homogenization in Argentina's leading print and online newspapers', *Political Communication*, 24: 2, pp. 167–80.

Chadwick, A. (2011), 'The political information cycle in a hybrid news system: The British prime minister and the "Bullygate" affair', *International Journal of Press/Politics*, 16: 1, pp. 3–29.

Chyi, H. I. (2005), 'Willingness to pay for online news: An empirical study on the viability of the subscription model', *Journal of Media Economics*, 18: 2, pp. 131–42.

Conboy, M. and Steel, J. (2009), 'The future of newspapers: Historical perspectives', in B. Franklin (ed.), *The Future of Newspapers*, London: Routledge, pp. 21–32.

Deuze, M. (2007), *Media Work*, Cambridge: Polity Press.

Engebretsen, M. (2006), 'Shallow and static or deep and dynamic? Studying the state of online journalism in Scandinavia', *Nordicom Review*, 27: 1, pp. 3–16.

Franklin, B. (2008) (ed.), *Pulling Newspapers Apart: Analysing Print Journalism*, London: Routledge.

Greer, J. D. and Mensing, D. (2006), 'The evolution of online newspapers: A longitudinal content analysis, 1997–2003', in X. Li (ed.), *Internet Newspapers: The Making of a Mainstream Medium*, Mahwah, NJ: Lawrence Erlbaum, pp. 13–32.

Hamilton, J. T. (2004), *All the News That's Fit to Sell: How the Market Transforms Information into News*, Princeton, NJ: Princeton University Press.

Hamilton, J. T. (2007), 'News that sells: Media competition and news content', *Japanese Journal of Political Science*, 8: 1, pp. 7–42.

Hotelling, H. (1929), 'Stability in competition', *The Economic Journal*, 39: 153, pp. 41–57.

Kautsky, R. and Widholm, A. (2008), 'Online methodology: Analyzing news flows of online journalism', *Westminster Papers in Communication and Culture*, 5: 2, pp. 81–97.

Keith, S., Schwalbe, C. B. and Silcock, B. W. (2010), 'Comparing war images across media platforms: Methodological challenges for content analysis', *Media, War & Conflict*, 3: 1, pp. 87–98.

Kind, H. J., Nilssen, T. and Sørgard, L. (2008), 'Business models for media firms: Does competition matter for how they raise revenue?', Working Paper No 21/08, Bergen: Institute for Research in Economics and Business Administration, Norwegian School of Economics and Business Administration.

Lowe, G. F. (2011), 'Respecting the PSB heritage in the PSM brand', *International Journal of Media Management*, 13: 1, pp. 21–35.

Mensing, D. (2007) 'Online revenue business model has changed little since 1996', *Newspaper Research Journal*, 28: 2, pp. 22–37.

Messner, M. and DiStaso, M. W. (2008), 'The source cycle: How traditional media and weblogs use each other as sources', *Journalism Studies*, 9: 3, pp. 447–63.

Meyer, P. (2009), *The Vanishing Newspaper: Saving Journalism in the Information Age*, 2nd edn, Columbia: University of Missouri Press.

Neuberger, C., Tonnemacher, J., Biebl, M. and Duck, A. (1998), 'Online – The future of newspapers? Germany's dailies on the world wide web', *Journal of Computer-Mediated Communication*, 4: 1, pp. 1–24.

Neuendorf, K. (2002), *The Content Analysis Guide Book*, Thousand Oaks: Sage.

Nguyen, A. (2008), 'Facing "the fabulous monster": The traditional media's fear-driven innovation culture in the development of online news', *Journalism Studies*, 9: 1, pp. 91–104.

Oblak, T. (2005), 'The lack of interactivity and hypertextuality in online media', *Gazette*, 67: 1, pp. 87–106.

Opplag.no (2010), Opplagstall, http://www.opplag.no/opplagstall. Accessed 30th November, 2011.

Picard, R. G. (2009), 'Shifts in newspaper advertising expenditures and their implications for the future of newspapers', in B. Franklin (ed.), *The Future of Newspapers*, London: Routledge, pp. 75–87.

Porter, M. E. (1985), *Competitive Advantage: Creating and Sustaining Superior Performance*, New York: Free Press.

Porter, M. E. (1998), *On Competition: Updated and Expanded Edition*, Boston: A Harvard Business Review Book.

Propaganda (15th September, 2011), 'TV-reklame øker mest' [Increase in TV advertising], http://www.na24.no/propaganda/article3230586.ece.

Quandt, T. (2008) '(No) news on the world wide web? A comparative content analysis of online news in Europe and the United States', *Journalism Studies,* 9: 5, pp. 717–38.

Quinn, S. (2005), 'Convergence's fundamental question', *Journalism Studies*, 6: 1, pp. 29–38.

Singer, J. B. (2004), 'Strange bedfellows: The diffusion of convergence in four news organizations', *Journalism Studies*, 5: 1, pp. 3–18.

Sjøvaag, H. (2012), 'Revenue and branding strategy in the Norwegian news market: The case of TV 2 news channel', *Nordicom Review*, 33: 1, pp. 53–66.

Song, Y. (2007), 'Internet news media and issue development: A case study on the roles of independent online news services as agenda-builders for anti-US protests in South Korea', *New Media and Society,* 9: 1, pp. 71–92.

Stahl, F., Schäfer, M-F. and Maass, W. (2004), 'Strategies for selling paid content on newspaper and magazine web sites: An empirical analysis of bundling and splitting of news and magazine articles', *International Journal on Media Management*, 6: 1–2, pp. 59–66.

Thurman, N. and Herbert, J. (2007), 'Paid content strategies for news websites: An empirical study of British newspapers' online business models', *Journalism Practice*, 1: 2, pp. 208–26.

van der Wurff, R. (2005a), 'Online competition and performance of news and information markets in the Netherlands', *Gazette*, 67: 1, pp. 9–26.

van der Wurff, R. (2005b), 'Business magazine market performance: Magazines for the agricultural, business services, and transportation sectors in the Netherlands', *Journal of Media Economics*, 18: 2, pp. 143–59.

van der Wurff, R. (2008), 'The impact of the internet on media content', in L. Küng, R. G. Picard and R. Towse (eds), *The Internet and the Mass Media*, Los Angeles, CA: Sage, pp. 65–85.

van der Wurff, R. and Lauf, E. (2005) (eds), *Print and Online Newspapers in Europe: A Comparative Analysis in 16 Countries*, Amsterdam: Het Spinhuis.

Varadarajan, R., Yadav, M. S. and Shankar, V. (2008), 'First-mover advantage in an internet-enabled market environment: Conceptual framework and propositions', *Journal of the Academy of Marketing Science*, 36: 3, pp. 293–308.

Weare, C. and Lin, W-Y. (2000), 'Content analysis of the world wide web: Opportunities and challenges', *Social Science Computer Review*, 18: 3, pp. 272–92.

Zott, C., Raphael, A. and Lorenzo, M. (2011), 'The business model: Recent developments and future research', *Journal of Management*, 37: 4, pp. 1019–42.

Notes

1   This is a slow move. Impressive annual growth figures for online advertising aside, the printed newspaper remains by far the largest advertising medium in the media sector in Norway. Online advertising takes 14% of the total media advertising market for 2011, while newspapers make up 23.9% and television 34.8% (Propaganda 15.09.11).

2   The codebook can be obtained by request to the authors.

3   The coding scheme was developed inductively based on observations of the news media surveyed, and based on the research questions.

4   A reliability test was performed on 100 items, from the printed newspaper edition of *Dagens Næringsliv* from 11 October 2011 (48 items) and the printed edition of *Finansavisen* from 12 October 2011 (52 items). Disagreements were primarily related to the issue of when to apply the 'other' category. As Cohen's kappa is a conservative measure, any measure above .70 is considered acceptable (Neuendorf 2002: 143).

5   Except in the case of TV 2 News Channel. Here, every news item has been logged whether new/unique or repeated. This is due to the nature of the editing practices of the news channel format. Editing practices are not the same in the online context. Here, an article's content is assumed to remain unchanged unless the headline is changed. In online cases where the headline has been updated but the subsequent text remains static, the updated story was logged and the overlapping story was removed to avoid sample duplication.

6   Removed from the analysis are hence reports considered outside the definition of financial news, such as 'breaking news' segments on TV 2 News Channel, listed stock prices in the printed newspapers and advertising in the online editions.

7   Dine Penger is also published in printed magazine format with 15 issues annually. As the printed version is a monthly edition, we chose not to include it in the sample.

Chapter 7

Covering the crisis: Politics and culture

Jostein Gripsrud

The media constitute the core infrastructure of the modern public sphere. They are the key suppliers of the information and analysis citizens need to understand unfolding situations and the central arenas for the collective discussion of possible responses based on 'the public use of reason' (Kant [1784] 2010) that lies at the heart of Enlightenment models of the democratic process. Consequently, when major political decisions are to be made on pressing social issues, democracies have come to rely to a great extent on media to promote the public understanding required to underpin political participation.

But as Michael Schudson (1999) has suggested democratic theory's utopian ideal of the all-knowing autonomous citizen is unrealistic and should be abandoned in favour of a more modest figure: the 'monitorial citizen'. Like parents at a community pool with their kids, 'monitorial citizens' are seemingly passive but actually scanning the scene in order to act swiftly if anything serious happens. Faced with the scale of the economic crisis that has marked Europe and North America since 2008, monitorial citizens urgently need reliable and comprehensive information and analysis, first, to form a considered opinion on the overall situation and, second, to take purposeful action, both personally, in their own specific situation, and politically on the economic and social issues at stake.

The western democracies struggling to overcome the overwhelming economic problems at hand are, however, societies where (somewhat varying degrees of) freedom of expression is combined with a marked stratification in both the production and reception of public discourse. One influential version of these dimensions was introduced by Nancy Fraser (1990) when she distinguished between 'strong' publics with the power to shape events and 'weak' publics without such power, such as various social movements and other civil society publics. There is abundant research evidence to show that these variations in influence are consistently translated into differential access to media, with government ministers, elected politicians and leading representatives of major economic and academic 'power elites' being significantly more likely to be cited as news sources or invited to contribute op-ed pieces to newspapers or appear on television discussion programmes or in documentary films. In contrast, as the Occupy Wall Street Movement and the militant street demonstrations in Greece demonstrate, 'weak publics' often need to resort to theatrical protest to gain a public hearing for their views. In these instances, the public sphere acts, in Jürgen Habermas's useful phrase, as a 'sounding board' of discontent, needs and demands from below (c.f. e.g. Habermas 1999, Chapter 8 and an interesting discussion of the sounding board metaphor in Hove 2009). But the ability to shape the terms of debate continues to lie with the members of 'strong publics'. This does not mean that elite discourse is univocal. On the contrary, the financial crisis has generated a crisis in the economics profession, with neo-liberals promoting responses based on savage cuts to public welfare budgets and public austerity and supporters of revivified variants of neo-Keynesianism advocating public investment in infrastructure and skills.

Divisions in access to public voice are replicated in the sphere of reception. Much economic commentary presupposes a mastery of concepts and terms confined to those with an extended education and the capacity to act on the information provided by, for example, shifting investments or paying down debts. Coverage aimed at those lacking cultural and economic capital is likely to be much skimpier. As we shall see, whereas Norway's equivalent of the *Financial Times* carried 22 items on the financial crisis during the sample period selected for analysis here, and the quality subscription title, *Aftenposten,* had 19, the leading tabloid, *VG,* had only 4.

It is not only the amount of information on offer and the conceptual frames that underpin it that are at issue. A full understanding also requires histories to be linked to biographies by demonstrating the concrete human consequences of impersonal forces. Here again, different media forms make these connections in different ways. Some offer insights into the suffering inflicted on ordinary people, others privilege the misfortunes and dilemmas of those inside the system, and others fail completely to put a human face to events and processes.

It is against this background that this chapter will discuss the ways in which mass media have handled the economic crisis and contributed to citizens' capability to act politically. While most media and communication scholarship tends to focus exclusively on journalistic media, the intention here is to also include media and genres that are located in the cultural part of the public sphere. Despite its pivotal role in linking histories to biographies the cultural public sphere has routinely been overlooked in public sphere theory and in most contributions to political philosophy more generally. It is therefore still very rare that the relations between journalistic and aesthetic/fictional treatment of the same issues are looked at in one and the same piece of scholarly writing.

1

The intention here is not to give a full account of how the media in a particular country has covered the current crisis and contributed to our understanding of it. Rather by way of an analysis of selected examples the aim is to suggest certain possibilities and limitations in some of the main genres employed in both journalism and the arts.

I will be looking at two documentaries about the 2008 crash in the financial sector, one Norwegian and one American, and two Hollywood feature films concerned with the financial crisis and the subsequent economic downturn. The American documentary is *Inside Job*, which won the Academy Award for best documentary in 2011. The Norwegian film is Hans Petter Moland's *When Bubbles Burst* (2012). The feature films are *Margin Call* (2011), 'easily the best Wall Street movie ever made' (Denby 2011), loosely based on the collapse of Lehman Brothers and *The Company Men* (2010), a film about 'downsizing' and unemployment. Two of these films are discussed from different perspectives elsewhere in this volume, by John Corner and Anja Peltzer. My analysis centres on their status as contributions to public discourse on the financial crisis: What do these films actually contribute? Can they be said to argue for a certain view of or political position on the crisis? What are the limitations, not least in terms of their genre(s), as contributions to the formation of public opinion and political action?

This chapter is written in the hope that it may shed light not only on the ways in which the media, seen from a Norwegian position, have handled the challenge of representing the current crisis, but also more generally on how key genres in the political and cultural public sphere all play a role in forming the ways we monitorial citizens perceive, understand and develop a basis for acting politically on our respective situations.

But we start, as most analyses do, with press coverage, looking at the articles retrieved from the Norwegian database for all newspapers' texts, *Retriever/A-tekst*, employing three search terms: 'euro crisis', 'financial crisis' and 'debt crisis' to four national Norwegian newspapers from the first full week of March and the first full week of September 2012.

According to Statistics Norway, 77% of those aged between 16 and 24 read at least one newspaper either on paper or in a web edition on 'an ordinary day' in 2011. This figure rises to 82% of those aged 25–44, 85% of those between 45 and 66 and 90% of those aged 67–99. According to the most recent World Press Trends survey, Norway is the third in the world (along with Sweden and Switzerland) in terms of newspaper readership, only Iceland (no. 1) and Japan (no. 2) have higher percentages. Daily newspapers, including their online editions, are thus key sources of information for the Norwegian public.

The newspapers in our sample are politically and otherwise diverse.

Klassekampen used to be Western Europe's only Maoist daily, but has now for 10 years or so been a broader left-socialist daily newspaper very widely read (in terms of political orientations) and generally respected for its journalism. It has been growing fast in circulation but is still quite small, also in terms of the number of pages on most days of the week.

VG is a tabloid-format newspaper that has been leading in terms of circulation since the 1970s. It is in part sensationalist and oriented towards celebrities and entertainment, but has also established itself as a resourceful, journalistic medium that has considerable political influence. Many politicians of different orientations favour it when they want to publish an op-ed article on something or other. The paper's own political line is largely marked by right-wing social-democratic leanings.

Aftenposten is the subscription-based ex-broadsheet (now in tabloid format) with the largest circulation of any 'quality' title the country. Traditionally a conservative paper it has moved towards the centre of the spectrum over the last decade or so.

DN is a business daily concentrating on economic and financial reporting but also carrying general foreign news, prize-winning investigative journalism and daily pages on the arts, media and cultural industries that are read by most of those employed in those sectors – plus media scholars and politicians interested in the field. These pages were originally the creation of the present editor of *Klassekampen*, Bjørgulv Braanen, who worked at *DN* 1990–2000. Politically – in its editorial and most of its editorial commentaries – it is right wing or liberalist in terms economic policy, and liberal when it comes to issues such as immigration, gay rights and the like.

What I will be looking for in the reporting and commentary gathered are the ways in which the crises are understood, how they are linked (if at all) and which political solutions are proposed.

2

The weeks selected for study were not chosen on the basis of particular events. I wanted to get at the everyday coverage, the ways in which newspapers inform their readers on a regular basis in a situation of prolonged developments. Most people will – at least until they are directly affected – get their information on a process like the financial crisis through a series of news items in broadcast media and newspapers. But a significant segment of the citizenry will also look for and read additional and background information as well as relevant knowledge in newspapers, magazines and a variety of online sources. What such people would find in the Norwegian newspapers studied is the subject of the following paragraphs.

In quantitative as well as qualitative terms, the first striking fact is the difference between the 'quality tabloid' *VG* and the three other papers. According to our searches, *VG* contained only four items, all of which were published in our September week. One of the articles (4th September) is devoted to the steep increase in Norwegian housing prices and references to the international financial crisis are only used to highlight the relative uniqueness of the very satisfactory economic situation in Norway. On the same day, there is a well-informed commentary on the upcoming Dutch parliamentary election, focusing on the coming together of the far left and the far right in critiquing the EU and its crisis policies. A third item (6th September) is a short speculative editorial comment on the meeting of the board of the European Central Bank taking place that day, which, interestingly, presupposes that the paper's readers actually know what buying state debt means. Finally, there is the 7th September editorial commentary on the outcome of the ECB's board meeting the day before. This is longer and explains more fully what buying state debt is about. After describing the political situation, it argues that ECB's unlimited buying of debt is 'like curing gangrene with paracetamol' and that 'the euro crisis is political': The EU as a solidarity project can only solve the Eurozone's problems by a thoroughgoing policy of financial and tax integration.

The comment, by a member of the paper's editorial staff, shows that *VG* does seem to have qualified journalists for competent economic coverage. On the other hand, the meagre outcome of our searches also indicates that this is not a prioritized subject. Moreover, there is a total lack of coverage concerning the effects of the crisis for ordinary people in the EU.

The searches provided very different results in the case of *Aftenposten*, the Oslo moderately conservative subscription, 'quality' daily: 19 items, 12 of which appeared in our March sample. The numbers should perhaps be reduced since 4 items were published together on 7th March as reports on south Europeans arriving in Norway looking for work, including interviews with some of them where the situation in their home countries is described. But the quantitative difference remains striking. The 7th March reports in themselves mark a qualitative difference from *VG*'s coverage, where this aspect of the crisis was missing. On 8th March *Aftenposten* reports more broadly (and yet concretely) on the situation of 'Euro-refugees' in the Norwegian labour market. On 6th September they carried a report on North-African and other immigrants in Greece, and on 8th September a report on the problems of ordinary people in Spain.

Aftenposten also covered related political events, including a press conference in Berlin with the German foreign minister Guido Westerwelle, where he was questioned by Greek journalists (6th March). The title is 'Cultural collision in Europe' and the journalist includes quotes from the somewhat heated exchange between Westerwelle and the representatives of Greek media. The report refers also to the EU parliament's president, the social democrat Martin Schulz, and his visit to Athens the week before. It ends by pointing towards a recent op-ed piece in *The Guardian,* where two German researchers advocated a more holistic European approach that would include delegating more power and financial resources to the EU system. This piece is a good example of the extended reporting made possible by the paper having a qualified correspondent in the German capital who also reads the British press.

Aftenposten furthermore covers the crisis from a specifically Norwegian point of view detailing gains and losses. On the one hand it recounts that export industries in Norway fear a stronger Norwegian currency vis-à-vis the euro will make sales in Europe more difficult (5th March). On the other, it reports on how much less expensive buying a house in the south of Europe has become for well-off Norwegians (8th March) and carries a piece on how Norwegians still flock to Greek islands in their summer vacations (10th March).

Finally, there are brief but insightful commentaries by members of the editorial staff on both the economic and political dimensions of the crisis. Of particular interest is the longer piece by Kristina Overn on 7th September. Overn, who after 5 years as a journalist in *Aftenposten* completed her MSc degree in European Political Economy at the London School of Economics in 2012, starts from the 'Outright Monetary Transactions' decision of the European Central Bank but goes on, referring to recent LSE research, to develop perspectives on the crisis as primarily a deep political and social crisis that is centrally about citizens' confidence in the existing political institutions.

The coverage in this subscription-based general interest newspaper thus appears well informed, competent and many-sided. With the at least partial exception of Overn's article of 7th September, it is, however, difficult to find examples of analytical overviews, especially ones that end in suggestions for concrete political actions.

Dagens Næringsliv (DN) is Norway's parallel to the *Financial Times*. It published a number of reports and commentaries containing our search terms – 22 in total, 11 in our spring week and 11 in the autumn one. Six articles are mainly about sectors of the Norwegian economy and their relations to the international crises. Eleven are competent reports or comments by the editorial staff and correspondents on particular events in Europe. They include interviews with certain international actors or commentators and one report on the trial of Iceland's former prime minister Geir Haarde concerning his role in the country's financial disaster. One item is a long form reportage of the Madoff swindle – as seen through the eyes of Ruth Madoff, the crook's wife. The rest are mostly more general commentaries on the situation. One, interestingly, is a review on 6th March of the Norwegian documentary on the 2008 financial crisis by Hans Petter Moland, *When Bubbles Burst* (which I will examine in more detail presently).

This ambitious film starts out by asking what happened when several Norwegian municipalities invested in rotten financial constructions sold to them by a Norwegian banking group but actually coming out of the United States. It contains interviews with authoritative economic analysts including Nobel laureate economist Joseph Stiglitz and one of the leading commentators in the *Financial Times*, Martin Wolf. The reviewer is a regular liberal-right commentator in the paper and he is critical of the film's perspective and of its lack of an answer to the initial question asked.

A quite different view is formulated in a syndicated commentary by Howard Davies, a professor at Sciences Po in Paris, formerly an executive at the Bank of England, director of the London School of Economics and chairman of the board of the Financial Services Authority. He discusses the problems with the dominant models used in economics, ridicules the Chicago School's liberalist idea of perfect markets and argues that new, more realistic, models are necessary so that a new, stricter regulatory regime can be established.

This piece is a good example of the way that media outlets aimed primarily at economic and political elites provide a platform for intra elite arguments over how best to address pressing issues that may threaten their continuing domination. Davies' former role as a regulator coupled with the prestigious positions he has occupied within academia place him at a certain distance from the captains of finance and provide him with political and cultural capital that allows him to mount an authoritative challenge to their view that there is no effective alternative to business as usual.

The most striking difference between this newspaper and *Aftenposten* is, however, telling: There are no concrete reports on the agonies of ordinary people affected by the crisis. The space in which elites argue amongst themselves is not a space where interviews with Spanish people desperately looking for work in Norway are most likely found. The victims remain objects rather than subjects. They are the faceless, collective, targets of policies or plans for intervention rather than named individuals with lives, hopes and views that deserve to be recorded and respected.

At the other end of the political spectrum, the reporting in *Klassekampen*/'The Class Struggle' (KK) was marked by the paper's scarce resources and their inability to employ foreign correspondents supplying independent views from the key centres of decision-making in Europe. Most items are thus based on readings of other media, international at least as much as national, normally presented in ways that reflect the paper's general left-wing critical stance (it was established by the Maoist movement), which in Norway includes an absolute resistance to membership in the European Union and even the European Economic Area. In fact, most of the 20 items generated by our searches are commentaries that are quite explicit in their critical perspective on the ways in which the EU and various member states try to handle the crisis. Telling examples of titles (in my translation) are 'Women are worst hit' (10th March), 'The EU accepts lobby demands' (10th March), 'The rule of industrial capitalism' (6th March), 'The EU attacks workers' (8th September).

Given the paper's political stance this is not very surprising, but it is unique in our sample. KK has grown a lot in terms of circulation over the last 10 years due to its status as an important source for often well-founded critical perspectives that are missing in the rest of the daily press, and it enjoys a wide-reaching respect from actors in the public sphere with quite different political views. It thus serves to confirm the basic idea behind the government's system of press subsidies, which is not least intended to secure the public's access to a wide variety of perspectives on political and cultural matters.

KK is also the only newspaper where satirical fiction is employed – a pseudo report from a press conference with IMF boss Christine Lagarde, including her backstage comments and toasting in champagne (10th March).

A somewhat surprising lacuna in the paper's coverage, though – as represented in our sample, it must be added – is the lack of concrete, human interest-like reporting on the situation of individuals and families in southern Europe. Nor, in contrast to the stories of migrants in *Aftenposten* is there any coverage of people arriving in Norway from the hardest hit countries looking for work and a new life for themselves and their families. The effects of the crisis on everyday life are thus clearly given a lower priority than the directly economic and political dimensions. We might suggest several explanations for this absence: the paper's lack of resources, a political orientation focused on the corridors of power, and the fact that because it is normally the second or third choice of paper for its readers it concentrates on views that the other papers neglect expecting its readers to get other kinds of coverage from other sources. This absence of flesh and blood individuals from the pages of a paper that presents itself as championing the 'people' against the centres of power plays into the hands of critics of the left who have long accused them of loving the idea of the workers but not wishing to actually meet them.

The sketchy overview presented above indicates that readers of the tabloid VG, though far more serious than equivalent British tabloids, are offered almost little or no information or explanatory material that would enhance their ability to understand what goes on, why it goes on and what can be done to improve the situation. In contrast, readers of the (once broadsheet) subscription-based *Aftenposten* would be reasonably well informed on key events in the day-to-day key development of the economic crises and offered insights into the perspectives of citizens in the hardest hit European countries, including some of those who seek work in Norway. For more specialized information and debate largely from a business point of view and with a leaning towards liberalist policies, they could turn to DN.

For leftist views on what goes on, there is KK. In both these politically opposite papers, though, there is little or nothing on the concrete everyday experience of hard hit ordinary people.

Overall, two types of material are missing from the newspaper coverage considered here: historical overviews that provide comprehensive information on the forces at work and their connections to day-to-day events, and specific information and arguments on the actual or possible options open to decision-makers nationally as well as internationally. A third element is touched upon by *Aftenposten*'s reports on the unemployed: material that would enhance or produce empathy for those suffering from the crises and, potentially generate an emotional motivation for political engagement with the issues in question.

As we argued earlier, access to these informational, analytical and empathetic resources is essential if citizens are to act effectively, even if we settle for Schudson's more modest ideal of engaged 'monitoring'. So are they available elsewhere, from other cultural forms? To explore this question let us look first at one of the other major fact-based genres, documentary film.

3

The documentary *When Bubbles Burst* premiered in the cinemas of major cities in Norway on 23rd March, 2012, and was aired by the public service broadcaster NRK later in the year. It is an attempt by the well-established Norwegian director of feature films, Hans Petter Moland, at making the international financial crisis understandable for a general audience. It starts out by telling the story of the small municipality Vik in western Norway that invested 10 years of future income from its hydroelectric resources in US sub-prime-based financial products (created by Citibank) sold to them by a major Norwegian financial enterprise, Terra, which had been recommended to them by the local bank. Their hope was that this would help finance a much needed road tunnel but it ended up as an immense debt when the value of their investment suddenly dropped to zero. Moland sends two representatives of the municipality on a journey to discover the causes of their situation. They go to the United States where they visit Detroit, and get an overwhelming impression of the colossal decay and decline from the city's glorious growth in the golden decades after the Second World War. They then go to New York where they visit Wall Street and get to talk to a number of specialists from both the financial sector and Academia. The dominant voice amongst the latter is Nobel laureate Joseph Stiglitz, whose basically Keynesian views are supported in various ways by other voices, primarily the Norwegian economist Erik Reinert and his colleague at the Tallinn University of Technology, in Estonia, the Venezuelan social scientist Carlota Perez (who also has links to the University of Cambridge and other UK universities). She talks mostly about her theory that major crises, including the current one, are tied to changes in technological paradigms so that the electronic, digital revolution that she sees starting with the invention of the microchip now needs to be replaced by a new revolution tied to 'green' technologies. The film historicizes the crisis in a surprisingly thorough way, going all the way back to Mesopotamia (!) and on to the many financial crises in the early days of western capitalism. Wonderfully illustrated with anything from several hundred years old prints to clips from the Great Depression and today's America, it presents a long string of talking heads that address the ways in which financial speculation has become progressively cut off from its ties to the real economy generating a near total collapse that affected, amongst many, many millions, the inhabitants of Vik, Norway.

Ninety-two minutes suffice to give a vivid impression of the historical and systemic nature of the current crisis. A Keynesian approach, rejecting austerity measures and advocating public spending and stricter regulation of the financial sector, is clearly privileged in terms of pointers towards a solution. At the same time, Perez' neo-Schumpeterian fatalism (on the inevitable 'creative destruction' produced by technological shifts) and the often difficult-to-follow expert attempts at explaining the financial system leave the audience at a loss when it comes to concrete alternatives for action. It is not surprising that the two men from Vik towards the end of their journey can only conclude that honesty is a necessary virtue.

It is, however, clear that a documentary such as this one provides space for an overview of the crisis and sustained argumentation on its causes and cures from particular perspectives, which are largely missing from daily newspapers because of limitations in their news-based format. The visual representations of decay, particularly from Detroit – where, amongst other things, the film shows a former grand building with wonderful ceiling décor converted into a parking structure – are stunning. The historical clips showing anything from 1950s US TV commercials to a famous Roosevelt speech ('nothing to fear but fear itself') are fascinating. Still, outside of a few people from Vik and homeowners hit by the loan crisis in Detroit, there are few representatives of the myriad victims of the crisis who might provide opportunities for empathy and potentially for solidarity. The representatives of the financial sector are all critical of the business they know from the inside, but none of them talk about the motivations or individual experiences of those actually involved in the construction of toxic products such as those bought by the municipality of Vik.

The 2011 winner of the Academy Award for best documentary feature *Inside Job* is discussed by other contributions to this volume, so I want to simply make some points related to my general argument.

Its start at the periphery of the financial centres of the world economy, Iceland, is reminiscent of the Norwegian film's start in Vik – but also very different, since Iceland actually produced an enormous financial bubble all by itself through mindless liberalization of the banking sector and a naïve optimism as to the sustainability of a financial economy based on massive debt. The film then moves to New York and investigates the 2008 financial crisis in depth, arguing convincingly through interviews and a variety of factual information, how the crisis resulted from the reckless speculation and outright fraud that thrived under conditions marked by the markedly more lax regulatory system that had developed since the 1980s. The film could well be considered a bit of a rhetorical masterpiece, where very cinematic footage, especially from Manhattan, interweaves with highly informative, concise and often dramatic and revealing interviews that may remind some viewers of Michael Moore's confrontations with his suspects. The ordinary viewer however will have to take notes or watch the film more than once in order to get all the complex information on procedures and products in the financial industry correctly. What remains in the mind after a first viewing is the impression of massive fraudulent behaviour supported by scholars closely tied to the industry who have been well paid for their services. The film also makes clear that these academics and the leading executives in the industry have been extremely well placed politically, having been called upon for government service by a string of both democratic and republican presidencies.

Inside Job enjoyed on the whole a very favourable critical reception, as indicated by the Oscar that it was awarded. Unsurprisingly, right-wing writers and media were not happy with it. But the fact that the film was both convincingly argued and hard-hitting, while refraining from Michael Moore's more theatrical devices (Peter Bradshaw of *The Guardian* described it as 'a Moore film with the gags and stunts removed'), made it a uniquely acclaimed and internationally successful rendition of the crisis and its construction in the corridors of financial and political power.

These two documentaries were available in cinemas and to Norwegian newspaper readers over roughly in the same timeframe (2011–2012) as the coverage represented by our spring and autumn samples of press coverage. They were discussed in various forums, online and offline, but never succeeded in attracting an audience comparable to the newspapers' readership. What most citizens then missed was the chance to acquire the deeper and longer form of historical and political understanding of the financial crisis provided by these 92- (*When Bubbles Burst*) and 120-minute (*Inside Job*) films. The only alternative, in practice even less available to most people, would be to read one or, preferably, more of the many books published on the subject. Norwegian media did not exactly overflow with reasoned recommendations for such books – and so only those with a particularly keen interest, international connections and a good command of at least English could be expected to search for and find such recommendations – and act upon them.

Once again we see a sharp stratification in access to essential cultural resources for effective 'monitorial' citizenship, with *Inside Job* requiring precisely the prior familiarity with economic terms and arguments that most viewers would be unlikely to possess and *When Bubbles Burst* failing to foreground the full human and social costs of the crisis. But what of mainstream Hollywood movies with plot lines constructed around the human consequences or public events? The question is, again, what kinds of input to the public's understanding are supplied by this (kind of) material.

4

I want to concentrate on two relevant US films here, one about the 2008 financial crisis and one about a key consequence of this crisis: unemployment. Writer-director J. C. Chandor's film *Margin Call* (2011) has, as indicated in the Internet Movie Database's collection of 'external reviews', been almost unanimously, critically acclaimed as a very realistic, nuanced representation of what went on during the 24 hours in 2008 in a financial institution very reminiscent of Lehman Brothers immediately before its collapse. According to Christopher Orr in *The Atlantic* (21st October, 2011), who thought the movie was one of the best made that year,

> Chandor's film is less a portrait of individual malfeasance than of systemic, cultural failure. His characters have made their moral compromises gradually, selling off bits of themselves at a loss, piece by piece, until they find that their debts outweigh their assets and the only evident way out is to keep going.

The film was nominated for the Academy Award for best original screenplay and also for the Golden Berlin Bear and other highly respected prizes. Despite these accolades, it never gained a cinema screening in Norway, which is surprising since all major Hollywood movies normally open very early in Norway. This decision, by the Swedish-owned distribution company SF Film, was based on a purely commercial judgement that classified the film as an 'art house' production with only limited mass audience appeal. It was, however, issued on DVD in June 2012 and has been on offer by streaming services such as Comoyo, owned by the dominant Norwegian telecom corporation Telenor. According to SF Film's marketing director for home entertainment, the DVD and Blu-Ray editions had sold 6,300 copies by January 2013, which is considered reasonably good.

The film's intensity as a drama springs from its animating plot device that shows the real, catastrophic situation of the firm being discovered almost by accident late in the evening by a young employee, working on data provided by a downsized risk manager. The ensuing struggle over how to handle this revelation takes place over the next 24 hours. The question is whether the company should try to sell as many as possible of their worthless financial constructs to their regular customers or not. They do try, confirming a moral bankruptcy that some of the characters have problems with. The audience is invited to identify primarily with those who have some scruples, primarily Kevin Spacey's character, Sam Rogers, but excellent acting in all major parts along with the dark, almost noir'ish night time *mise-en scène* contribute to an experience of nuanced, psychologically believable drama.

But what the film also does is construct a story where most of those involved did not know what they were doing before the sudden discovery of catastrophic prospects. The ethical collapse is portrayed as a response to a more or less unforeseeable situation. It is as if the company, and by extension, the US financial industry, moved from respectability to fraudulent practices only very recently. There are, as we now know, reasons to doubt this story.

The second film I want to examine, *The Company Men* (2011), also never got a cinema showing in Norway (according to personal communication from Nordisk Filmdistribusjon). This in spite of its star cast and the fact that it was critically acclaimed in the United States. The 'external reviews' listed on the International Movie Database show this – from Roger Ebert in the *Chicago Sun-Times* to the critics at the *New York Times* and the *Village*

Voice. The general opinion was that the film is a believable and interesting portrayal of the painful drop from way up high that business executives experience when they fall victim to financially motivated downsizing. The film's 'potentially noxious message' is, according to *Village Voice* critic Karina Longworth, that 'The bad economy is hard on rich people, too'.

Ben Affleck's character is a cocky MBA who lives in a huge house, drives a Porsche to work and spends a lot of time and money on golf. The audience is invited to sympathize with this character and feel sorry for his loss of a lifestyle more suitable for people who make far more than the 160,000 dollars a year he claims is his income as sales manager in the transportation business he works for. After unsuccessful attempts at getting another job suitable for an ambitious MBA he ends up working for his brother-in-law's small construction company. He is a lousy carpenter, but gets to experience hands on the production of something concrete and useful under the grumpy command of his brother-in-law, played by Kevin Costner. The number two man in the transportation corporation, played by Tommy Lee Jones, is one of its founders and the number one owner-executive's best friend. He also ends up losing his job after opposing the latter's downsizing strategy, which is motivated primarily by a wish to improve stock value before an expected takeover. There is also a third executive who gets fired, played by Chris Cooper, a man pushing 60 who has worked his way to the top from a start as a welder. There is a scene where Tommy Lee Jones walks with Ben Affleck in a deserted shipyard and talks about the good old times when the company they used to work for produced real, useful things – largely, it seems, various vessels for the US Navy. The film has an optimistic ending where all the laid off people get together under Tommy Lee Jones' leadership and set up shop again: reopening shipbuilding with the expressed intention of beating the Chinese and other foreign competitors.

The movie is well acted and has some positive realist features often associated with high-end television drama. The writer and director John Wells was an executive producer on two of the most acclaimed shows of recent years, *The West Wing* and *ER*. The characters and their relations appear believable up to a point. But on closer inspection, one wonders how it is possible that Tommy Lee Jones' character could have maintained his alleged best-friends relationship with the ruthless co-founder of the company for so long (since they were college roommates) and how such a self-indulged hyper-ambitious MBA as Ben Affleck's character would have chosen such a kind and cute-but-plain wife from such an humble background. In contrast, Tommy Lee Jones has a monstrously big spending wife who becomes sore when she is not permitted to use one of the corporate jets to go shopping in Florida (they live in Boston).

The Company Men opens with TV clips from news coverage of the financial crisis. But thematically it is more concerned with the problems of manufacturing in a globalized economy where production is increasingly is moved to low-cost areas overseas and where executives' strategies are more concerned with stock prices than anything else. It can therefore be said to paint a picture of just how central financial markets have become in today's western capitalism, a useful background for understanding the nature and significance of the financial crisis in itself. But the film's main message is that the solution is a return to the values of hard work, honesty and team spirit. Underneath, there is also, as pointed out by *Village Voice* critic Karina Longworth, a theme of unemployment as a form of emasculation:

> What still rings true, however, is the symbiotic link between money and masculinity. Not exactly dude-friendly (the pyrotechnics are all actorly, and emasculation is as pervasive as the defense-mechanism body humor in a bromance), *The Company Men* is maybe best understood as a chick flick about dicks: Before its too-easy conclusion, the movie offers a multifaceted glimpse at what can happen when the connective tissue between a man and his source of income is cut, and rarely suggests that it could be anything less than excruciating to stop the bleeding.

This is a particularly interesting claim since unemployment as emasculation was a recurrent theme in the analysis I did some 30 years ago of Norwegian novels on unemployment produced in the 1930s. But while the lack of income was an important aspect of unemployment in these representations, especially since it meant one was unable to form a family, the feeling of being useless because of the lack of work as a productive, creative activity, in most cases physical, was much more important than it is in *The Company Men*.

Both of these Hollywood representations of the crisis ask the audience to sympathize or at least empathize with white collar, upper middle and upper class people, their hardships and moral scruples. They both tell a story of a capitalism that has gone wrong due to uninhibited greed, an extreme emphasis on paper pushing instead of 'real' productivity and radically increased social differences in terms of economic resources. But they never refer to lax regulation, non-existing unions or any other politically challenging reasons for and potential solutions to the issue at hand. The crisis is understood as primarily rooted in the morality of individuals and so its solution also must be found in a kind of moral rearmament. As Frank Buchman put it in the speech that started the Moral Re-Armament movement (the 'Oxford Group') in 1938: 'The crisis is fundamentally a moral one [...] Moral recovery is essentially the forerunner of economic recovery. Moral recovery creates not crisis but confidence and unity in every phase of life' (Buchman 1955: 46).

5

The newspapers, documentaries and feature films we have considered here all provide citizens with information about, and a variety of perspectives on, the current economic crisis but as resources for 'monitorial' citizenship, they are limited in two important ways. First, the cultural forms they work with organize the possible ways that events and issues are represented in crucial ways. They construct patterns of spotlights and shadows that are then mediated by the ideological dispositions of particular media organizations and the productive resources at their command. Second, although a media system that keeps a diversity of cultural forms in play may offer a degree of plurality and comprehensiveness, citizens' effective access to this resource base remains strongly stratified by the differential command over economic and cultural capital.

Newspapers generally require brevity and exclude extensive formats outside of their weekend magazines. The findings from our press sample suggest that broader, historical and explanatory expositions of the causes and trajectories of the western financial crises and the links between its various aspects are missing. Attempts at something like this might have occurred outside of our sample's papers and periods, but it seems this is a space where documentary makers have come up with the most ambitious contributions aimed at the general public.

Both the examples presented here are critical, not only of the dispositions of financial institutions immediately before the 2008 crash but also of political authorities for withdrawing from regulation, academic economics for excluding the financial sector from dominant models of the economy, and prominent scholars for being too closely tied to the financial industry. These films not only suggest empirically founded ways of understanding the causes of the crisis but also point to areas for further critical debate and action. But while newspapers are extremely widely read in Norway (readers of papers like *Klassekampen* and *Dagens Næringsliv* will normally also read a [former] broadsheet like *Aftenposten* every day), documentary films have a radically smaller audience. This is so even if they are broadcast as *When Bubbles Burst* was. A 1-hour version was aired only on the 'elite' channel NRK2 only while *Inside Job* was never broadcast to my knowledge, and it seems its only cinema screening in Norway was at the Bergen International Film Festival.

The two feature films considered above provide believable psychological perspectives on the motivations of actors in the financial industry and their moral challenges on the one hand, and the situation of laid-off executives in manufacturing industries on the other. This experiential insight is a useful addition to the perspectives available in the other media but it remains problematic from a social point of view that Hollywood does not seem capable of producing films that invite audiences' empathy with people at the lower end of the social pyramid who suffer the most severe consequences of a large-scale financial crisis such as the present one.

It seems, though, as if even these gentle fictional representations of high-end aspects of the crises have severe problems in reaching a Norwegian audience. In spite of both films having star-studded casts and garnering a very positive critical reception in the United States and elsewhere, neither ever opened in Norwegian cinemas! Even though over half of Norwegian cinemas are still municipally owned – a unique system inherited from the 1920s – they rely largely on commercial distributors who evidently did not see sufficient profit potential in screening them.

So we arrive at a situation where neither an Academy Award-winning documentary on the causes of the crisis or two well-regarded mainstream Hollywood feature films exploring aspects of its moral dilemmas and social impacts could secure a general cinema release in Norway, and where the major local documentary anchoring the general crisis in a specifically Norwegian experience was relegated to a minority television channel and shown only at a local film festival. The economic crisis has consequences that reach into every life but the evidence presented here suggests that sustained engagement with its causes and consequences is seen as a minority rather than a general interest.

This same commercial judgement also underpins the dearth of coverage in the major tabloid newspaper, *VG*. In contrast, the paper directed at the country's economic elite, *DG*, offered a steady stream of relevant information and analysis on responses to the crisis by leading financial and political actors but not a single item on its impact on ordinary people. The only human interest story is a feature on the fraudster Bernie Madoff, recounted from the perspective of his wife, an exclusively 'insider' viewpoint mirrored in the two Hollywood feature films discussed here.

The only media outlet in our sample that offered both commentary on the course of the crisis and coverage of its dire impact on the lives of those most exposed to its impacts was *Aftenposten*. However, while its continuing economic base in reader subscriptions provides a buffer against the demands of advertisers and the ascendency of commercial calculation, it also restricts its social reach.

We therefore end up with the profound paradox that access to the resources of information, analysis and empathetic insight needed to understand and respond to the most serious economic crisis in Europe and North America since the Great Depression are themselves stratified in crucial ways by the differential economic and cultural capital available, first, to media workers operating with particular genres and within particular markets and, second, to readers and viewers in different social locations. The findings presented here suggest that those most severely affected by the crisis in their everyday lives are least likely to have access to readily intelligible accounts of its causes and possible solutions while those most involved in addressing problems with the present system are least likely to be aware of the scale and scope of the human devastation that has followed in its wake. This damaging disjunction poses major challenges for the democratic process. Analysis without empathy does little to address the irresponsibility of those at the top. Hurtful experiences uncoupled from sustainable explanation lays the ground for a resurgence of populist politics.

References

Fraser, N. (1990), 'Rethinking the public sphere: A contribution to the critique of actually existing democracy' in Craig Calhoun (ed.), *Habermas and the Public Sphere*, Cambridge MA: The MIT Press, pp. 109–142.

Habermas, J. (1996), *Between Facts and Norms: Contributions to a Discourse Theory of Law and Democracy*, Cambridge MA: The MIT Press.

Hove, T. (2009), 'The filter, the alarm system, and the sounding board: Critical and warning functions of the public sphere', *Communication and Critical/Cultural Studies,* 6:1, pp. 19–38.

Kant, I. (2010 [1784]), 'An answer to the question: 'What is enlightenment?'' in Jostein Gripsrud, Hallvard Moe, Anders Molander, and Graham Murdock (eds), *The Public Sphere Volume 1: Discovering the Public Sphere,* London: Sage Publications, pp. 5–11.

Schudson, M. (1999), *The Good Citizen: A History of American Civic Life,* Cambridge MA: Harvard University Press.

Part 3

Screen talk

Chapter 8

No guns, no rules, just pure capitalism! Hollywood's portraits
of Wall Street

Anja Peltzer

Introduction

On 8th December, 2012, the *Frankfurter Allgemeine Zeitung* devoted several columns to Sarah Wagenknecht's statement on the current crisis, in which she argued that it is still, at root, a financial crisis. The German politician's article was illustrated with a film still taken from *The Dark Knight* (Christopher Nolan, 2008), displaying Batman's merciless opponent the Joker burning several million dollars. This is by no means an isolated example. The adoption of the fictitious world of symbols and codes made in Hollywood in the context of the factual coverage of the financial and the initially mentioned states crisis can be found regularly in print media publications. On 11th October, 2010, for example, Gordon Gekko (alias Michael Douglas), the notorious speculator from Oliver Stone's *Wall Street* movies (*Wall Street*, Oliver Stone, 1987; *Wall Street: Money Never Sleeps*, Oliver Stone, 2010), made the cover of the news magazine *FOCUS* whose central feature addressed the role of speculators during and after the financial crisis 2008/2009. In April 2010, the *Economist* borrowed a reference from the monumental Vietnam War film *Apocalypse Now* (Francis Ford Coppola, 1979), to depict German Federal Chancellor Angela Merkel as the renegade Colonel Kurtz in the context of the debate over the crisis in Greece.

All three publications – The *Economist*, *FOCUS* and *FAZ* – resorted to the fictitious inventory of Hollywood's film world to put a human face on the abstract processes of the financial economy. This recirculation of movie characters underlines the fact that screen heroes not only have an impact in theatres, they also remain present as highly resonant icons and collective symbols that can be drawn on in media narratives and everyday life (see Wulff 2001: 150). 'The repertoire of cinematic icons has long since become an integral component of cultural memory' (Röwekamp 2004: 114) and fictional entertainment media have become a central dimension of public communication (see Görke 2002: 66). The integration of fictional icons into factual reporting, as illustrated here, assigns a significant role to the medium film in the public communication of today's developed societies: 'This is a visual, cinematic age' (Denzin 1991: viii).

Hollywood's presence in financial-economic coverage leads to the two initial key reflections of this article: that films are both mediators and archivists of their social environment. They do not emerge without ties to society – quite the contrary – they are 'reactions to the social environment, in which they develop' (Everschor 2003: 205).

Figures 8.1–8.3: The *Economist* (29th April, 2010); *FOCUS* (11th October, 2010); *FAZ Feuilleton* (8th December, 2011).

However, they do not just simply depict it, but – depending on their style – convey a specific interpretation of social reality (Schroer 2007: 7) and thus provide 'interpretation options, which have changed and continue to change the conditions of social reality as they are being adapted by a scattered public' (Keppler 2006: 46). What develops in consequence is an interplay between everyday social life and cinematic features (see Winter 1992). From this decidedly film-sociological perspective, this chapter thus focuses on how cinema represents the financial economy. Or following the title-metaphor of this book: How does cinema make money talk?

In the case of financial economics, questions about its cinematic translations offer a special trick, since one of the basic features of financial markets is the abstraction of trade from 'those "material values", which before were considered guarantors of economic operations' (Stäheli 2007: 11). Material values are translated into shares and traded as fictitious capital on de-territorial stock markets. This abstraction already contains aspects of the 'de-economization' of the stock market, which go beyond the usual 'semantics of production, exchange and labour market' (Stäheli 2007: 11). Ever since its establishment at the turn of the last century, the financial sector has been trying to compensate for its own de-economization with a 'legitimate economic way of communication' (Stäheli 2007: 11). Just as financial speculation situates itself between economic abstraction and popular speculation, its communication is always both economic and uneconomic at the same time (Stäheli 2007: 10 et seq.). One consequence of this is the production of a strongly metaphorical vocabulary in the semantics of the world of financial economics: Bubble, Boiler Room, Lady Credit, Poison Pill. Cinematic representations are therefore facing the task of having to retranslate the abstract, already fictionalized processes of the financial sector. The abstractness of financial economics and its omnipresent consequences for everyday life challenge the film medium not only as an entertainer, but also in its social function as a translator and mediator in current times of social crises.

Cinema is thus, of course, much more independent in its interpretation of the stock market than actuality media coverage: 'The point is, ladies and gentlemen, that greed, for lack of a better word, is good. Greed is right. Greed works. Greed clarifies, cuts through and captures the essence of the evolutionary spirit' (*Wall Street*, Oliver Stone, 1987). Gordon Gekko's sermon on the rules of capitalism is a real classic in movie history. Not only does it mark the broker as the bad guy, it also presents the cinematic discourse about the stock market as explicitly normative. Of course, greed is not good – quite the opposite: It is one of the seven deadly sins. The abstractness of the stock markets, as well as the normative expression of their medial translations raises the following the research question: How does cinema depict the financial markets and their impact on modern capitalist societies? Which symbols, metaphors, allegories are and have been chosen by Hollywood cinema? How are they judged or valued? Which strategies of justification are offered by these movies?

The good, the bad and the broker

Hollywood started to depict the stock exchange long before Gordon Gekko's times. As early as in 1920, *The Saphead* (Herbert Blaché, 1920) was released to cinemas as an evening-filling silent movie with Buster Keaton in the lead. Since then, Wall Street has again and again provided the scene for Hollywood productions, irrespective of whether the pictures were tragedies, psycho-thrillers or comedies. The role of the stock exchange varies extensively from film to film. Sometimes it is no more than a dramaturgic accessory, as in the slapstick comedy *Tower Heist* (Board Ratner, 2011) or the psycho-thriller *American Psycho* (Mary Harron, 2000). Sometimes, however, the market and the investment banking sector, in particular, are right at the heart of the story showing the full spectrum of trading, speculating, losing and winning. It is these films, which place the stock exchange centre stage, that I want to focus on here. I will be looking particularly at five films: *Margin Call* (J. C. Chandor, 2011), *Wall Street: Money Never Sleeps* (Oliver Stone, 2010), *Boiler Room* (Ben Younger, 2000), *Wall Street* (Oliver Stone, 1987) and *The Saphead* (Herbert Blaché, 1920).

The first analytic approach to the films is provided by the character of the speculator, '[combining] two almost contradicting systems of logic: on the one hand a no longer calculable imagination of and intuition for the market ("market feeling"), on the other hand control of these figments of imagination by rational processes which reach from instruments of mathematical modelling and the sophisticated techniques of chart analysis, up to cognitive and emotional self-control techniques' (Stäheli 2010: 356). The speculator's interface role between economic rationality and the speculative element links successful speculation on the global financial markets both with economic expert knowledge and enough courage to take risks. It represents two sides of the same coin: economic calculation on the one side and taking the risk to gamble on the other. It is precisely this area tension and potential of conflict that has characterized criticism of the stock exchange since the very beginning of its existence: It has been seen as nothing other than 'gambling which wears the mask of business' (Gladden 1884: 624). This kind of criticism is currently more topical than ever. In the coverage of the financial crisis the terms 'casino capitalism', 'gambling' and 'financial jugglers' are frequently used. No one seems to have anything good to say about speculators any more – neither in the news, nor in the arts. In consequence, the literature scientist Joseph Vogl summarizes the characteristics that have constantly accompanied the financial and stock exchange speculator for at least two centuries as follows: 'Endowed with the legend of ruthless efficiency, predator instincts, and with the reputation of individuals – young, smart and raised by wolves – who embody the dangerousness of financial capitalism, he becomes part of a series reaching from Balzac's "Condottieri", "pirates" and "werewolves" of the money business, over Marx' vagabonding knighthood of credit up to the *mad dogs*, *rogue traders* and "wolf packs" of today's foreign exchange markets' (Vogl 2011: 11). It might seem easy to criticize the 'bankster'; however, there are at least two profound arguments supporting him. On the one hand, speculation does not only destroy, it also leads to real economic production. On the other hand, trading also entails a democratic chance: everyone can win. This combination of democratic chance, capitalistic maximization ideals, preparedness to take risks and the 'good-for-nothing' character in the person of the broker supplies Hollywood with a story ideally suited for the cinema but also a dilemma because one can become a millionaire, without ever having washed a single dish. Hollywood's answers to this dilemma are now explored using five movies as examples.

The Saphead: **The contingency of speculation**

In *The Saphead*, shot in 1920, Buster Keaton plays Bertie van Alstyne, the only son of Nic(holas) van Alstyne, a Wall Street tycoon. Wall Street is introduced on the intertitle as 'A little street where money is everything and everything is money' [00: 02.26]. Thanks to his productive gold mine Henrietta, Old Nick has made a fortune and is almost completely at peace with himself and the world. The only fly in the ointment is Bertie's pronounced tendency towards gambling and his extravagant lifestyle. However, Bertie does not spend his nights out for mere pleasure. To his sister by blood, Rose, he confesses: 'I'm leading a fast life, because I'm in love with Agnes'. This strategy was recommended by the guidebook *How to Win the Modern Girl* and Bertie wishes nothing more for himself than to win the love of his stepsister, the adopted Agnes and thus to be able to marry her. But the strategy does not work. On the contrary: due to his immoral life, both Agnes and Old Nick are abandoning him more and more. And it gets worse, since Rose's husband Mark Turner – who 'had succeeded in marrying Old Nick's daughter, but had never succeeded at anything else'– manages to set Bertie up with his illegitimate daughter, the outcome of a brief affair Mark had with the dancer Henrietta. The fact that both the sinful dancer and the blessed gold mine have the same name is important for the story. The illegitimate child is the final straw: Old Nick breaks all ties with his son Bertie and shows him the door. Old Nick now introduces Mark, the son-in-law and broker, to the business instead of Bertie. Mark sees his chance when his father-in-law sets out on a journey and entrusts him with the management of his business for one week. He steals

Figures 8.4–8.6: Stills taken from *The Saphead*: At the stock exchange (Fig. 8.4), 'I'll take it' (Fig. 8.5) and after close of trading (Fig. 8.6).

Old Nicks Henrietta Mine securities and sells them off. This causes the stock to plummet. Mark plans to become rich by buying back the stock when it reaches a bottom low. Only, his plan is foiled when the rejected Bertie, visiting the stock exchange for the first time, is advised by his dad's broker to buy back the stock – all without realizing what he is doing. The result is, Bertie saves his dad from bankruptcy, becomes rich overnight and wins the girl.

The picture's semiotic play with the contingence of speculation – the pretending – unfolds in particular in the last scene on the trading floor of the New York stock exchange. There, *Bertie* displays full commitment in attempting to stop the group of brokers calling the name of the calamitous Henrietta and thus literally 'gets things going on the floor'. According to his father's broker, the phrase Bertie needs to use to silence the men is: 'I'll take it'. By following this advice, Bertie – who has meanwhile assumed an aggressive pose – buys his father's mine Henrietta back without suspecting anything of the kind. Everyone calling 'Henrietta' gets tackled by Bertie: 'I'll take it!' (Fig. 8.5). Bertie's combative-provocative pose is an appropriately ironical representation of speculation, which from the beginnings of the stock exchange has been described as 'looking out for trouble' (see Stäheli 2010: 355). Bertie's extensive gambling experience seems to have prepared him excellently for the hustle and bustle on the floor. With great physical effort, he throws himself into the group of traders, sliding over the floor, so that there is not much left of his suit at the end (Fig. 8.6). In Bertie's case the trading on the floor is staged as 'hands-on work'. This is a crucial element, because by plunging into the turmoil with the intention to silence the crowd, he not only saves his father's company while being completely ignorant of the fact that that is what he is doing, but also fulfils the material-economic as well as typically American ideal of the 'hands-on mentality'. Whoever gets his hands dirty increases the gross national product and is thus rewarded: The value of the mine rises. The film thus evaluates two different things at the same time: Bertie's physical efforts are rewarded in full compliance with the American dream *anybody can make it big* and the contingence of speculation is unmasked.

The combination of ignorance, readiness for action, coincidence and monetary background – Bertie still has some money left from a paternal inheritance – in this example not only leads to a successful market performance, but also to an ambivalent attitude on the part of Hollywood towards the speculator. On the one hand, the stock exchange is staged as a space of turmoil and trading as contingent. On the other hand, it is exactly the radically democratic potential, as well as the abstraction of values at the stock exchange, that enables Bertie to save his father's company and his own future. This ambivalent attitude towards the speculator is increased, since not only Bertie speculates at the stock exchange, but also his opponent, the good-for-nothing Mark Turner. This way, the film not only provides an evaluation of the speculator, but presents two types of speculators: Mark as the lazy speculator destined to fail and Bertie as person with moral integrity who succeeds. While Mark will never trade again, Bertie remains in the game. This does not condemn speculating as such, but only its fraudulent form. This is a normative stance that remains topical in today's cinematic stock market depictions, typified by Oliver Stone's two *Wall Street* pictures.

Gordan Gekko: The temptation of speculation

In interviews on the *Wall Street* films, such as the press conference on occasion of the premiere of *Wall Street: Money Never Sleeps* in Cannes (www.arte.tv) Michael Douglas keeps mentioning how he has been confronted again and again by people who told him that their decision to work in the investment sector was inspired by Gekko. His objection that he was playing the bad guy was vehemently objected to by bankers saying they had never perceived him as such. 'So it was all very seductive I guess' (www.dailyrecord.co.uk). The fact that Gekko played the role of the 'villain' certainly did not harm the attractiveness of the financial sector to aspiring employees (Verdicchio 2006: 61). Quite the opposite: Gekko became a role model for stock brokers who imitated his habitus even literally quoting his lines such as 'lunch is for wimps'. The seductiveness is an effect of the relationship between Bud Fox and Gordon Gekko, since Gekko's strength is based in particular on Bud's weakness. How come, the paths of these two characters cross?

Bud Fox comes from a working-class family, his father is a flight mechanic with 'BlueStar Airlines' and a trade union chairman. Bud works as a stock broker in New York and trades via phone. But he wants more. He wants to make big bucks, just like his role model, the trader Gordon Gekko. Week for week, day after day, Fox calls Gekko hoping to finally meet with him. One day he succeeds. He is granted an audition and reveals sensitive insider information he has obtained through his father in order not to immediately get thrown out of Gekko's office again. Gekko and Fox are in business, but that is not all. Gekko becomes Fox' mentor and standard for trade ethics, clothes, women and hairstyle. Gekko makes good money from Fox' eagerness, as he continues to provide valuable insider information – often illegally. When Bud's father's airline faces difficulties, he suggests that his mentor buy and reorganize the company. Gekko agrees. However, Bud soon realizes that he made a mistake. Gekko will liquidate this company as he has others. Bud feels betrayed and swears revenge. With the help of Gekko's arch rival Sir Larry Wildman and the tricks he has learnt from Gekko, Bud manages to save BlueStar and spoil the deal for Gekko. Immediately, after having severed ties with Gekko, Bud is arrested in his office for insider trading. He is willing to cooperate to get a conviction for Gekko and to reduce his own sentence at the same time. The film ends as the Fox family is on its way to court, where both Gordon Gekko and Bud Fox have to face judgement for their actions.

According to popular Hollywood patterns, the story of Gekko and Fox is character-centred cinema (Bordwell 1985: 13). The basis for such a story is a concrete problem in the form of a natural catastrophe, an accident, an unknown person or a special assignment. The protagonist has to tackle an issue – which at this point at the latest has turned into a concrete goal – advancing the film plot (Eder 2000: 82). This is the case in *Wall Street*: Fox gains access to Gekko's trader universe and gets more and more familiar with his business, while accelerating the story. This feature of the narrative recalls the many sport films made in the same production decade such as *The Color of Money* (Martin Scorsese, 1986), *Days of Thunder* (Tony Scott, 1990) and *The Karate Kid* (John G. Avildsen, 1984). A new talent becomes a winner under the wings of an experienced coach. The goal of these recent arrivals is to become 'the best'. But what is Bud Fox's goal? This is revealed in the last scene when he faces Gekko.

After Gordon Gekko has been fleeced by Bud Fox's trading efforts and Fox has agreed to cooperate with the authorities to convict Gekko, there is a showdown between the former mentor and his renegade apprentice, who is now wearing an FBI wire. It rains. Fox and Gekko are facing each other in Central Park, off Wall Street. Gekko wears light-coloured clothes and is both in the centre of the shot and the action. Fox is dressed in black and walks towards him. Similar to a western shoot-out, the two opponents face each other in the street dressed in long coats, with the difference that the alleged villain is dressed in white and the alleged good guy in black. In its setup, this scene clearly differs from the rest of the film. The reduced number of cuts (no more than 10 during the entire 2-minute scene), the constant camera close-ups and the shaky hand-held camera suggest the high authenticity of the scene. Gekko gives free reign to his rage and disappointment. He insults Fox and hits him in the face several times. Bud does not resist. Gekko dominates. He is primarily depicted in bird's eye view or in over-the-shoulder shots. Bud, in contrast, is shot from a worm's eye view, from the rear or from ground level. Only once he is at eye-level with Gekko – Wet and with a bloody nose, he replies to Gekko's angry question asking why he had stabbed him in the back with the 'BlueStar' deal: 'I don't know. I guess, I realized I'm just Bud Fox. As much as I wanted to be Gordon Gekko. I'll always be Bud Fox'. This statement encapsulates Bud's passivity. Not only the choice of terms from the word field of uncertainty ('I don't know'; 'I guess'), but also the fact that he formulates imitation as an identity goal and does not provide an independent statement, makes him fail both as apprentice of Gekko and as hero of popular Hollywood cinema. The alternative course of action to Gekko's pursuits therefore presented – to put it bluntly – as Bud's identity stagnation. The immoral, but authentic Gekko is compared to the failed and passive Bud who is forced to act morally and literally looks pale. It is not Bud who advances the story, but Gekko. The hero, who remains standing in the dramaturgic sense, is no one else than the villain himself. This is one of the reasons for the seductiveness of Gekko's character, but there is another.

Figures 8.7–8.9: Stills taken from *Wall Street*: At *Gekko*'s office (Figs. 8.7–8.8), 'Let me show you my charts' (Fig. 8.9).

'It's not a question of enough, pal. It's a zero-sum game. Somebody wins and somebody loses' [1: 29'24–1: 29'28], he explains to his apprentice. Gekko's dialogues are filled with capitalistic passwords, characterizing him as a ruthless, full blooded, trader. But the villain's semiotic capital is not only fed by the capitalistic repertoire: The Mephisophelean rhetoric 'I create nothing. I own. We make the rules, pal' – and the visual presentation make Gekko both charismatic and diabolic.

This becomes apparent, for example, when Bud meets Gekko for the first time and Gekko is sitting in his red leather armchair, cigarette smoke ascending in front of his face (Fig. 8.8) while a 'blazing' Manhattan appears behind the enormous windowpanes of his office (Fig. 8.7) or when Gekko lures Bud with his charts in the semi-dark (Fig. 8.9). Gekko's actions are characterized by both genial and cunning and unscrupulous. The Mephisto quotes in Gekko's staging are the strongest arguments against him – being the classical villain. In Goethe's portrayal of Mephisto it is the 'scoffer' ['*Schalk*'] who provokes activity and development, because 'ever too prone is man activity to shirk' (Goethe 1966 [1808]: 18). And in the end it is Mephisto who convinces his lord to take the bet. In this construction, speculation is not only an evil of the financial markets, but also a condition for the economy continuing to grow. The staging of traders as Mephisto hits a sensitive spot in modern capitalistic societies and makes the film a moral play. The question is: growth yes, but at what price?

In answer to this question, *Wall Street* offers two types of action: On the one hand, there is Gordon Gekko, the ingenious as well as unscrupulous, full blooded capitalist, always at full throttle. He knows, how the game works, because he plays it according to his own rules. 'He's a mixture of ruthless venality and roguish charm' (Arsenault 1998: 23) and as Oliver Stone puts it: 'He's a fascinating buccaneer' (Riordan 1995: 226). On the other hand, there is the dewy-faced Bud Fox, an over-ambitious youngster, who keeps chumming up to Gekko, until explicitly asked to stop doing so by him. Even when Bud sacrifices his former mentor, he is not intrinsically motivated, but forced into action by the pressure put on him by the police and the supervisory body. His passivity – as counterpart to Gekko – undermines the construction of *Wall Street* as an anti-capitalistic morality play. *Wall Street* does not criticize Gordon Gekko, but offers the new broker generation no alternatives to Wall Street's established action patterns.

Oliver Stone's sequel, *Wall Street: Money Never Sleeps*, also raises the question of an alternative. Gordon Gekko is back, and this time is accompanied by Jake Moore – a young broker, who is – in addition – engaged to Gekko's daughter Winnie. Gekko has spent

8 years in prison for insider trading and on the day of his release, there is nobody there to pick him up, not even Winnie. She blames her father for her brother's drug-related death and has broken all ties to him. But Gekko finds his way back into business fast and in that context meets Jake. Both have a thirst for revenge on the same person, Bretton James, a rival CEO – Gekko, because Bretton betrayed him and delivered him to the police, Jake, because Bretton is responsible for the death of his paternal mentor, Louis Zabel. Both are thus united by a hardly philanthropic motivation: revenge. Just like Bud Fox, Jake believes for a long time that he and Gekko have the same objective. But then Gekko abandons him and Jake seems to lose it all: his relationship with Winnie, his money as well as his credibility as a broker.

A remarkable feature of *Wall Street: Money Never Sleeps* is that the film represents the interdependence between financial market and everyday social life with various staging strategies. In the picture's opening sequence two of these elements are already being established. After the pre-sequence, Gekko's release, the film's intro shows shots of Manhattan from different perspectives. From the Hudson River, a long slow camera pan along Manhattan shifts to fixed perspectives of the city, in time-lapsed quick motion, while the New York's skyline is shown as a white curve diagram – which appears in the upper part of the screen as Dow Jones Industrial Average, a cinematic statement regarding the inter-connection of financial-economic processes and social reality (Fig. 8.10). From this external perspective on the city, camera focus then shifts to the private sphere, the two-story penthouse of Jake and Winnie, to finally pan directly to a renewable energy plastic model in the form of wind turbines (Fig. 8.12), after a short scene at Jake's workplace, easily recognizable by the six monitors displaying market data (Fig. 8.11). With the pan, the film not only intertwines speculation and real economic projects, but also investment in long-term, socially useful, research. The young committed trader Jake Moore embodies the action model of meaningful speculation. Here the stock market not depicted solely as a self-contained arena, obscure and removed from the lives of normal people. Speculation is presented as a necessary condition of sustainability and progress. The film thus raises the crucial question of any free market: Does the end justify the means?

In *Wall Street: Money Never Sleeps* both heroes and villains speculate, but some do it for a 'just cause', such as renewable energies. The normative pattern provided by *The Saphead* thus seems to repeat itself here at first. There is the good and there is the bad broker. In the second part, however, Gordon Gekko is not the one being sacrificed as the 'bad broker', but the aforementioned Bretton James. Gordon and Bretton know each other from the old days.

Figures 8.10–8.12: Stills taken from *Wall Street: Money Never Sleeps* (Oliver Stone, 2010).

Gekko fills in his future son-in-law about his opponent by explaining that 'James is a player, just like me. And he has an ego as big as Antarctica. Just like me'. Bretton James loses the game against Gekko and is taken to court for share manipulation and tax evasion. Gordon Gekko and Jake Moore, however, remain in business. Gekko from London, continuing to play the game according to his own rules and Jake from New York, investing in renewable energy. The normative picture of good and bad broker is here extended by Gordon Gekko, the player. The incalculability, in the form of Gekko, is simply a fixed component of the stock market.

The picture's final shot depicts a family celebration over the roofs of New York. Winnie and Jake are celebrating their son's birthday, and everyone is there: Gordon Gekko, the fusion scientist, Jake's Wall Street colleagues, Jake's mother, the failed and highly indebted real estate broker, and Winnie's colleagues from the left-wing website Frozen Truth, which ultimately toppled Bretton James. The excessively harmonious final renders the crucial capitalistic question as positively answered undermining the film's critical construction of the stock market and the figure of the investment banker. At the same time, it raises the possibility of shifting criticism to everyone involved in the money business. After all, the final shot of the family celebration is also a social inclusion metaphor. The thesis of the film is: the financial market is not a decoupled parallel world, but an omnipresent power in today's capitalistic societies, requiring everyone to act 'responsibly'.

Boiler Room: **Playing the players**

In *Boiler Room* (Ben Younger, 2000), the 19-year-old Seth tells the story of his Wall Street experiences. All the newspapers and TV shows had urged him to join the show: and so he did, as a broker. 'And that's exactly what I wanted to do: get in. I didn't want to be an innovator, I just wanted to make the quick and easy buck'. His employer is the brokerage firm J.T. Marlin, located 'a good hour from the New York stock exchange'. The situation of the company is its programme: a miss is as good as a mile. First, Seth is irritated by the dubious working atmosphere at J.T. Marlin, but the fast and easily made money via phone convinces him. However, he soon finds out about the secret of J.T. Marlin's success and the above average commissions. He and his colleagues sell shares in companies that – in fact – do not exist. The shares ultimately belong to Marlin itself. The sales department creates artificial demand and as soon as all shares are on the market – selling is stopped. But it is not only Seth who uncovers the company's illegal practices. The FBI is also on them and when he agrees to cooperate with the authorities, the days of the company are numbered.

When Seth has its first interview with J.T. Marlin he notices that all the employees act as if they were at Wall Street in spite of the spatial distance an assumption reinforced by the advice the chief instructor, Jim Young, offers Seth and the other broker apprentices: 'Act as if!'. This paradigm also allows the company to rid itself of any social responsibility. The question of what was real becomes obsolete. The 'act as if' policy has replaced striving

Figures 8.13–8.15: Stills taken from *Boiler Room*: Seth's backroom casino (Fig. 8.13), gambling at bar (Fig. 8.14) and at office (Fig. 8.15).

as the productive mode of the American Dream, a premise that is consistently staged at a variety of levels throughout the movie. On the phone, for example, when the young brokers use other names to be able to sell all the shares faster, or in Seth's backroom casino for students, where they gamble, as if they were in Las Vegas (Fig. 8.13). The most significant 'act as if' scene however is shot at Greg's, Seth's team leader with J.T. Marlin. The J.T. Marlin boys watch a movie with pizza and beer. It is *Wall Street* by Oliver Stone. Seth enters the room at the point when Bud and Gekko meet for the first time. When Gekko appears the boys demand absolute silence and synchronously repeat the dialogue: each text line, both individually and even as a whole group. The 'act as if' habitus accompanies the J.T. Marlin brokers, irrespective of the duration of their service, throughout the entire picture. This is illustrated by their belief that if they can talk like Gordon Gekko they can also crack the stock market, by the fact that they immediately stand out in New York's broker bars, because they are unaware of the dress code and because they do not notice, until the very end, that they do not operate in the real stock market. Instead they work one hour away from Wall Street and are being used to manipulate shares of worthless or fictitious companies.

By constantly staging the 'act as if' or the 'playing of the player' motto, the picture not only comments on the risks of a de-regulated financial economy, but also points out the close relationship between gambling and speculation, casino and stock market. A metaphor, by the way, all stock market movies presented here have in common. To quote Gordon Gekko once again: 'It's not about the money – It's about the game'. When he joined J.T. Marlin, Seth was by no means a novice when it came to handling the money of other people. After abandoning college, he ran an illegal casino for students in his home (Fig. 8.13). *Boiler Room* systematically develops the parallels between gambling and the stock market. The motivation to get rich fast is behind both enterprises. Every moment is used to make money, no matter how (Figs. 8.14 and 8.15). While the speculator, as a privileged figure of economic subjectivity, is characterized, in the fight to distinguish gambling from speculation (Stäheli 2006: 38), economic competence no longer plays a role in J.T. Marlin's picture. Ultimately, the speculator is nothing more but a player.

Boiler Room offers no comprehensive judgment on the stock market and speculation. Only the hustlers are criticized. The movie's thesis is thus based on one of the oldest requirements speculators ever had to meet. As Max Weber (1894) stated: 'Speculators should have more to offer than just a pencil, a note pad and a big mouth' (Weber 2000 [1894]: 647).

Margin Call: **Fathers and mercenaries**

One of the more recent Wall Street fiction films is *Margin Call* (J. C. Chandor, 2011). It is the year 2008. Asset managers, brokers and financial advisers are still juggling with large amounts, generating dizzying profit margins without any bad conscience. But the financial crisis has already arrived and the investment sector has had to let people go on all hierarchical levels. Eric Dale, the boss of the risk department of a large investment company, is made redundant as well. Before he leaves the company, he hands a memory stick containing the results of his last calculations to his young colleague, Peter Sullivan who continues Dale's work and finds out that the company's end is near. The bank holds an enormous asset volume, which – in the near future – will turn out to be worthless and thus unsaleable. The bank's losses, however, will be substantially higher than the worth of the whole enterprise. The situation is critical and time is of the essence, a fact that is recognized immediately by everyone informed of Sullivan's discovery from the head of the department, the managers, to the directors. Now, there are two possibilities. Either a possibly terminal crisis for the firm is initiated by accepting bankruptcy or all the shares are offloaded as soon as possible. This second option will create a crisis for investors persuaded to buy them, since they will be left holding toxic assets. The company's management finally decides to sell all assets immediately, regardless of the consequences.

Margin Call's screenplay is mainly set at night and almost exclusively in the offices of the enterprise. Monitors are reflected in the office windows, so that the external existence of the financial world recedes into the background and the system is confronted with its own reflection. The picture not only presents the financial sector as a deregulated market, but as largely self-referencing entity. In *Margin Call* the function of windows is substituted for by monitors. The cosmos of the financial markets revolves exclusively around these monitors (Fig. 8.17). The conventional conceptions of space have become outdated. The global financial economy is 'inside' and the real economy is forced to remain 'outside'. This spatial reversal already formulates a first fundamental warning to the system, rendering the view through the window, which culturally and historically has always also been the view of realization and enlightenment, obsolete. The classical establishing shot on New York, which is the picture's first shot, is consequently not sharp, but distorted by a fisheye lens. New York is at the heart of the financial bubble (Fig. 8.16).

Figures 8.16–8.18: Stills from *Margin Call*: the establishing shot (Fig. 8.16), the monitor-window (Fig. 8.17), the escalator (Fig. 8.18).

When comparing the stock market films portrayed here, it is remarkable that in parallel with the money plot, they all systematically develop father-son relationships. In *The Saphead,* it is Bertie, who is first kicked out by his father, the Wall Street tycoon, but then – more or less consciously – manages to rehabilitate himself. In *Boiler Room,* it is the relationship between young Seth and his father, the judge Marty Davis. In the first Wall Street movie, Bud Fox (played by Charlie Sheen) has to choose between the two father figures Gordon Gekko and his natural father, the unionist Carl Fox. The fact that Carl was played by Sheen's own natural father, Martin Sheen, might be seen as a subtle semiotic suggestion as to which of the two father figures can be regarded to be the only true one. And, if we wished to follow the threads of intertextuality through which images and actors carry the baggage of connotations they have accreted into the present, we might notice that Martin Sheen was the main protagonist of Francis Ford Coppola's, *Apocalypse Now* (1979), which, as we saw at the outset of this discussion was featured on the front cover of *The Economist,* to typify the crisis. *Margin Call* also features the father-son motif.

While the issue of what to do with the toxic assets of the investment company has been discussed, morning has broken and the day of the sell-out is impending. Peter Sullivan, the 28-year-old rocket technician, runs into his superior Sam Rogers, the director of the trading department, outside the building. The discussion develops rather coincidentally and takes place outside the office, on the street. There is no other scene in the picture with more spatial proximity to social life. The setting of the scene thus provides all the conditions required for clear, direct face-to-face communication. During the discussion, however, both participants are always depicted in the same frame, but most of the time, throughout the scene, are never in full focus. Already the cinematic staging prevents any possibility of social interaction at eye level. In this scene, Peter, who is as old as Rogers' son, asks the more experienced Rogers for his assessment of the situation, and/or his paternal advice. Rogers answers him with blunt honesty. He neither conceals everyone's forthcoming dismissal, nor his own uncertainty regarding the decisions of the management. He turns out to be experienced but ignorant and therefore does not fulfil the role of the father providing advice. While the other films have at least one solid father model, *Margin Call* operates with a seeming father role, again and again shirking his responsibilities. While, the role of the father can be understood as a role model, which – based on his own experiences – can forecast future actions, the thesis of the film *Margin Call* is that there is no 'role model' for the speculator. Here, the film recalls a statement on the speculator by the cultural sociologist, Urs Stäheli:

Especially since the speculator always expects that everything is about to change, the construction of his identity is neither supported by historical narrative traditions or stories of establishment. Thus a daring social figure is established – a social figure with a highly flexible identity. The speculator has to re-invent himself over and over; he ultimately becomes a bottomless second-order observer.

(Stäheli 2010: 358)

The only role model Rogers offers is the one of the mercenary. Even if Rogers at first opposes the company's chosen strategy, he finally gives in. The pay-off cheque promised by the head of the company, John Tuld, serves its purpose. After all, every man has his price. Peter thus remains faithful to his role model Rogers, even if he ultimately signs a new work contract with Tulds and does not turn his back on the company. The interesting aspect of Rogers' and Peter's decision is that the film grants discretion in decision-making to both characters. Especially in Rogers's case – for a very long time – the expectation of him not being willing to agree to the merciless sell-out of the toxic assets is created. By showing that both characters use this room for manoeuvre for rather than against the system, *Margin Call* impressively illustrates the powerful appeal of the stock market and the capitalistic principle that underpins it. Their decision to endorse the system is anticipated at the end of the discussion scene mentioned earlier, when, on their way back to the offices, both characters are absorbed by the escalators conveying them onwards and upwards (Fig. 8.18).

Conclusion: Beyond Wall Street?

The stock market has furnished Hollywood with material from the very beginning. All of the films analysed in this article have depicted different aspects of its organization and dynamics. *The Saphead* stages the stock exchange as contingent slapstick. In both *Wall Street* films it is both a place of chance and temptation. *Boiler Room* displays it as a casino and *Margin Call* as a self-referenced micro-cosmos, a time bomb ticking inside any capitalistic society. These different forms of representation are connected in turn to various justification strategies for the stock trading business.

In 2006, in his article on cinema's representations of the financial sector, Dirk Verdicchio argued that a film like *Wall Street* does not criticize capitalism as such, but rather depicts two different types of economy, production economies that are presented as the 'good' economics and financial economics that appear as the 'bad' economies. This confrontation with the honest and innovative 'real' economy remains a central theme in public talk critical of the present organization of financial capitalism. The stock market films analysed here, however, offer a different duality centred on the confrontation between 'good' and 'bad' financial economics. What is 'good' is the financial sector, which understands itself as productive and formative (The Green Wall Street). 'Bad' are the people driven by greed acting purely for their own benefit. *Boiler Room, The Saphead, Margin Call* and *Wall Street I & II* are not attempts to settle the score with the stock market, but only with the people not playing by the rules. The claim of all the films for more know-how and social responsibility on part of the brokers leaves at least two conceptions untouched. They do nothing to challenge the central features of the stock trading business. On the contrary, by presenting it as an arena in which, despite the risks, everyone could be a winner, they reinforce one of the main sources of its enduring attraction. Added to which, they silence any sustained interrogation of an alternative economics to an ethics based on the motto 'the end justifies the means' is being abandoned.

The interdependent links between the financial market and the social lives of citizens demand informed citizens who see themselves as participants in a political system as well actors, and victims, within a market. The films analysed here fail to provide this essential perspective.

References

Arsenault, R. (1998), 'The stockbroker's son and the decade of greed', *Film & History*, 28: 1–2, pp. 16–27.

Bordwell, D. (1985), *Narration in the Fiction Film*, Madison: University of Wisconsin Press.

Denzin, N. K. (1991), *Images of Postmodern Society. Social Theory and Contemporary Cinema*, London: SAGE.

Eder, J. (2000), *Dramaturgie des populären Films. Drehbuchpraxis und Filmtheorie*, Hamburg: Lit Verlag.

Everschor, F. (2003), 'Hollywood als politische Macht', in F. Everschor (ed.), *Brennpunkt Hollywood. Innenansichten aus der Filmmetropole der Welt*, Marburg: Schüren, pp. 205–07.

Gladden, W. (1884), "Three dangers", *Century: A Popular Quarterly,* 28: 4, pp. 620–27.

Goethe, J. W. (1966 [1808]), *Faust. Der Tragödie erster und zweiter Teil, Urfaust*, Hamburg: Christian Wegner Verlag.

Görke, A. (2002), 'Unterhaltung als soziales system', in A. Baum and S. J. Schmidt (eds), *Fakten und Fiktionen: über den Umgang mit Medienwirklichkeiten*, Konstanz: UVK, pp. 61–73.

Keppler, A. (2006), *Mediale Gegenwart. Eine Theorie des Fernsehens am Beispiel der Darstellung von Gewalt*, Frankfurt am Main: Suhrkamp.

Riordan, J. (1995), *Stone: The Controversies, Excesses, and Exploits of a Radical Filmmaker*, New York: Hyperion.

Röwekamp, B. (2004), 'Ein Zitat ist ein zitat ist ein ziTAT. Anmerkungen zum Filmzitat', in B. Röwekamp and M. Steinle (eds), *Selbst/Reflexionen. Von der Leinwand bis zum Interface*, Marburg: Schüren, pp. 113–26.

Schroer, M. (2007) (ed.), *Gesellschaft im Film*, UVK: Konstanz.

Stäheli, U. (2007), *Spektakuläre Spekulation. Das Populäre der Ökonomie*, Frankfurt am Main: Suhrkamp.

Stäheli, U. (2010), 'Der Spekulant', in S. Moebius and M. Schroer (eds), *Diven, Hacker, Spekulanten: Sozialfiguren der Gegenwart*, Berlin: Suhrkamp, pp. 353–65.

Verdicchio, D. (2006), 'Finanzökonomie im Film: Monstrosität als Inklusionsmodus', *KultuRRevolution: Zeitschrift für angewandte Diskurstheorie*, 50, pp. 58–63.

Vogl, J. (2011), *Das Gespenst des Kapitals*, Zürich: Diaphanes.

Weber, M. (2000 [1894]), 'Die Börse II. Der Börsenverkehr', in M. Weber (ed.), *Gesamtausgabe, Abt. 1, Bd. 5.2, Börsenwesen. Schriften und Reden 1893–1898*, Tübingen: Mohr, pp. 619–57.

Winter, R. (1992), *Filmsoziologie. Eine Einführung in das Verhältnis von Film, Kultur und Gesellschaft*, München: Quintessenz Verlag.

Wulff, H. J. (2001), 'Konstellationen, Kontrakte und Vertrauen. Pragmatische Grundlagen der Dramaturgie', in *Montage/av 10/2/2001*, pp. 131–54.

Internet

Press Conference, 'The premiere of *Wall Street: Money Never Sleeps* in Cannes', http://www.arte.tv/de/2151166,CmC=3219704.html.

Interview with Michael Douglas on www.dailyrecord.co.uk (29th September, 2010), http://www.dailyrecord.co.uk/showbiz/celebrity-interviews/2010/09/29/michael-douglas-i-had-no-idea-my-wall-street-character-gordon-gekko-would-turn-out-to-be-an-icon-86908-22594657/.

Films cited

American Psycho (Mary Harron, 2000)
Apocalypse Now (Francis Ford Coppola, 1979)
Boiler Room (Ben Younger, 2000)
Days of Thunder (Tony Scott, 1990)
Margin Call (J. C. Chandor, 2011)
The Color of Money (Martin Scorsese, 1986)
The Dark Knight (Christopher Nolan, 2008)
The Karate Kid (John G. Avildsen, 1984)
The Saphead (Herbert Blaché, 1920)
Tower Heist (Board Ratner, 2011)
Wall Street (Oliver Stone, 1987)
Wall Street: Money Never Sleeps (Oliver Stone, 2010)

Chapter 9

System down! Three documentary accounts of crisis

John Corner

A systemic crisis like the financial collapse of 2008 presents documentary production both with an opportunity and a challenge. The sheer scale of events provides unusually high levels of significance, bordering on the apocalyptic, which recruits viewing attention at the levels both of civic concern and of spectatorial 'awe'. However, at the core of events there are the abstractions of market structures and techno-economics rather than, say, the physical intensities of armed conflict, natural disaster or climatic shift. How to use audio-visual resources to connect with these? Documentary has always displayed a tension, often a discursively productive one, between its interest in using film and television to 'photograph the living scene' as John Grierson called it, as part of 'showing the real', and its interest in making claims *about* aspects of reality, claims that have much more to do with 'telling' than 'showing', whatever illustrative aids they deploy.[1] With its generic appeal and status grounded in what is offered to the eye, documentary often also needs to present a great deal to the ear in order to do the tasks it sets itself. Unlike the mediations of audio-visual news forms, features and current affairs, these tasks allow for considerable space and time to place and consider a topic, drawing on a range of contexts and generating an expositional flow less urgent and foreclosed than most news accounts, able to take side-roads and come at questions from several angles. Even when working as a mode of 'long-form' journalism, documentaries can also employ the symbolic resources more closely associated with fiction. These include extensive use of music, a connotative resonance in shots and sequences and a narrative pacing and density that have time fully to enlist the imagination of the viewer, including by devices of mystery and puzzle, drawing them into the thematic worlds depicted.

I want to discuss how three documentaries go about the job of portraying what happened in 2008, exploring the often very different ways that they use image and sound. The selected films are Michael Moore's *Capitalism: A Love Story* (2009), Charles Ferguson's *Inside Job* (2010) and the first episode of Adam Curtis' three-part series *All Watched Over by Machines of Loving Grace* (2011). All three were high-profile productions, receiving a wide range of appreciative as well as critical commentary. Some of the routes taken by them are predictable, if no less effective for that – the close examination of 'typical' cases, a focus on the 'human story' as a tale both of 'victims' and 'villains', the drama of the confrontational interview, a closing in on key documents – but others show the distinctive originality of viewpoint and approach behind their production.

Rather than dealing with each one separately, at the beginning of this discussion I want to move across them, making comparisons and contrasts. First of all, however, a few points about each are necessary to establish them properly in my account.

Capitalism: A Love Story continues Moore's signature style of polemical engagement, assumed naivety, comedy and interventionism for which he has become internationally famous. Perhaps surprising here is the extent to which he makes positive connections with Christian teaching in his exploration of the ethical deficits of the dominant economic system and also with the unfulfilled hopes of post-war social democratic development to be found in the final speeches of President Franklin Roosevelt. Once more weaving a biographical element into his account, as a personal journey of discovery in which disgust at what has happened is relayed through a relentlessly ironic perspective (the persona of the 'critical clown'), he is joined by his father for a section of the film dealing with the closure of GM motors at Flint, Michigan (the focus of his first documentary success, *Roger and Me*, 1989).

Inside Job operates for a large part within the framework of conventional documentary exposition, although towards the end the commentary (one projected more strongly for many viewers by its being spoken by the actor Matt Damon) shifts in tone from the investigative to the openly critical and accusatory. More than either of the other two films, it attempts to engage seriously with the complex technical character of the economic instruments and practices that lay behind the collapse, to this extent contrasting with the largely comic approach to economic technicality taken by Moore. However, like Moore (and as its title clearly suggests) it is concerned to emphasize the 'criminality' of what went on and does so with sustained effectiveness through archive footage of the proceedings of various committees of enquiry and a number of tough interviews. Its expositional structure is emphasized by a numbered five-part scheme ('How we got here', 'The Bubble', 'The Crisis', 'Accountability' and 'Where we are now').

Episode one of Curtis's series *All Watched Over By Machines of Loving Grace*, called 'Love and Power' (the main title is taken from a poem by Richard Brautigan), has a much broader expositional remit than the financial crisis. The main theme of the series is the various employments of computers as tools of elite power and social control and this first episode has an initial focus on the influence of the ideas of thinker and novelist Ayn Rand. However, in the second half it places economic breakdown at the centre of the account, initially as part of the story of the rise to prominence of the economist Alan Greenspan and the ideological constellation (involving Rand) which he represented. Curtis situates the events of 2008 within the context of shaping ideas about technology, political economy and contemporary consciousness as well as recent world history. Grounded in the confident exposition of its sober if often ironic commentary, although using a range of other material including interviews, it is the most theoretically ambitious of the three films, locating its topics explicitly within an intellectual as well as socio-political landscape.

I want to organize my account first of all thematically and then in relation to form, even though there is an inevitable and often close interconnection between these. Thematically, I want to look at 'places', 'faces and voices' and 'causes' as three different aspects of the way in which the films organize their substantive account, using the specific resources available to documentary production. I then want to take one scene from each of the films for closer scrutiny in a way that not only connects with the categories of my earlier discussion but also gives a more continuous and sustained sense of the identity of each documentary, however difficult it is to do this given their internal variety of theme, form and tone.

Places

At the centre of all three films is Wall Street's architecture of power, both neoclassical stone and glistening towers. This is the locale both of crisis and criminality, the 'ground zero' of 2008 whose Manhattan activities are often in shady relationships with what is going on in the familiar white edifices of Washington. *Capitalism*, in a typical piece of interventionist theatre close to its conclusion, has Moore taping-off several of the main buildings of Wall Street as a crime scene. *Inside Job* starts its account in Iceland and stays for a while with the outlines of the Icelandic bank-collapse story of the same year, told against the austere beauty of mountain and sea, until it moves to New York, seen initially in sustained aerial shots underneath a surging musical score that convey an emphatic sense of a dramatic narrative turn ('from the periphery to the centre', as it were).[2] In *All Watched Over* there is little sustained sense of place since Curtis' visual approach is essentially that of montage (also a feature of Moore's aesthetic), running together diverse images drawn from archive footage, including that of feature films, so as to construct a flickering flow of often subliminal associations. The places, times, actions and people, sometimes seen only in the briefest of shots, constitute a pattern of continuities and shifts over which a musical soundtrack cues a varying sense of mood and (an often frenetic) tempo to accompany Curtis' commentary as he builds his steady exposition. Only occasionally does this sense of 'placelessness' shift to something more stable and referential, as in the more sustained sections of news clips marking important events and developments in the political and economic world and in the interview sequences, for the most part conventionally set in offices and apartments.

Capitalism differs markedly from the other two films in giving extensive time to the places and spaces of the dispossessed, literally so insofar as a number of sequences involve the eviction of people from their homes as well as a struggle by workers at a Chicago factory to receive payment of their wages following redundancy. This concern not only with deficits of the system but with the impact of these deficits upon particular lives in particular places provides Moore's account with a degree of humanitarian indignation that frames the whole of it. By taking his film radically outside the spaces of high politics and high finance for extended sequences, Moore introduces points of strong spatial contrast with the power duality of 'Washington and Wall Street'. These are deeply social contrasts that, by their very physicality of portrayal, support the abstractions of the moral case about inequality he wants to make. *Inside Job* also connects at points with the experiences of victims of events (including a sequence of interviews in an urban 'tent city' in which people who have lost their jobs or their savings speak of their situation), but *Capitalism* establishes dispossessed space as the ground of its own point of view rather than simply another point of reference.

Faces and voices

Here, perhaps the first point to make is that throughout *Capitalism*, we are constantly being returned to Moore's face, sometimes directed straight at the camera as he performs his actions and his speaking, sometimes in interview questioning, sometimes in open confrontation and sometimes in modes of reaction (puzzlement, incredulity, open hilarity). As in other films by Moore, this strongly presentational, performative approach makes watching the film a matter of a personalized alignment with the filmmaker, an alignment that will be variously negotiated or perhaps even refused by viewers. The other two films are 'faceless' in their authorial function, although both are strongly voiced within a more formally scripted language than that employed by Moore and thus, although they carry more impersonal and distant tones, they have a more dense and elaborate vocabulary in which to describe, explain and judge. Both, like the Moore film, have a number of faces assembled within them, some of which are immediately recognizable as the faces of power and some of which are there to testify, drawing on personal experience and on various kinds of expertise to do so. In all three films, there is extensive use of two distinctive framings of face and voice – that of the archive footage of leading figures in the story of the crisis, especially news footage, and that of the interview, including interviews conducted specifically for the films. Again, in all three films there emerges a cast of 'the guilty', those elite managers of the economy about whom serious questions are raised. Prominent here in all of the films is Alan Greenspan, the US economist who served as Chairman of the Federal Reserve from 1987 to 2006. With variations, his thinking about the financial system in relation to geopolitics and the US social order is viewed as central to what went wrong. Hank Paulson, US treasury secretary during the crisis and a major organizer of the 'bailout' (see below) is also a principal character, not only in what went wrong but in what went wrong in trying to put it right.

Some of the interviewees recruited to the films are there largely to lend support for the developing evaluation. They are in a sense, even if implicitly so, 'witnesses for the prosecution' in the accusations that all three films in their different ways are concerned to make. Other interviews are positioned more as 'witnesses for the defence', attempting to present a more positive account than the film (and the interviewer questioning) suggests. These interviews, not surprisingly, often develop into confrontations and this is particularly true of *Inside Job*, which contains revealing and often comic moments of tortuous self-justification and 'forced errors' by elite interviewees in response to sustained and quite aggressive questioning. Some of these scenes are contained within the archive footage of sessions of committees of enquiry but the most significant are within interviewees conducted by the production team. In them, it is not only what is said that is revealing but also the changing expressions on the respondent's faces, underlining the strength of documentary as a genre for watching as well as listening, even where what is being watched is as pictorially conventional as an interview. I shall select one of these sequences for attention later.

Causes

To look at how the three films engage with questions of causality moves my discussion from the physical world of documentary's images and sounds to the abstract world of the propositions carried in their commentary and interviews. Among the questions at issue here is one I shall return to in the next section and in my conclusion – how far does what went wrong indicate a deficit *in* the system itself, perhaps even the failure *of* that system or how far is it a matter of abuse, mismanagement and criminality? This is, of course, a continuingly significant question in relation to all accounts of the problems of the world economy in the aftermath of 2008, carrying implications for the level and scale of the remedies proposed. Two of the films, *Inside Job* and *Capitalism* contain, as I have indicated, a strong charge of criminal behaviour. This is presented most graphically in Moore's attempt to recover the 'bail out' money from the relevant banks by turning up outside them with sacks, together with his taping off of Wall Street as a crime scene (an act prepared for right from the opening sequence of *Capitalism*, which involves footage from surveillance cameras showing bank robbers in action). In *Inside Job*, it is made clear in a comment like this from the narrator:

> Since deregulation began, the world's biggest financial firms have been caught laundering money, defrauding customers, and cooking their books; again and again and again.

All Watched Over works with a more abstract, theorized framing of dominant ideological formations than either of the other two. Although it 'personifies' the crisis through key figures who have acted largely in protection of their own interests it wishes to offer an explanation less at the level of 'crime' than at the level of elite self-deception, as the extract in my next section will show. *Inside Job* provides the most sustained 'technical' explanation of the financial practices and instruments (including derivatives, collateralized debt obligations and credit default swaps) that lay behind the crisis. It locates the primary source of the collapse in corrupt practice resulting from the search for maximized profit within an under-regulated system receiving White House blessing. It thus poses serious questions at the systemic level as well as identifying criminal activity, although it is the latter that provides it with the focus cued by its title. In what might be seen, in context, as a somewhat beside-the-main-point issue, it gives attention to high-class prostitution and drugs as one aspect of the lifestyle of a section of the financial elite, adding a further, noirish tinge to the account of their corruption. For Moore in *Capitalism*, the essential criminality *is* the system, the charge thereby going well beyond the indication in *Inside Job* that the prosecution of specific individuals should be sought but that so far no action to achieve this has been taken. What happened in 2008 is seen as something deeply written into the DNA of the dominant economic order, an order against which moral values rather than economic argument offer the primary line of opposition. It is here that Moore makes strong and sustained connection with the views of the church, accessing the views of a Roman Catholic Bishop among others.

Both *Capitalism* and *All Watched Over* are concerned with not only the factors that contributed to the collapse of 2008 but also the extent to which the Federal 'bail out' agreed after extensive lobbying pressure in October was a *continuation* of the corrupt alignment between Washington and Wall Street rather than any shift to a revised order (which *Capitalism* suggests might have followed a bailout refusal). The 'remedy', with its massive pay-offs to the banks and little clear accountability as to how the money was used, is thus viewed as a product of the same systemic weaknesses as the 'problem'.

Three scenes

I noted that selecting three scenes for closer analysis does an injustice to the variety and complexity of each film, both thematically and formally. However, it has the advantage of allowing an examination, albeit selective, of the specific image-flow and language at work in the accounts. There is a temptation to select material from the same stage of each film, the opening or the conclusion being obvious choices, but I have resisted this in order to bring a variety of discursive forms into focus in my discussion.

The conclusion of *All Watched Over*

There is a good sense in choosing this sequence, since it exemplifies the abstract propositional drive of the commentary, which is the defining feature of the series, as well as the busy flow of connected and disconnected images that serve sometimes to 'illustrate' and sometimes to act as connotative support or counterpoint to what is being said. The text below ends the film:

> The Chinese money had led America into a dream world. But the reason so few bankers and politicians questioned it is because of their faith in computers. They were convinced that it was the computer that had brought stability to the system. The machines created mathematical models, parcelled out the loans and then hedged and balanced them so that there was no risk ... But then in 2008 that dream collapsed. Alan Greenspan's vision of a new planet and Gordon Brown's promise of no more boom and bust were revealed to be fantasies built on a wave of financial speculation. That speculation had happened because those running the financial sectors in American and Britain had promised that they could create a new type of market democracy that would be stable. But again and again it had led to the opposite, chaos and instability around the world. And finally that had happened at the very heart of the west. But yet again just as in South East Asia ten years before those running the financial sector now mobilized political power to rescue themselves and protect their supremacy. They asked the politicians to bail them out and they agreed. And again, just as in South East Asia, the price was being paid by the ordinary

people of the country. But we are now entering a very strange moment. We know that the idea of market stability has failed. But we cannot imagine any alternative. The original promise of the Californian ideology was that the computers would liberate us from all the old forms of political control and we would become Randian heroes, in control of our own destiny. Instead, today, we feel the opposite. That we are helpless components in a global system, a system that is controlled by a rigid logic that we are powerless to challenge or to change.

This spoken account is accompanied by a soundtrack that mixes surging rock riffs, the sprightly elegance of chamber music and 'disturbing' electronic tones, bangs, snarls and whooshes. From the start of transcript above, the image track runs roughly as follows:

1. Corridors and doors in an office building rapidly passed through in forward and reverse.
2. Computer mainframe units in a large room seen in slow-motion and through diverse angles of camera.
3. The NY stock exchange trading floor in a flurry of anxious activity.
4. A world leaders' economic summit. Barack Obama with other leaders at a conference table.
5. Drunk man (with face pixelated) attempting to get money from a cashpoint and having great difficulty in standing up and performing the required actions.
6. Chairman of Federal Reserve Ben Bernanke entering US Treasury Building along with aides.
7. Politicians going up steps and into buildings on Capitol Hill prior to meetings.
8. Storm violently blowing trees at night, shadows on buildings with lit windows.
9. New York stock exchange trading floor. Anxious faces and phone-calls.
10. A crowd assembled in a dark hall watching a gigantic early videogame play out on a large screen.

This combination of sound and image follows the pattern that Curtis has established as his own signature style – a series of confident, formally phrased claims, inclining towards the curt, placed across a rapidly changing series of images that combine a denotative function with strong and shifting associational meanings. Here, the drunk trying to get money from the cashpoint is a typically inspired piece of found footage.

The argument carried in the commentary is essentially quite simple but worth paraphrasing in its main points. What has happened is the product of self-deception (a 'dream world') about the capacity of computers to bring economic and political stability. Instead, radical instability has followed, but the elite of the financial sector have been bailed-out from the consequences of their illusion by their continuing alliance with political power. As for ordinary people, they are the ones who will suffer but 'we', who once thought we might be liberated and control our own destiny through the use of computers, have instead recognized that we are trapped within a system from which we cannot escape and to which there is no imaginable alternative. There is some uncertainty here around the pronominal usage. While initially it appears that it was an elite that was self-deceived, it now appears that a much greater grouping ('us all') at least partly succumbed to the liberatory fantasy too. 'We' believed that increased freedom from political control would follow from computer applications but 'we' now realize that, instead, we are politically helpless.

There are at least two elements that weaken this closing account. First of all, the emphasis on the naïve faith in computers works to displace direct engagement with the political and economic motives and interests lying behind the crisis (both of which are fully dealt with in the other two films). This emphasis follows from the fact that film's main theme concerns the way in which computers have exerted a treacherous pull over the imagination (and the fantasies) of the political and corporate elite. However, to carry this theme so uncompromisingly through the section on financial crisis seriously limits the explanatory scheme. Secondly, the explanation offered is organized as a grand melodrama of reversal, in which 'we' who expected liberation are instead further confined. This has strength as a trope of narrative design, certainly. But the relationship between the self-deception of the elite and the delusion of the larger group ('us') is left implicit and no evidence is offered anywhere in the film to support the idea that 'we' ever did seriously believe in such generalized liberation, or indeed that all sections of the elite ('they') ever did either. In order to give edge and impact to his history of ideas, Curtis is guilty of reductionism both in his identification of beliefs about computers as the principal factor at work in the creating of the 2008 crash and in his assertions about a widespread not simply elite faith in their benign potential, one that has now to be exchanged for despair. The story of the crisis as a story of delusion ending in terminal entrapment is too vulnerably a rhetorical construct – one dependent upon strategic exaggerations and omissions around a narrowly selective line of causality.

Key interview sequences in *Inside Job*

In some contrast, both formally and thematically, with the above are the following two sequences of exchange in which Charles Ferguson pursues his enquiry with interviewee Frederic Mishkin, who is not well prepared either for the content or the tone of the questioning.

Extract 1. Ignoring of warnings about the dangerous level of loans.

NARRATOR:	One of the six Federal Reserve Board governors serving under Bernanke was Frederic Mishkin, who was appointed by President Bush in 2006.
FERGUSON:	Did you participate in the semiannual meetings that, uh, Robert Gnaizda and, and, uh, Greenlining had with the Federal Reserve Board?

MISHKIN:	Yes I did. I was actually on the committee that, uh, that was involved, involved with that; the Consumer Community Affairs Committee.
FERGUSON:	He warned, in an extremely explicit manner, about what was going on; and he came to the Federal Reserve Board with loan documentation of the kind of loans that were frequently being made. And he was listened to politely, and nothing was done.
MISHKIN:	Yeah. So, uh, again, I, I don't know the details, in terms of, of, uh, of, um – uh, in fact, I, I just don't – I, I – eh, eh, whatever information he provide, I'm not sure exactly, I, eh, uh – it's, it's actually, to be honest with you, I can't remember the, the, this kind of discussion. But certainly, uh, there, there were issues that were, uh, uh, coming up. But then the question is, how pervasive are they?
FERGUSON:	Why didn't you try looking?
MISHKIN:	I think that people did. We had people looking at, a whole group of people looking at this, for whatever reason –
FERGUSON:	Excuse me, you can't be serious. If you would have looked, you would have found things.
MISHKIN:	Uh, you know, that's very, very easy to always say that you can always find it.

Extract 2. The 2006 study of Iceland.

FERGUSON:	In 2006, you co-authored a study of Iceland's financial system.
MISHKIN:	Right, right.
FERGUSON:	Reads out 'Iceland is also an advanced country with excellent institutions, low corruption, rule of law. The economy has already adjusted to financial liberalization – while prudential regulation and supervision is generally quite strong.'
MISHKIN:	Yeah. And that was the mistake. That it turns out that, uh, that the prudential regulation and supervision was not strong in Iceland. And particularly during this period –
FERGUSON:	So what led you to think that it was?
MISHKIN:	I think that, uh, you're going with the information you have at, and generally, uh, the view was that, that, uh, that Iceland had very good institutions. It was a very advanced country –
FERGUSON:	Who told you that?
MISHKIN:	– and [they had not] –
FERGUSON:	Who did, what kind of research –
MISHKIN:	Well, it –
FERGUSON:	– did you do?

MISHKIN:	– you, you talk to people, you have faith in, in, uh, the Central Bank, which actually did fall down on the job. Uh, that, uh, clearly, it, this, uh –
FERGUSON:	Why do you have 'faith' in a central bank?
MISHKIN:	Well, that faith, you, ya, d-, because you ha-, go with the information you have.
FERGUSON:	Um, how much were you paid to write it?
MISHKIN:	I was paid, uh, I think the number was, uh, it's public information.

{ON SCREEN CAPTIONS: FREDERIC MISHKIN WAS PAID $124,000 BY THE ICELANDIC CHAMBER OF COMMERCE TO WRITE THIS PAPER.}

FERGUSON:	Uh, on your CV, the title of this report has been changed from 'Financial Stability in Iceland' to 'Financial Instability in Iceland'.
MISHKIN:	Oh. Well, I don't know, if, it–, whatever it is, is, the, uh, the thing – if it's a typo, there's a typo.

In both these sections of interview, filmed with the interviewee (behind a desk) as the only person in shot, a senior financial advisor and Federal Reserve Bank governor, who is also an elite economics professor, is put under sustained and firm questioning as to what he knew and what he did. In both sections, the weakness of his defence, both in substance and in delivery, is clear, becoming close at times to an open admission of guilt. Ferguson is frequently direct and hostile (e.g. 'why didn't you try looking', 'you can't be serious', 'who told you that') is a way that clearly throws Mishkin's phrasing into disarray. Throughout, the camera shows the deeply uncomfortable experience of the interview for him, using regular close-ups of his face as he listens to the questions and attempts answers.

It is interesting to contrast the method and effect here with the confrontational exchanges that Moore sets up (mostly on the street or on the steps of corporate institutions) in *Capitalism*. These are certainly not without their effect too, often combining comic theatre with visually strong images of 'authority', but Moore rarely gets an answer to his most pressing questions. The refusal even to attempt an answer or to respond at all is, in a sense, the result that his film expects and is seeking.[3] Here, in *Inside Job*, the interviewee, presumably expecting a rather different agenda to be followed, is forced into a performance that is as revealing in its verbal content as it is viewable in the visible humiliation it exacts.

Supportive testimony in *Capitalism*

The interview above can be contrasted with the way in which Moore uses interview comments from two priests and a Bishop to develop his ethical critique of capitalism, subsequently working off the idea of 'propaganda' to present a graphic, and characteristically funny, account of how capitalism has become accepted as a 'good thing' by the American people.

MOORE:	Is Capitalism a Sin?
FATHER DICK PRESTON:	(in a chapel setting, with stained-glass windows and candles).

Yes, Capitalism for me, and for many others, at this present moment is evil. It's contrary to all that's good, it's contrary to the common good, it's contrary to compassion, it's contrary to all the major religions. Capitalism is precisely what our holy books, our holy books in particular remind us is unjust and in some form or fashion God will come down and eradicate somehow.

MOORE:	This was Father Dick Preston, the priest from Flint who married my wife and me.
PRESTON:	Capitalism is wrong and therefore has to be eliminated.
MOORE:	Eliminated! That might be a little harsh. So I decided to go and talk to the Priest that married my sister and brother-in-law. I'm sure he would have a more balanced approach when it came to Capitalism.

(Priest putting on full vestments in church)

Father Peter Dougherty Catholic Priest for 45 years (captions)

DOUGHERTY:	(now sitting on a chair in tee shirt): It is immoral, it is obscene, it is outrageous you know. It is really radical evil, radically evil.
MOORE:	Wow! Does their boss know their talking like that? I thought it best to go and check this out with the Bishop.

Bishop at desk, walking through Church.

Bishop Thomas Gumbleton Archdiocese of Detroit (captions)

GUMBLETON:	The system does not seem to be providing for the well-being of all the people. And that's what makes it almost in its very nature contrary to the Jesus who said 'blessed are the poor, woe to the rich'. That's right out of St Luke's Gospel.

Moore now with Peter Dougherty.

MOORE:	How have we put up with this system for so long?
DOUGHERTY:	The system has built into it what we call propaganda. I'm in awe of propaganda. The ability to convince people who are victimized by this very system to support the system and see it as a good.

(Monochrome archive footage, man speaking direct to camera)

We know that American capitalism is morally right, because its chief elements, private ownership, the profit motive and the competitive market, are wholesome and good. They are compatible with God's laws and the teachings of the bible.

MOORE:
(Old film, magician waving hands to hypnotize man)
For as long as I can remember, I've been told that competition and profit are good things.

(Echoing voice over images of hypnosis) They are compatible with God's laws and the teachings of the bible.

MOORE:
(over images of swirling vortex) And if increasing profits means locking up a few kids or cashing in on the death of an employee [reference to earlier sections of the documentary].

(Deeper toned echo effect) They are compatible with God's laws and the teachings of the bible.

MOORE:
(over image of white-coated man hypnotizing woman on couch). it is morally right to provide for the stockholders

(Echoing voice, with even deeper tones, over close-up images of hypnotic eyes and woman's face) They are compatible with God's laws and the teachings of the bible.

MOORE:
(over images of a staring man swaying a pendant hypnotically) Debt, eviction and exploitation.

(Voice, deeper still) They are compatible with God's laws and the teachings of the bible.

MOORE:
What were we really pledging our allegiance to? (shot of classroom and children pledging allegiance with hands on chests).

(Deep echo voice) The profit motive.

This movement across three interviewees followed by commentary over archive film and the use of distorted voice effects shows the sociability, and the accessibility, of Moore's approach, both contributing to the strong entertainment experience that his work offers alongside its expositional throughput. There is a relaxed 'openness' of structure about the way in which Moore registers to the viewer his surprise and doubts about the testimony of the priests and decides to 'check it out' with the Bishop. His established persona as the naïve 'little guy' who is just trying to figure things out through a folksy process of trial and error, while it has annoyed some viewers and critics, is here at work in involving the viewer in a journey of discovery that takes little for granted by way of prior knowledge. What the priests supply to the film is accredited moral condemnation, although the very uncompromising terms in which this is done, with suggestions of the 'elimination' of the system (by God) not accompanied by further details, risks a problem of credibility on the 'solution' side if not in the terms in which the 'problem' is characterized. There is, perhaps, some irony in a Roman Catholic priest giving focus to the idea of 'Propaganda' (given the strategic role of this term in the counter-reformation of the early seventeenth century) but it is an idea that Moore is able to use effectively, employing old movie footage and repeated phrasing with distortions to generate a sense, only partly playful, of mass indoctrination. At this point, his account veers close to themes in *All Watched Over*, although this is only a phase in his film, which has multiple strands of argument. Nevertheless, the idea that capitalism has been accepted by the US population because of a false belief that it is 'compatible with God's law' is a proposition whose weakness in socio-historical terms, whatever its comic yield, does little to develop the film at the level of a serious diagnosis to run alongside the condemnation.[4]

Conclusion

These three films all mix a range of documentary approaches to offer both a pictorial rendering of financial crisis and a variously-sourced account of what happened and why.[5] They all work with a documentary aesthetic that seeks to hold the viewer through strong visual engagement as well as clear and sometimes surprising testimony.[6] Both *Capitalism* and *Inside Job* make good use of the camera's focusing in on the highlighted text of key documents, text that is also read out in voiceover, thereby thickening their accounts with a more literally 'documentary' source of evidence. In all three, a musical score is, at least for certain passages, a key ingredient in infusing drama and an appropriate sense of mood and of mood shift into what is watched.[7] *Capitalism* and *All Watched Over* operate more at a 'total system' level than *Inside Job* that, while it contains systemic analysis, particularly in its conclusion, spends a lot of its time at the level of the crime within the system rather than the criminality of the system, to use the rather vulnerable distinction I drew earlier. None of the films has much to offer by way of suggested alternatives and this is only to be expected given their primary work of exposition. *Inside Job* finishes with what is, even in the context of its own arguments and evidence, a rather unpersuasive claim that 'at tremendous cost, we've avoided disaster and are recovering', despite the lack of criminal prosecutions, the low chances of recovering a proportion of the 'bail out' money and the continuation of the climate of deregulation. In this context, it is an understatement for its final words to note that getting 'change … won't be easy'.[8]

Although Moore goes further than the other two projects in addressing deficiencies in the principles of the underlying model, these deficiencies are seen as moral more than they are economic and there is a final narrowing towards the 'financial sector' as the specific criminal group that, if only slightly, displaces the focus upon the broader economic order. In *Capitalism*, the question of why the economy broke down is returned again to the idea of corruption combined with the end of the 'unfair advantage' for the United States in world commodity production, just as the question of why the model has been popularly accepted for so long is answered by the idea of propaganda. Moore, at the end of the film, can look back 70 years and see how things might have been very different had President Roosevelt's vision, building on his New Deal principles of economic regulation, social equity and international cooperation, come to pass. This presents, at best, a revised version of American capitalism rather than any alternative. Nevertheless, Moore also inserts into his film testimony and evidence about the power of popular protest, even if the way that this is seen to be effective in localized dispute rather than in systemic change makes any indication of revolutionary possibility rather muted. That said, a sense that ordinary people have started to see the system for 'what it is' adds a positive dynamic to his final section and prevents it from carrying the terminal pessimism that runs through *All Watched Over*. I noted how *All Watched Over* also places a strong emphasis on the role of propaganda, but the idea of 'system' here extends well beyond the specific financial order to connect with a broader set of ideas about control and consciousness.

In all three films, the ways in which the flows and circuits of money have brought about a crisis is presented through depictions of people, institutions, practices and structures. A rich documentary discourse is used to deliver these accounts, offering a varied range of viewing satisfactions. Matters economic have been a longstanding strand of documentary portrayal but the current visibility of systemic weaknesses and the deep uncertainties of policy that surround them are providing an urgent and continuing point of reference for documentary's civic commitments and its capacities both for showing and telling.[9]

References

Austin, T. and de Jong, W. (2008) (eds), *Re-Thinking Documentary*, Maidenhead: McGraw-Hill/ Open University Press.

Bruzzi, S. (2006), *New Documentary,* 2nd edn, London: Routledge.

Corner, J. (1996), *The Art of Record*, Manchester: Manchester University Press.

Corner, J. (2002), 'Sounds real: Music and documentary', *Popular Music,* 21: 3, pp. 357–66.

Hardy. F. (1966) (ed.), *Grierson on Documentary*, London: Faber.

Nichols, B. (1991), *Representing Reality*, Bloomington and Indianapolis: Indiana University Press.

Renov, M. (1993) (ed.), *Theorising Documentary*, London and New York: Routledge.

Winston, B. (1995), *Claiming the Real: The Documentary Film Revisited*, London: British Film Institute.

Notes

1   The quote from Grierson comes from his 1932 article 'First Principles of Documentary' (1932, see Hardy 1966). There is now a large literature on documentary theory and practice, amongst which the books of Nichols (1991), Renov (1993), Winston (1995), Corner (1996), Bruzzi (2006) and Austin and De Jong (2008) figure significantly, alongside a vast number of journal articles.

2   Ferguson has described this segment as a 'rock video' element in the film that, while a calculated overstatement, catches at something of the flourish of its visual and aural power.

3   The idea of a quest, known in advance to be futile, to get answers from key individuals (or even get a chance to put questions) is a narrative device in a number of documentaries. Moore's *Roger and Me* (1989) is a significant example, as its ironic title suggests, while Nick Broomfield's *Tracking Down Maggie* (1994) is another example of the 'stalker' structure.

4   Moore's attempt to explain popular acceptance of the system is in interesting contrast with that of BBC correspondent Robert Peston. In his December 2011 two-part documentary, *The Party's Over: How the West Went Bust*, Peston worked with an explanation in which consumer greed and naivety, attributed within his inclusivist populist address to 'us', were significant parts of the problem. As well as the title's suggestion of previous (irresponsible) 'good times', Peston was quite emphatic in his opening commentary – 'Many of us were complicit … No one forced us to binge on spending and borrowing'.

5   A useful comparison could be made with work in other media, including not only newspaper and magazine articles but books designed for a general readership, of which there have been a great many, including John Lanchester's *Whoops* (Penguin, 2010) and Andrew Sorkin's *Too Big To Fail* (Penguin, 2010).

6   All three documentaries received a good level of critical praise alongside strands of disagreement with parts of their analysis. *Inside Job* won the 2011 Oscar for best documentary. Predictably, expressions of doubt were raised about the general integrity of *Capitalism* as the continuation of Moore's project of polemical (and populist) filmmaking. *All Watched Over* confirmed for some the distinctive and praiseworthy commitment to complex ideas shown by Curtis while for others it showed a suspect tendency to overstate and simplify, using a limited and repetitive set of visual and verbal devices.

7   The role of music within documentary design remains a vital and still under-explored aspect of the 'control' of viewing engagement (see Corner 2002).

8   However, mention has to be made of the way in which *Inside Job*, in its final stages, gives extensive space to the complicity of the US academic establishment, including top Economics departments, in the formation of neo-liberal strategies. This includes not only the academic 'validation' of policy at the level of 'rubber-stamping' but involvement in reduced oversight procedures, both for considerable fee rewards. In this way, the diagnosis moves out from the activities of the financial sector per se to identify some core problems with dominant forms of 'economic knowledge'.

9   A classic example would be Basil Wright's *Song of Ceylon* (1934), which is both about local culture and the impact upon it of imperial trade.

Part 4

Everyday talk

Chapter 10

'I just hope the whole thing won't collapse':[1] 'Understanding' and 'overcoming' the EU financial crisis from the citizen's perspective[2]

Andreas Hepp, Swantje Lingenberg, Monika Elsler, Johanna Möller, Anne Mollen and Anke Offerhaus

The EU 'financial crisis' from a citizen's perspective

What has come to be called the 'EU financial crisis' has not only been an important focus of media coverage in Europe and beyond, it has also been the subject of a concerted intellectual debate conducted in printed media and across the Internet. Together with demands for deeper European integration, these interventions share a common critique of the 'lack both of dynamic leadership and of democratic legitimacy' (Giddens 2012: 3). Spurred on by this conviction, the leading German sociologist, Ulrich Beck, has become politically active in spearheading an initiative for a 'bottom-up Europe', in which citizens' 'uncertainty, anxiety and indignation' becomes a core reference point (Beck 2012: 14), a project that has attracted support from a wide range of leading politicians and intellectuals including, Zygmunt Bauman, Jacques Delors and Richard Sennett (c.f. Delors et al. 2012). The problem is that we know very little about the way people, in their role not as national consumers but as citizens of Europe (Canclini 2001), talk about, understand, and engage with the idea of Europe and with the public sphere where its future is deliberated. We have general opinion data generated by large scale surveys such as Eurobarometer (2012) and generalizing interpretations based on them (Risse 2010) but few studies of people's everyday struggles to make sense of the situation and the shifting mixes of doubt, anger, and empathy that inform their attempts. Focusing on responses to the financial crisis, this chapter tries to fill at least some of the gaps in this research deficit.

Drawing on in-depth interviews conducted in Austria, Denmark, France, Germany, Poland and the United Kingdom, our aim is to explore the 'citizens' perspective' on the crisis. All the research presented here is based on a collaborative investigation carried out within the project 'The Transnationalization of Public Spheres in Europe: Citizens' (re)actions', which is part of the Collaborative Research Center 597 'Transformations of the State' at the University of Bremen and funded by the German Research Foundation (DFG). Since 2003 we have been researching the possible articulation of a European public sphere on the levels of media content, media production, and now media appropriation.[3]

Georg Vobruba (2012) has argued that 'citizens' constructions of European society are largely utilitarian and built around 'their own economic interests' (Vobruba 2012: 274). In contrast, for the 'professionalized European integration elite' – a group, to whom we can also add academics like Beck as involved intellectuals –'European society' is what *inevitably* has to be built to secure freedom and welfare in Europe. While 'national political elites', who are the principal target of the criticisms levelled at the EU system by the intellectuals, having their national competencies, responsibilities and elections in mind, construct Europe as simultaneously an arena that they are involved in and an intervention into national politics. As a result of these contrasted constructions, we are confronted with complex processes of struggle and conflict over the meaning and constitution of European society.

Mediatized 'communicative constructions' of Europe (Hepp 2012; Knoblauch 2013) play a central role in this struggle since for most people, the array of available media will be both their principal source of relevant information, analysis, and argument and potential spaces of active engagement. Citizens are not just an 'audience' that 'receives' media 'contents'. They are actively involved in processes of communicative construction: They appropriate media coverage as they locate and make sense of it in their everyday practices. And they articulate their own positions, usually in everyday interchange but possibly also 'in the media' when they write blogs, submit online comments or post comments on Twitter. In short: citizens *act* as well as *react* and in so doing they become part of the communicative construction of Europe and its public sphere.

One useful starting point for unpacking citizens' (re)actions is the concept of 'public connection', the idea that linking themselves to an imagined public, whose interests they share, is a precondition of democratic engagement (Couldry et al. 2007: 5). By building up a European public connection, both through their media use and their social interactions, they communicatively construct themselves as European citizens.

The so-called 'financial crisis' has been widely and variously commented on by leading intellectuals. For the British sociologist and Labour appointee to the country's second legislative chamber, the House of Lords, it is the result of the missing pan-European state reforms when the euro was introduced (Giddens 2012: 1–2). For Ulrich Beck it is not 'a debt crisis' but a struggle for solidarity (Beck 2012: 23f). And for Germany's best-known social philosopher, Jürgen Habermas, it points up the need for a post-or-supranational Europe as part of a world society (Habermas 2011). These arguments, and variants on them, circulate within the European public sphere where they compete for attention with the news and documentary accounts analysed in earlier chapters. But if we are interested in the full range of processes entailed in the communicative construction of the crisis, we also need to analyse citizens' constructions. Only by doing so can we arrive at an overall understanding of how this 'crisis' becomes concrete.

Bearing in mind Antonio Gramsci's argument (1971: 178) that a crisis is a process of struggle, including struggles over its definition, we want to focus here on the ways that people in different social locations, with different stocks of practical experience and different patterns of media engagement, negotiate the array of available constructions and the competition between them. For practical reasons, we will use the term 'EU financial crisis' without quotation marks. Nevertheless, it is important to bear in mind that we are speaking here about certain constructions of what is *called* 'a crisis' – not about a given definition.

In approaching citizens' constructions we need to distinguish two dimensions. First, there is the question of how people construct their 'understanding' of the crisis and its causes.

Here we are confronted with perplexity, anxiety and speculation. Second, there are ideas about how to 'overcome' the crisis. At this point, our interviewees organized their thinking and argumentation around three possible responses: a national way, a European way, and something we might call a 'new' way, based on *re-negotiating European cooperation*.

The research reported here is based in six different EU countries: Austria, Denmark, France, Germany, Poland and United Kingdom. Originally, the intention was to select two of the core funding members of the EU (France, Germany), two smaller countries (Austria, Denmark) and Great Britain, a country dominated by rather critical orientation to the EU. This sample was later extended to include Poland in order to have one important new Eastern-European member state in the sample.[4] While one might criticize this sampling for omitting a southern European state, up to now this comparative design has worked well, also in relation to other studies on the European public sphere (Wessler et al. 2008; Hepp et al. 2012a). In each of the researched countries we were looking for participants with strongly contrasted ages, life backgrounds, media uses and political orientations towards the nation-state and Europe.

Our research is based on qualitative in-depth interviews with 30 citizens in each of the six sampled countries. These included a semi-standardized section on socio-demographic background (which was additionally documented by post-interview protocols and case profiles), supplemented with qualitative network maps (interviewee's drawings of their communicative networks) and media diaries (interviewee's documentations of their media use over a period of one week). Fieldwork was conducted from September to December 2011, a period when discourses surrounding the 'EU financial crisis' reached a first peak, reflecting speculation that Greece might withdraw from the Eurozone, something that has not happened until now.

Having questions of public connection, media appropriation and public engagement in mind, we asked our interviewees about their personal life and biography, their media use and communicative networking, their possible access to the national and (mainly through that) to the European public sphere, their participation in the European public sphere, as well as their political identifications and understandings of political legitimization. Fieldwork was undertaken in two phases of six weeks, each investigating three countries at the same time and accompanied by a shared interpretative discourse among the research team. For practical reasons we had to limit the duration of our fieldwork to 3 months in total. What follows is a preliminary analysis of citizens' constructions of the 'EU financial crisis' as communicated to us in interviews.

'Understanding' the crisis: Perplexity, anxiety and speculations

Across Europe, the citizens we interviewed saw the financial crisis as a serious matter. When articulating their disorientation, the pattern of understanding characteristically widens: first of all, from *wondering* about how it all begun and what is going on, leading to *worrying about its possible effects* on both their personal lives and the future of Europe, and then to *speculation* about the complex nature of the crisis.

As a 50-year-old university project manager from London noted: 'It's just way too complicated and unwieldy for most people to understand. You know, what you get off the news is, the more you know the less you understand' (Jessica Parker,[5] 50). Similarly, a young man from France articulates his anxiety about the consequences of the crisis by stating that 'the big question is what happens if the crisis cannot be solved', and he continues, 'this unsettles me a lot, and therefore I try to follow the developments' (Roberto Zero, 25).

Perplexity: Grasping the crisis

Above all, the interviewees are puzzled by the crisis. They construct it as complex in its economic and political nature and consider it difficult to understand in detail. In trying to make sense of it and its likely impacts, they rely on the information they acquire from the media they use as well as their everyday interchanges with friends and family. They then relate this information back to their everyday lives as well as to what they perceive as a broader European context.

For example, Amina Zündler, a 28-year-old woman from Austria who works as a manager for cultural projects, perceives the Greek crisis as bewildering and states that she cannot understand: 'How can a whole country fail?' (Amina Zündler, 28). In her eyes, the economic aspects of the crisis are obscure and opaque, so that she feels completely mystified. She is joined by a 50-year-old woman from London who states that 'this whole sort of economic mechanism is just too complicated for anybody to understand now. […] you know, the top economic brains in the world don't know how to fix it. And […] governments are just incapable of knowing what to do about it' (Jessica Parker, 50). Similarly, Dennis Cooper, aged 29, a political science student from North London, states: 'The European financial crisis, I've been following that quite a bit. I think I don't know nothing about, I don't know anything about economics' (Dennis Cooper, 29). To resolve this deficit, he follows media reporting on the financial crisis. He tries to find out more about the crisis, mostly online, via BBC News, Twitter and blogs, including the blog of Chris Delow, an economist who is writing a lot about the financial crisis and the problems in Greece. Likewise, for Angelie Toulon, a 21-year-old French student of agronomy, the crisis reveals both that the topic is very complicated and that she simply is not educated in economics. To compensate for this, she tries to understand what is going on and what the impact of the crisis might be by following the reporting of *Le Monde*, her favourite newspaper that she receives for free at her faculty department. However, she does not always succeed: 'Sometimes I understand something and one second later I don't understand anything anymore' (Angelie Toulon, 21).

Another way of dealing with the uncertainty is to talk about the crisis within one's circle of friends and family. Here, we hear from the French retired pharmacist Karlotta Sapon, aged 65, that she is presently talking about it a lot with her husband, as the crisis is 'the big, our big worry' (Karlotta Sapon, 65). For Stéphane Trufon, aged 27, a psychologist living in Paris, it is his girlfriend who turns out to be his personal expert in this matter, as she studies International Relations.

To summarize, the interviewees share the experience that their common knowledge of economic topics proves insufficient when it comes to such a complex matter as the EU financial crisis. One frequent but not always sufficient way to remedy this is to stick to media coverage. Another is to make use of personal networks.

Anxiety: Worrying about the future

The interviewees are highly concerned about the possible impacts of the crisis. On the one hand, their worries are on a personal level, as they articulate anxiety about rising unemployment rates, the risk of inflation and depreciation of their savings. On the other hand, in the interviewees' eyes the whole EU project is at stake. Seeing the EU's *raison d'être* first and foremost as an instrument for creating and maintaining peace, prompts fears that an economically flagging EU might once more result in terror and war.

When it comes to the personal life of our interviewees, the crisis turns out to be an important topic of conversation in the family circle. For example, the 50-year-old Britain Jessica Parker talks about how her family feels directly affected by the crisis:

> [M]y daughter has just finished her undergraduate degree and then my auntie's son has as well, so we worried about finding jobs. […] Ehm, you know, they're both looking for jobs and not finding it very easy not to pass on your mind at the moment.
>
> (Jessica Parker, 50)

Similarly, the currently unemployed 21-year-old Steven Corner from Plymouth in Southern England states that the crisis 'does impact my family […] as my mother might lose the house' (Steven Corner, 21).

However, worrying about the personal impacts of the crisis is not limited to job-related concerns. It is also threatening in terms of money. On the one hand, there is Herbert Sennenberger, a 65-year-old retired design draughtsman from Austria, who fears that the crisis might lead to inflation, something that he associates with his parent's generation's experiences: 'Even if we returned to gold, then I'd give a gold dollar for a kilogram of bread, and the gold is all gone either way' (Herbert Sennenberger, 65). Besides worries about the costs of every day basic needs such as food, there is also concern about financial investments. Our French interviewees Karlotta Sapon and her husband, for example, fear that the money they have invested at the stock exchange might be endangered by the crisis.

Besides personal worries, the interviewees are also concerned about the future of the EU. Here, the spectrum of worries varies. There are unspecific concerns, as we can hear from Jacques Ardèche, a 64-year-old French manager, from Angelie Toulon, who finds it hard to view the future of the EU optimistically, or from Stéphane Trufon, who, in the light of the crisis, does not expect the EU to get anywhere. For some, these general doubts about the impacts of the crisis and the chances of overcoming are reinforced by a perception that it is characterized by the manifoldness of the EU's many different cultures, as the Austrian student of agriculture and nutrition science Kilian Wedekind, aged 26, puts it.

However, our interviewees do not agree about the extent of attention given to EU crisis. Some argued that the crisis has attracted either too much or too little attention. For example, 23-year-old Maria Rudler, an Austrian student of political science, complains that due to the crisis various issues such as foreign affairs and environmental and cultural aspects are being eclipsed. Another interviewee, Simon Gärtner, a 37-year-old gardener from Germany, rather suspects that politicians even stoke conflicts like xenophobia and risk of terror in order to distract from the actual dimensions of the financial crisis. In contrast, other interviewees were troubled by suspicions that the situation might be even more serious than it appeared at first sight. For Danish pensioner Bjørn Æby, aged 64, a former blacksmith, the implications of the crisis are not at all clear yet. Despite the fact that he does not feel affected personally, as he considers himself economically secure, he perceives the crisis as 'the worst thing he has experienced in Europe in his whole life' (Bjørn Æby, 64). His greatest fear is that some other EU member states from Eastern Europe might join Greece and Italy in their financial problems. Eventually, the separation of a few or more countries from the Eurozone would lead to chaos. This ultimate, almost apocalyptic scenario also haunted other interviewees. For example, 25-year-old agriculture engineer Roberto Zero from France wonders what would happen if no solution to the crisis could be found: 'Everything can collapse, dissolve, and this makes me very uneasy' (Roberto Zero, 25). Likewise, Hilde Haltenberger, an Austrian retired foreign language correspondent, aged 56, hopes 'that the whole thing will not collapse' (Hilde Haltenberger, 56). Or, as another Austrian pensioner, a former nurse, Friede Kerner, aged 59, worries 'something even worse might break out, something like war' (Friede Kerner, 59).

As we have seen then, while it is common for our interviewees to be worried about the EU's financial crisis both the extent and the causes of their concern vary: from the individual to the collective level, from a general feeling of discomfort to fundamental fear for Europe's future.

Speculations: How the crisis came about

Although the interviewees construct the crisis as difficult to understand, they are not shy of speculating about the reasons for it. The explanations they present are all permeated by the perspective that the economic problems have been predictable and, in parts, avoidable. The failure to address them is located either within national misgovernment, or within the EU's system. At first glance, the interviewees' willingness to apportion blame seems inconsistent with the impression that they are confused by the crisis. But a closer look reveals that both attitudes can coexist, inasmuch as our interviewees try to overcome their disorientation by constructing individual explanations. On the basis of this, we have identified three approaches to speculation about the causes of the crisis: an economic perspective, a focus on national misgovernment and an approach concentrating on the structure of the EU.

One way of reasoning about the financial crisis is to appraise it from a perspective that assigns a central role to economic actors and institutions. For example, 58-year-old jobless Lucas Almenos from Marseille states that the problem is that the banks rather than the politicians govern the world. Noah Moulin, a 28-year-old IT-security engineer from Paris is employed in the financial industry himself. During his daily work, he 'watch[es] the financial markets breaking down'. He 'notice[s] many billions, billions and billions being transferred in order to help Greece, or to help Portugal' (Noah Moulin, 28). In his opinion Greece should not be in the Eurozone since small countries, such as Greece, with a generally weak economy need financial flexibility. For him the euro is a part of the problem for Greece rather than being a part of the solution. Another interviewee, Kurt Binder, a 60-year-old pensioner from Germany, insists that the crisis originated in the US financial system. He sees it as having no relation to the euro in particular or the EU in general. The 33-year-old Danish street newspaper seller Anders Hansen cannot identify a specific location for the crisis but suspects that 'someone' is holding the 'cash box' and needs to be made to 'give back the money not only to Greece, but to Europe as a whole' (Anders Hansen, 33). Despite these variations of emphasis all these accounts are united in focusing solely on economic aspects, allowing the complex issue of the EU financial crisis to be more easily understandable but at the same time reducing them to a simplified level.

A second explanatory approach developed by our interviewees shifted the focus to the failings of national governments. Here we have, for example, Lone Søndergaard, a 24-year-old Danish student of education, who states that the Greek financial crisis does not necessarily have anything to do with the EU. On the contrary, she regards the whole problem as being caused by misgovernment on the part of Greek politicians and the inability of the people of Greece to call them to account. The same argument can be heard from Max Rost, a 33-year-old Austrian electrician, who suspects that the crisis has been caused by national political 'disorder' (Max Rost, 33). Another Danish interviewee, Mads Jespersen, a 50-year-old architect, admits that while it is clearly a problem if the Greeks are not willing to pay their taxes one has to ask why they refuse to do so. In his view, it is all based in mistrust of 'the central power', stemming from Greece's recent history that was overshadowed by military dictatorship. On the basis of this, he considers the Greeks to have every reason to fear that their taxes would not be used to the benefit of the collective good.

What is characteristic for this set of explanations is that they perceive the crisis as grounded in failures of national – Greek – politicians, all too long condoned by the people of Greece. In this perspective responsibility, if not delinquency, lies squarely within the national field of accountability.

A third explanatory approach offered by our participants is grounded in the perception that it is inefficiency and mismanagement within the EU itself that either caused the crisis or at the very least been unable to prevent its fall out from having serious consequences for its (weaker) member states. For example Edgar Davis, a 71-year-old consultant from Great Britain, regards the euro as a disaster and expects the EU to 'go down the drain' (Edgar Davis, 71). For a Danish interviewee, Poul Omegn, a sales promoter who is currently unemployed, aged 44, the EU had recently grown too big too fast, with the enlargement following the incorporation of the Eastern European countries. Concerning the accession of Greece to the EU, Mads Jespersen, the 50-year-old architect from Denmark, tells a remarkable narrative. In his point of view, Greece was assisted by the EU in manipulating its facts and figures. The objective, he suspects, had been to support the young democracy, and he concludes that these superordinate political intentions were to 'woo them into the warmth'. Another interviewee, the 65-year-old French Clément Sapon, a retired executive, argues that the crisis would not have affected Greece and Portugal so much, 'if there had been a European economic government providing harmonisation […] – Taxes, expenditures, laws, and tolls need to be harmonised' (Clément Sapon, 65). Fabrice Girard, a 45-year-old French consultant, adds:

> We don't have a European defence policy, no European economic union, there's no one who represents us against the global lobby. Well, and now we face the disaster, as it is us who have to solve Greece's problems now. […] We don't have a European government, and this is the catastrophe.
>
> (Fabrice Girard, 45)

'Overcoming' the crisis: Ambivalent ways out

Our interviewees did not confine themselves to trying to understand the present situation, they also proposed solutions that might lead Europe out of the crisis. Some suggested *national solutions*, emphasizing Greece's national responsibility to solve 'their' problems on their own and rejecting the idea of helping them out financially. As a young Danish woman, a student of education living in Copenhagen, emphasized, Greece has 'made its bed, and now must lie on it' as 'there is no money to be grabbed' from the other EU member states (Lone Søndergaard, 24). In contrast, other participants advocated *European solutions*. Some supported absolute solidarity with Greece as a member of the European community, because otherwise 'there is no point in the EU at all' (Louis Barney, 21). Others argued for greater European integration in order to have better institutional instruments at hand to solve the financial crisis. For them 'more EU and not less EU' (Mads Jespersen, 50) was the political answer to the crisis. In addition to the articulation of national and European ways out the crisis, a third pattern that can be extracted from the interviewees' statements is the hint of an *alternative* based on the need to re-negotiate European solidarity with Greece in the light of the actual circumstances of the current crisis.

Yet, before presenting the three different ways out of the crisis articulated by our interviewees in detail, we want to shed some light on their perceptions of the key political actors in the crisis. Remarkably, most saw national rather than European politicians as the principal actors. Whereas European politicians are dismissed as invisible and ineffective, national actors are seen as to fill the vacuum.

For example Fabrice Girard, a French freelance business consultant who lives in Paris, but commutes to London to work for one week per month, regrets that only two political actors seem to be assuming responsibility for tackling the financial crisis and visibly fostering political solutions: Angela Merkel, the German chancellor, and Nicolas Sarkozy, the then French president: 'It is a shame that they [Merkel and Sarkozy] are doing this job alone, that there are no other countries who feel responsible to act. The others, they just twiddle their thumbs and watch, they just watch' (Fabrice Girard, 45). Nevertheless, he admits, it 'would be much more complicated to discuss all this with 15 or even 27 member states'. In a similar vein, a Danish interviewee, Faris Hom, a young man with family roots in Somalia who is currently preparing to be a taxi driver, states 'there are many countries [in the EU] that don't help. I think if everyone had helped like Angela Merkel does, then this problem here would have been solved a long time ago' (Faris Hom, 25). And Poul Omegn, a 44-year-old, currently unemployed sales promoter from the Copenhagen suburbs, misses 'official EU politicians' acting as strong crisis managers: 'Rompuy [head of the European Council] does not act as a visionary, he doesn't do anything. There is always Angela Merkel, Berlusconi and Sarkozy' (Poul Omegn, 44).

Beyond these perceptions and evaluations of national and European politicians acting or not acting in order to 'overcome' the actual EU financial crisis, as we noted above, our interviewees constructed three different routes out of the crisis, namely national, European and new.

The national way: Solving a nation's problem

For some of our interviewees, it is above all maladministration flanked by corruption and unreasonableness that has played a major role in the case of the financial crisis in general and Greece's economic problems in particular. Consequently, they suggest that each aggrieved party should be left to solve their problems on their own. For example, Herbert Sennenberger, a 65-year-old retired design draughtsman from Austria uses the term 'dissoluteness' arguing that Greece 'crept into the EU by faking facts'. He compares Greece, Germany and Austria to neighbouring families, with two of them being hard workers and one of them being dissolute and having squandered all his money. Against this background he cannot approve supporting Greece. For him, the crisis is not only the fault of the Greek politicians and banks but also of an upper class that 'has cheated on the state' (Herbert Sennenberger, 65). Similarly, Ismael Brooker, a former engineer who migrated to the UK from Lebanon in the 1960s and now runs a coffee shop in Richmond near London, tends to see each EU member state responsible for its own economic problems, and concludes that the EU should not help Greece as long as it continues to pursue wrong policies. He compares Greece to a child who always spends all his pocket money and should therefore not be given any more:

> You know when you're raising kids [...], you give them pocket money; you have five kids, and one guy saves, [...] but one guy is a big spender and when the big guy spends money, you say, ok have some more. So it's not gonna fix his problem, and the same with Greece, it's not gonna fix anything. They don't care [...]. In my opinion this is what I think of the matter, why bring these countries, Lithuania for example, all these countries, why bring them around?
>
> (Ismael Brooker, 62)

Going along with these assignments of national fault and responsibility, many of our interviewees say they are not willing to transfer 'their' national taxes to Greece. For example, Kurt Binder, a German pensioner from a small town in the midlands of Germany, does not trust Greece to handle the European injections of cash responsibly. He fears that in consequence 'the German taxpayers have paid for it, and will in the end be burned one way or another' (Kurt Binder, 60). In a similar vein, Ismael Brooker states 'every single man is paying more taxes, because they [EU] didn't let them [Greece] go' (Ismael Brooker, 62).

From these interviewees' statements it becomes obvious that excluding Greece as a member state of the Eurozone may be considered as a radical, but nevertheless conceivable consequence and solution. For Lisa O'Connor, a 62-year-old woman, living in a rented castle in South Denmark and working as an arts and music manager, there is no alternative, one should 'send them to hell, sorry, them down in Greece. Well, if they do not stick to the rules we have here in the EU, then it's over, it simply is' (Lisa O'Connor, 62). Similarly, the Eastern German Joachim Gerke is obviously niggled that 'a whole country is flagging just because it is not able to, uhm, govern itself and to budget responsibly [...]. I cannot understand that there is still more and more money being invested into this country' (Joachim Gerke, 46). A somewhat double-edged attitude, as to whether the European community generally should interfere with national sovereignty or not, can be observed in the case of a Danish cleaning lady, Lina Rendersen, who on the one hand refuses the EU's right to 'dictate Danish interests', but on the other hand expects Greece to let the EU take over crisis' management, 'because if they want something from us, then they also have to give something' (Lina Rendersen, 58).

As these extracts from our interviews show, the national way as a solution to overcome the EU financial crisis is mostly being promoted by assigning responsibility to Greece for its problems. As a consequence, the Greek government is expected to solve the problems they have produced by national economic or political maladministration on their own. Against this background the interviewees articulate their reluctance to spend billions of euros to help Greece fix the problem. And even more, they do not trust Greece to handle any financial support provided by the EU responsibly ... Some even consider Greece's exclusion from the EU as a conceivable alternative.

The European way: Solidarity and intensified integration

In marked contrast to participants who advocated a national solution to the crisis other interviewees argued strongly for a solution on a European level. This construction was underscored by two arguments: *absolute solidarity* rooted in humanitarian considerations and the project of building a European community, and *intensified integration* on an institutional level on the other. In both these argumentations, we can identify a strong commitment to the essential *raison d'être* of the EU. As one interviewee put it: 'The Greek crisis can be seen as the European time of reckoning' (Mads Jespersen, 50).

Regardless of the assumed culpability of Greece's national government, these interviewees consider it to be a human imperative or a natural consequence of Greece's EU membership to show *solidarity*. The Austrian interviewee Fritz Kantler, who himself tries to eke out a living more or less unsuccessfully as a returned globetrotter with neither education nor employment, states penalizing the Greeks as unfair and considers the Greek people to be 'quite hard-pushed' (Fritz Kantler, 61). Louis Barney, a 21-year-old living at his parent's house in South England and studying history and political science at the University of Plymouth, states quite emotionally: 'What's the point of being in [the EU] if you're not getting that [financial] protection. It's necessary to help each other out. It's important for them [the Greeks] to know you want them to be back'. He continues, arguing that every EU member state 'has to give something back at some point', because the community makes it natural to help each other out and not to split up as soon as problems arise. As a consequence, 'everyone has gotta tighten their belts, and keep hoping. [...] The EU should be kept together [...] instead of splitting up and going back to say the Deutschmark or the Franc. [...] So just keep the economy strong and stick to it really' (Louis Barney, 21).

Likewise, 52 year-old Polish Barbara Szymańka, working as a cleaning lady in Warsaw, supports a common European effort to overcome the crisis even though she admits that she does not 'know what will be later, how we will have to pay off, how our children will feel' (Barbara Szymańka, 52). In a similar vein, 37-year-old biologist Simon Gärtner, who works as a gardener in a public park in the North German city of Bremen, advocates that Greece should stay in the EU: 'Europe as a whole deserves it to see this through' (Simon Gärtner, 37).

With regard to Europe as a political community, the Danish unemployed salesman Poul Omegn characterizes the current financial crisis as a European 'litmus test'. According to him, the question at stake is 'whether the European team spirit actually works' (Poul Omegn, 44). Consequently, he is in favour of absolutely sticking together in the EU – otherwise it would be like refusing help to a family member. For him, it is this reciprocal help for which the EU stands. Nevertheless, he sees financial help for Greece also being beneficial for the sponsoring body, like the Marshall plan after the Second World War. As he explains: 'This steel company will in the end profit from the fact that Greece gets financial help – because they will buy its steel products'.

European solidarity without conditions in times of crisis is also what Austrian agricultural and nutritional student Kilian Wedekind from Vienna advocates. He goes even further and accuses national politicians, who, in order to promote themselves in national elections, abuse the Greeks and their problems by saying 'we pay, we pay, we pay [for them] and in the end we do not get anything back'. For him it is a matter of principle, that 'countries who perform badly economically have to be supported' (Kilian Wedekind, 26). Similarly, British 50-year-old university project manager Jessica Parker argues that politicians should be careful not to stigmatize countries like Greece now:

> I think we gotta be prepared not to stigmatise countries that are, have been performing badly economically. I think we've gotta be careful that the stronger countries don't bully the weaker countries. I think we've got to put everything in historical atrocities that have happened, ehm, in these countries.

She goes on to state that even though 'there doesn't seem to be any real leadership' in the crisis, it would be problematic to have one single country taking over this leadership:

> We don't want to reach the point where one country has too much power in Europe. Because that's always been dangerous in the past. Ehm, but I think we've got to [...] appreciate that despite being in the EU the constituent member countries are very different and very unique. And they're not all gonna fit this one-size fit sort of type concept. [...] You know, Germany and France have had strong, [...] I mean, Germany has got an amazingly strong economy, ehm, you know, most countries in the EU never gonna match Germany in its efficiencies and strong economy. It's just never gonna happen. [...] I think it's a bit rich for countries in Europe telling, you know, telling Greece what to do at this time, because you know, Greece has never been a strong economy and there are others, other economies in Europe that are a bit dysfunctional as well. And, ehm, I just don't think they should be punished in this way, I just think this whole thing is problematic. [...] Ehm, I feel really sorry for Greece.
>
> (Jessica Parker, 50)

Other interviewees endorse this concern. Austrian Fritz Kantl, aged 61, living in 'precarious' circumstances himself and having been out of regular work for decades, expresses his 'appreciation and sympathy for the people' in Greece. From his perspective, they are 'in big difficulties [...], because the economic system, ehm, thus just horrible on the human level'. He associates his sympathy with the Greek people with his own stigmatization as a 'longhair and, eh, eh anti-social' (Fritz Kantler, 61).

The feeling that showing solidarity is a necessary prelude to addressing the crisis by finding a European solution is strongly bound up with the call for an extension of European cooperation on institutional levels. Our interviewees' expressions of absolute solidarity, rooted in a commitment to the European community or simply to humanitarian reasons, provide a foundation for suggestions for *deepening European political integration* as well as an *improvement to European institutions*.

On the basis of his perception that the EU financial crisis is a 'crossroads', leading either to a 'European federal state', a 'separation' of the EU member states or remaining at the 'status quo', Austrian political science student Manuel Vechter, aged 19, advances his 'ideal conception' leading to the 'United states of Europe' (Manuel Vechter, 19). In a similar way, French Roberto Zero, aged 25, 'hopes that […] the crisis allows Europe to foster integration even more' (Roberto Zero, 25).

Rather than promoting 'more' European integration, other interviewees argued that the EU must be improved with regard to its institutional functioning. We can refer here to an already quoted statement by Fabrice Girard, the French business consultant. He regrets that there is currently 'no European Economic Union […]. There is no European government, and this is the catastrophe. Europe, the next Europe that we will construct, must above all be political, so that the national governments will dissolve' (Fabrice Girard, 45). Similarly, David Weaver, aged 49, working as a freelance financial consultant and living just outside of London, argues that the EU needs central monetary control since:

> [T]his whole thing [the EU] seems a bit ill-conceived': 'If you've got countries like Greece and Germany, with Greece trying to run similar economic models and such, and you don't have central money control, then you're gonna have problems.
>
> (David Weaver, 49)

In addition to advocating a choice between European and national ways out of the EU financial crisis our interviewees also proposed a third option: the re-negotiation of European cooperation.

New ways: Re-negotiating European cooperation

This 'new' solution contradicts neither the national nor the European way of overcoming the crisis, but rather forms an integrative alternative to both solutions. It calls for a re-negotiation of the way the EU is handling the current crisis as well as the way European solidarity should be handled with regard to countries like Greece in the current EU financial crisis.

The 44-year-old Danish man, Poul Omegn, living in Copenhagen's suburbs and usually working as a marketing assistant but temporarily unemployed, states that European solidarity must have certain limits. For him, the case of Greece brings to light where these limits are, so that they can be discussed and re-negotiated again. Similarly, 56-year-old Cornelia Sucher from Austria states that European solidarity with countries like 'Ireland, Greece [might] be an extra topic' (Cornelia Sucher, 56), because corruption, which is assumed to be part of everyday life in those countries, cannot be supported by the EU. Other interviewees stressed that countries wanting to receive financial support from the EU in times of crisis need to 'do' something in return. For Lina Rendersen from Denmark, aged 58 and working as a cleaner, the Greek people as well as the Italian people need to work for the financial help they receive. And another interviewee from Austria, Hilde Haltenberger (56), hopes that the European community will not collapse in the course of the current financial crisis but insists that the EU should have a say 'when spending billions' of euros on countries like Greece.

The crisis as a problem for the EU and its public sphere?

Summing up, our interviewees across all six countries construct their understanding of the EU financial crisis by actively following the media coverage and talking to friends and families about possible consequences for their personal lives as well as for the EU as a political community. They not only perceive the crisis as being a complicated matter from their citizens' point of view, but also discuss the perspective of economic experts and politicians who are meant to fix the problems.

In addition, the analysis of our interviews has shown that constructions on how to overcoming the EU financial crisis can be differentiated by an emphasis on national, European or new solutions. Interviewees advocating a national approach argue that countries like Greece who are facing severe financial difficulties should solve 'their' economic problems on their own, claiming that they have produced these difficulties themselves as a consequence of economic and political maladministration as well as corruption. In contrast, participants championing a European way out of the crisis either emphasize absolute solidarity with Greece because Greece is after all part of the European community, and the community spirit ought to be to help each other, especially in times of difficulties. Or they recommend improvements at the European institutional level as well as a deepening of European integration in order to have better EU political instruments at hand to manage and overcome the crisis. Situated between these two poles, other respondents articulated an alternative, 'third' way, stressing the need to re-negotiate the terms of European cooperation in response to the financial crisis. Interestingly, while most of these interviewees did not question Greece's membership of the European monetary union, they did not advocate solidarity with Greece regardless of the actual situation, nor did they support a deepening of European integration.

We can now relate these results back to the reflections with which we began this chapter. Fundamentally, we see a quite pronounced European public connection in relation to the crisis. Additionally, our analysis demonstrates that reflection about how to overcome the crisis is not just an elite debate on the part of well-known intellectuals but a prominent topic of people's everyday discourse. Analysing data like this is also remarkably helpful because it also offers a chance to deconstruct particular criticisms that are often *assumed* as a citizen's perspective. As we have seen, it is *not* the case that a national point of view is the only position. Our interview transcripts reveal more nuanced positions together with sustained reflection on European solidarity and shared interests.

On the basis of our findings so far we can argue that our respondents' perspectives on the EU financial crisis were organized around, both of the main dimensions of Europeanization identified by researchers: 'vertical' and horizontal' (Koopmans and Erbe 2004; Wessler et al. 2008: 10, 56; Koopmans and Stratham 2010: 41). Vertical Europeanization refers to the increasing 'monitoring' of Europe and the EU in the public sphere of each country. Horizontal Europeanization entails 'monitoring' and discussion with other European countries. Both these dimensions can be further subdivided, generating four distinct criteria for characterizing the Europeanization of national-mediated public spheres (Peters 2008: 200). The vertical dimensions can involve both the monitoring of EU governance and collective identification with Europe. At the horizontal level we can find both a pan-European discursive exchange, with for example, the same articles being translated and published in different languages, and a convergence of arguments within national public spheres.

Our interviewees' attempts to make sense of the crisis and its possible solutions ranged across all four of these dimensions. They monitored the EU governance of the crisis (dimension 1). With a varying degree we find a basic identification with Europe, not necessarily as the EU, but more with the fundamental idea of Europe (dimension 2). While only very world-oriented people monitor media coverage from other countries directly, there is at least an indirect discursive exchange of other European positions through national media that provide resources for perception and interpretation (dimension 3). And finally, we are confronted with some convergence of arguments when it comes to the three different possible ways of overcoming the crisis (dimension 4). This said, for sure we cannot argue generally for each individual that he or she defines him- or herself as being a 'European'. Also we do not have the historical interview data that would make it possible to develop a long-term view of change along these dimensions. Nevertheless, we can postulate a fundamental 'anchoring' of a European orientation, even in times of crisis. This does not mean that there won't be any criticism of the EU and its crisis management. But a fundamental legitimation of the European idea seems to be evident in spite of the EU financial crisis (c.f. Hepp et al. 2012b).

How do we evaluate research results like these? In our view, two points are striking.

First, our analysis shows that the financial crisis in general and the serious economic problems in Greece, and in other European countries, in particular, are of high concern to interviewees across Europe. The question of whether the crisis is perceived as a threat to the EU and will possibly end in the cessation of the EU remains open and is discussed ambivalently. However, the more striking point is that our participants not only have a European public connection, but are involved in a shared discourse on the crisis. Irrespective of their construction of how to overcome the crisis, this involvement can be understood as the core point. Referring back to pragmatic concepts of citizenship and the public sphere (Dewey 1927; Lingenberg 2010: 49f.), we can argue that our interview partners position themselves *as European citizens* insofar as they construct the European financial crisis as a problem affecting their own lives. In some cases, this citizenship might be highly situational and framed negatively but even so it serves as a foundation for a certain 'understanding' of the crisis and often also the wish to articulate ideas of how to 'overcome' it.

Second, our transcultural analysis demonstrates the complexity of crisis constructions. They do not follow solely national patterns. Despite the strong Euro sceptic current in contemporary English politics by no means all our English respondents articulated 'national' explanations and solutions to the crisis. Indeed, one of the strongest advocates of European solidarity was a political science student, Louis Barney, living in the south of England. His responses, and those of all our other participants, highlight the need for a much more fine-grained analysis to tease out the social roots and dynamics of different constructions and their complex interplay both with patterns of personal communicative activity and networking and 'media repertoires' (Hasebrink and Domeyer 2012). This said, even from the preliminary results presented here it is clear that national divisions within Europe are cross-cut in complex ways by transnational patterns of both segmentation and a shared sense of belonging and responsibility.

As we are still in the middle of the process that has come to be called the 'EU financial crisis', any statement of the eventual outcome is bound to be speculative. However, our analysis suggests that it could result in a deepening of European integration, not only at the level of institutions, but also in the everyday lives of citizens. Our participants seem to share an understanding of the present crisis as a 'common crisis' in Europe. If ways can be found to incorporate these citizens' perspectives and concerns into the mechanisms of deliberation and decision-making, against the odds the result of the crisis might be a strengthening of the Europe of citizens.

References

Beck, U. (2012), *Das deutsche Europa. Neue Machtlandschaften im Zeichen der Krise*, Berlin: Suhrkamp.

Couldry, N., Livingstone, S. M. and Markham, T. (2007), *Media Consumption and Public Engagement. Beyond the Presumption of Attention*, Basingstoke: Palgrave Macmillan.

Delors, J., Solana, J., Beck, U., Cohn-Bendit, D. and others (2012), 'Let's create a bottom-up Europe', *Guardian*, 3rd May, 2012, http://www.guardian.co.uk/commentisfree/2012/may/03/bottom-up-europe/print. Accessed 2nd December, 2012.

Dewey, J. (1927), *The Public and Its Problems: An Essay in Political Inquiry*, New York: Holt.

Eurobarometer (2012), Standard Eurobarometer 78. Autumn 2012: Public opinion in the European Union, First results, http://ec.europa.eu/public_opinion/archives/eb/eb78/eb78_first_en.pdf. Accessed 3rd January, 2013.

García Canclini, N. (2001), *Consumers and Citizens. Globalization and Multicultural Conflicts*, Minneapolis, MN: University of Minnesota Press.

Giddens, A. (2012), 'In Europe's dark days, what cause for hope?', *Guardian*, 25th January, 2012, http://www.guardian.co.uk/world/2012/jan/25/anthony-giddens-europe-dark-days-hope/print. Accessed 1st December, 2012.

Gramsci, A. (1971), *Selections form the Prison Notebook*, London: Lawrence & Wishart.

Gripsrud, J. (2007), 'Television and the European public sphere', *European Journal of Communication*, 22, pp. 479–92.

Habermas, J. (2011), *Zur Verfassung Europas. Ein Essay*, Berlin: Suhrkamp.

Hasebrink, U. and Domeyer, H. (2012), 'Media repertoires as patterns of behaviour and as meaningful practices: A multimethod approach to media use in converging media environments', *Participations: Journal of Audience & Reception Studies*, 9, pp. 757–83.

Hepp, A. (2012), *Cultures of Mediatization*, Cambridge: Polity Press.

Hepp, A., Brüggemann, M., Kleinen von Königslöw, K., Lingenberg, S. and Möller, J. (2012a), *Politische Diskurskulturen in Europa. Die Mehrfachsegmentierung europäischer Öffentlichkeit*, Wiesbaden: VS.

Hepp, A., Lingenberg, S., Offerhaus, A., Möller, J., Elsler, M. and Mollen, A. (2012b), 'Europe beyond the crisis? Citizens' (re)actions on the multi-segmentation of the European public sphere', in L. Morganti and L. Bekemans (eds), *The European Public Sphere. From Critical Thinking to Responsible Action*, Berlin, New York: Peter Lang, pp. 69–84.

Knoblauch, H. (2013), 'Communicative constructivism and mediatization', *Communication Theory*, 23: 3, pp. 297–315.

Koopmans, R. and Erbe, J. (2004), 'Towards a European public sphere? Vertical and horizontal dimensions of Europeanised political communication', *Innovation: The European Journal of Social Science Research*, 17, pp. 97–118.

Koopmans, R. and Statham, P. (2010), 'Theoretical framework, research design, and methods', in R. Koopmans and P. Statham (eds), *The Making of a European Public Sphere: Media Discourse and Political Contention*, Cambridge: Cambridge University Press, pp. 34–59.

Lingenberg, S. (2010), 'The citizen audience and European transcultural public spheres: Exploring civic engagement in European political communication', *Communications*, 35, pp. 45–72.

Peters, B. (2008), *Public Deliberation and Public Culture*, Basingstoke: Palgrave Macmillan.

Risse, T. (2010), *A Community of Europeans? Transnational Identities and Public Spheres*, New York: Cornell University Press.

Vobruba, G. (2012), 'The social construction of the European society', *Current Perspectives in Social Theory*, 30, pp. 263–79.

Wessler, H., Peters, B., Brüggemann, M., Kleinen-v. K. K. and Sifft, S. (2008), *Transnationalization of Public Spheres*, Basingstoke: Palgrave Macmillan.

Notes

1. Quote from an interview with a 56-year-old retired Austrian foreign language assistant living in a small village in the North of Austria.
2. An earlier version of this chapter was issued at Working Paper No. 168 at the Collaborative Research Centre 597 'Transformations of the State', at the University of Bremen (2013).
3. For more information on the Collaborative Research Centre 'Transformations of the State' see http://www.sfb597.uni-bremen.de, for more information on our subproject see http://www.zemki.uni-bremen.de/en/research/third-party-funds/dfg-project-public-spheres-in-europe.html.
4. For more details on our previous empirical design, see Hepp et al. 2012a: 49–62.
5. We have changed all our interviewees' names in order to respect their anonymity.

Afterword: Business as usual and its discontents

Graham Murdock

S urveying the financial sector in the spring of 2014, the Cambridge-based economist Ha-Joon Chang, a consistent critic of prevailing arrangements, could see little change to the system that had created the 2008 crisis. Its central actors remained wedded to the pursuit of short-term gains and convinced that while risks would be socialized, and funded from the public purse, costs would be privatized and fall most heavily on the least well-off.

> Our financial firms have become very good at generating high profits for themselves at the cost of creating asset bubbles whose unsustainability they obscure [and] when the bubble bursts, [they] deftly use their economic weight and political influence to secure rescue money and subsidies from the public purse, which then has to be refilled by the general public through tax hikes and spending cuts.
>
> (Chang 2014: 311)

Avoiding another crisis, Chang argued, requires government to impose much stronger curbs on speculatively activity. 'Unless we regulate our financial system much more strictly, we will see the repeat of crises … Many of the regulations … weakened or abolished since the 1980s need to be brought back or even strengthened' (Chang 2014: 311).

Calls for tougher curbs on financial activity have been resisted with particular force in Britain, where the City of London, which benefitted substantially from the concerted deregulation introduced under the Thatcher government, continues to exert a powerful influence on economic policy, supported by a 'revolving door' system that sees senior politicians recruited to lucrative City positions on leaving office. The privatization of Royal Mail demonstrates particularly clearly how personal connections and shared assumptions reinforce an 'insider' mentality that privileges corporate interests at the expense of the public good.

Two leading banks, UBS and Goldman Sachs, were appointed to organize the share sale, with Lazard & Co, appointed as the sole independent financial advisor, responsible for overseeing the process. The prospect of buying into Royal Mail promised investors substantial returns. It was an established and valued brand with a dominant market share in a key sector. As an added incentive the government had removed price controls and taken on responsibility for pension liabilities. In an effort to ensure that the sale was fully subscribed the float price was fixed at 330p, a figure that many analysts saw as artificially low. Barclays' equity division was typical in telling their clients that the shares were worth at least 420p, 27% more than the issue price (Warren and Mathiason 2014: 5). The two banks coordinating the float, however, recommended that the price should not increase by more than 20p, and received strong backing from Lazard & Co. Even this modest increase was rejected and the shares opened for trading at 330p. By the end of the first day the price had risen by 38%, and at 6 months was up 57%. The primary beneficiaries of this massive increase were the 16 'cornerstone' investors who had been accorded preferential share allocations on the understanding that they would be stable, long-term, investors. Within weeks of the flotation six had sold their entire stakes and another five had disposed of most of their allocation. By the end of January 2014, the 22% of shares originally allocated to them had fallen to 12%. Evaluating the sale, the National Audit Office estimated that the government's eagerness to push through the sale had cost the public purse £750 m on the first day of trading alone, concluding, with studied understatement, that the process 'could have achieved better value for the taxpayer' (National Audit Office 2014: 10).

Lazard's consistent refusal to recommend a higher issue price is partly explained by the fact that its fee as the independent advisor depended on a successful sale. But the more general impetus to privilege the interests of the financial sector points up the system's self-enclosure. Lazard's international chairman is Lord Mandelson, who had wanted to sell Royal Mail during his term as business secretary in the Labour government. Royal Mail's director of investor relations was a former corporate finance manager at Lazards, while two of the senior officials at the Shareholder Executive, the body that manages state-owned businesses, had also previously worked for Lazards. Given these cross-cutting ties, and the shared perspectives and priorities they cultivate, it is perhaps not surprising that Lazard's insistence on a low issue price and its obvious benefit to the inner circle of designated shareholders was accepted with so little argument. It offered another opportunity to consolidate business as usual. This same self-enclosure also characterizes the academic study of economics.

In 1821 the radical English poet Shelley ended his essay *A Defence of Poetry* with the claim that poets are the 'unacknowledged legislators of world', a thoroughly romantic conception of the power of the imagination to see beyond prevailing orthodoxies. He had reckoned without the ascendency of economic calculation. Paul Samuelson, who in 1970 became the first American winner of the Nobel Prize for economics, was in no doubt that his free market vision would dominate the way capitalist societies and their futures were seen and managed declaring, 'I don't care who writes a nation's laws – or crafts its treatises – if I can write its economic textbooks' (quoted in Chakrabortty 2014: 34). His best-selling text, *Economics: An Introductory Analysis*, which first appeared in 1948 and dominated post-war economics teaching, went a considerable way to making his wish come true. Despite the abject failure of mainstream economics to predict the crisis of 2008, it is once again business as usual in the academy. This restoration of economic orthodoxy has not gone unchallenged however. Students from 42 university economics associations in 19 countries have signed a manifesto calling for teaching to engage with a wider range of theories and approaches. As one of the British signatories to this call for a more plural economics points out:

The Financial Crisis in 2008 was a systemic crisis for mainstream economics. Five years later the debate has a distinct lack of economic alternatives or narratives. The debate can be exclusionary and misleading. This monoculture is damaging when the public relies on experts to mediate economic discussion. The state of the economy is central to society, which requires us to frame the debate critically and question the foundations, assumptions and practices.

(Rethinking Economics 2014)

This demand for a more open debate on economic affairs is supported by a number of critical economists including Thomas Piketty, whose landmark book, *Capital in The Twenty-First Century*, became an unexpected best-seller, topping the Amazon list in the United States in the spring of 2014. He dismisses mainstream economics' 'obsession' with mathematical modelling as 'an easy way of acquiring the appearance of scientificity without having the answer the far more complex questions posed by the world we live in' (Piketty 2014: 32) and argues for a return to the older tradition of political economy with its central moral concern with defining the 'good society' and exploring the role of the state in securing its conditions. His book is a magisterial illustration of this ambition in action, assembling an unprecedented array of historical and comparative empirical data to demonstrate beyond doubt that the neo-liberal reconstruction of the financial sector and the wider economy has reversed the advances in reducing inequalities of wealth achieved in the period between the 1930s and the 1970s. Research from the Organization of Economic Cooperation and Development bear him out, revealing 'a widening gap between rich and poor not only in some already high-inequality countries like the United States, but also – for the first time – in traditionally low-inequality countries, such as Germany and the Nordic nations' (OECD 2011: 22).

In Britain, the latest available figures (for 2010–2012) show that the wealthiest 20% of households command 105 times more aggregate wealth than the poorest 20%, up from 92 times in 2008–2010 (Office of National Statistics 2014). While the top 1% of taxpayers increased their share of post-tax income from 8.2% in 2012–2013 to 9.8% in 2013–2014, a year in which the top rate of income tax was reduced from 50% to 45% (Wintour 2014: 11). The huge bonuses paid to senior bankers have been a particular focus of anger. A recent European Union ruling has attempted to address the issue by limiting bonuses to one year's salary, with the option to pay two years' worth with shareholder approval. Banks however have immediately moved to evade this constraint by raising their senior employees' basic pay and giving them monthly allowances worth up to eight times their salaries.

It is against this assumption of the financial sector's entitlement to special privileges, both individually and institutionally, that Piketty's proposal to address this new regime of globalized financial capitalism with a progressive annual tax on wealth has met with a predictable chorus of dismissal from the system's guardians and cheerleaders. The *Economist*, the weekly parish magazine of the financial community, is typical. While it commends Piketty on his 'marvellous scholarship' and 'indisputably brilliant empirical sleuthing', and accepts that the evidence clearly shows that 'since the 1970s both wealth and income gaps have been rising back towards their pre-20th-century norms', it dismisses his proposal out of hand, claiming that it 'smacks of socialist ideology, not scholarship' (*Economist* 2014: 14). In fact Picketty is at pains to point out that having come of age to the sound of the Berlin Wall coming down, signalling the end of the Soviet Communist experiment, he was 'vaccinated for life against the lazy rhetoric of anti-capitalism' and has 'no intention of denouncing inequality per se' providing it can be justified and shown not to undermine a just social order (Picketty 2014: 31). The question of what conception of social justice is relevant under contemporary conditions and how best to translate it into practical policies goes to the heart of democratic debate.

Since the Enlightenment, public policy in Europe and North America has wrestled with the problem of how best to define and balance the three core demands of the French Revolution – Liberty, Equality and Mutuality. The Welfare variant of capitalism placed particular emphasis on promoting equality of opportunity and fostering a sense of collective responsibility through the extension of universal participation in a democratic process designed to decide on the optimum allocation of public resources. The neo-liberal era has seen these practical commitments to equality and mutuality progressively jettisoned, and 'liberty', redefined as the right of the already privileged to increase their share of wealth with the minimum interference from government. As US Supreme Court Justice Louis Brandeis famously said, 'We may have democracy, or we may have wealth concentrated in the hands of the few, but we cannot have both' (Oxfam 2014: 2). When wealth captures government policy and bends the rules to favour the rich the social solidarities and sense of collective responsibility on which democracy rests are comprehensively undermined as the privileged retreat to the protected enclosures offered by gated communities and off-shore tax havens.

As we have seen in the chapters collected here, wider questions of social justice are largely missing from news coverage of financial and economic affairs. The construction of economic and business news as a discrete, specialist, domain simultaneously reproduces the separation between economic analysis and ethical debate that characterizes mainstream economics and cements journalists' reliance on insider sources who almost all sing from the free market hymn sheet. The Irish housing bubble, which saw residential property prices triple between 1994 and 2006, provides a useful case study. As Julien Mercille has shown, right up until the market crashed in 2007, analysts from the financial and real-estate industries were maintaining that there was no bubble and predicting that the boom would end in a 'soft landing', and their upbeat message was being reproduced with little or no dissent in the major media. Both groups had a common interest in promoting Ireland as a 'Celtic Tiger' economy, cemented by close and long-standing ties between journalists and their sources, and in the case of the country's newspaper of record, the *Irish Times*, anchored in the expected gains from the property website MyHome, purchased in 2006 for 50 million euros (Mercille 2014). Robert Picard and his colleagues found the same reliance on insider sources in their study of reporting of the banking and financial sector in news organizations in four European countries between January 2007 and December 2013. On average 52% of the information about the banking crisis directly quoted in the coverage they sampled came from the banks themselves, with legitimated analysts/experts contributing a further 18% (Pickard, Selva and Bironzo 2014: 13). However, these figures may well underestimate the dominance of 'insider' sources since they exclude stories written by journalists, which do not mention a specific source but which, as the authors note, may well contain 'content suggested by third parties, or "inspired" by press release' (13). As Katherine Griffiths, the banking editor of the *Times,* London, told the research team, 'I like to speak to some people I can reach quickly. I know a few banking analysts very well and will phone them or others in banks. I've built up relations with analysts by ringing them over a long period of time … I trust their information' (27). Not only have the established insider circuits survived the crash, in many cases the accounts they provide are likely to be more carefully constructed. As another interviewee, Robert Bailhache, who has worked as both a journalist and head of press operations at HSBC Holdings, noted: '[T]he biggest lesson of the financial crisis for public relations officials is that it is imperative … to have a cogent narrative on and off the record' (5). The outcome of these established routines is once again to reinstate business as usual.

As people's first port of call for information and commentary on events and decisions that affect them, news has rightly been seen as an essential support for the deliberative process at the heart of democracy. But however well it performs this role it remains a relatively 'closed' cultural form (see Schlesinger, Murdock and Elliott 1983). Organizational imperatives coupled with professional routines and conceptions push news towards a focus on events rather than processes and a preference for sources drawn from political and business elites. There are exceptions, of course, when dissident voices are given a hearing, stories are told from the perspective of those at the sharp end of austerity policies and wrongdoing in power centres is uncovered. The research presented in this collection, and supported by other recent work, however, suggests that the routine coverage of economic and financial affairs continues to reproduce a 'business as usual agenda' with argument and opposition mostly confined to outlets read by the educated elite or produced by minority political and social movements. The effect is to reinforce a 'managerial' rather than a 'participatory' model of democracy in which extended debate is concentrated with elite circles. Participation becomes an extension of consumer choice in the marketplace of political brands.

That is why, in this collection, we have extended the scope of analysis and explored how the financial crisis has been represented in documentary and feature films that are arguably more 'open' as cultural forms. Released from the constraints of meeting the 24-hour news cycle and the need for compressed expression, they are able to work with a wider range of voices, experiences and ways of organizing narrative accounts. As a consequence, potentially at least, they offer additional, and readily available and accessible, resources for popular understanding and debate. The case studies presented here, however, suggest that this potential is more often than not subverted by the expressive conventions and commercial pressures that govern these forms. This is most obvious in the case of the major Hollywood feature films looked, with their concerted focus on the actions and motivations of those inside the financial system to the exclusion of any sustained portrayal of the impact of their decisions on the lives of those at the bottom of the social order. The representations offered by the documentary films contributors here are more diverse, with several notable attempts to tell the story of the financial crisis and its repercussions, from the point of view of the 'common man'. But again, compared with mainstream feature films, their circulation was often relatively restricted.

As noted in the Introduction, the studies assembled here are selective and partial, a first pass at an account, but taken together they point to important lessons for future work, not only on business and finance but on other major social issues.

First, the study of media representations needs to look behind media accounts to detail the ways evidence, talk and stories are organized and contested within the elite and expert circles that provide their major sources. The study of representations is not only about detailing how the knowledge and argument generated within restricted domains is reproduced and translated for general consumption, it is also about what is marginalized and dismissed and left unsaid and unreported.

Second, mapping the informational, analytical and empathetic resources available to citizens on key public issues requires research to go beyond news accounts and examine the organization of representation across the whole range of available media forms and platforms. It needs to look as carefully at popular fictions, advertising and video games as at news accounts, current affairs commentary and documentary. It needs to explore the new expressive forms being developed online – blogs and citizens' journalism. And most of all it needs to include all of these sources in the same study, examining where they overlap and reinforce each other and where they diverge and dissent.

Third, research needs to pay close attention to the ways access to the full diversity of resources for citizens' understanding is stratified by differential possession of economic and educational capital and to the complex interactions between people's media consumption ecologies, their circles of face-to-face conversation and argument, and their online and offline interactions, in shaping their constructions of issues and possible interventions.

Finally, in their role as engaged citizens researchers have a public responsibility to follow the implications of their research findings through into the political and policy arenas. Given that public decisions over how economic and financial systems do and should operate play a pivotal role in shaping living conditions and life chances, and the centrality of media in regulating access to resources for understanding and critique, research needs to reconnect the study of representation and reception to an analysis of the political economy of public communication. This task lay beyond the scope of the present volume but it is essential if the limitations of representations revealed in previous chapters are to be addressed in practical terms. The question of how best to guarantee a public communication system that provides citizens with the full range of informational and interpretive resources they need to participate fully in political debates on the future of economic life has been on the table since the advent of mass democracy based on the universal adult franchise. The research presented here reminds us forcefully of its continuing urgency.

References

Chakrabortty, A. (2014), 'Economics lobotomised', *Guardian,* 9th May, p. 34.

Chang, H.-J. (2014), *Economics: The User's Guide,* London: Penguin.

Mercille, J. (2014), 'The role of the media in sustaining Ireland's housing bubble', *The New Political Economy,* 19: 2, pp. 282–301.

National Audit Office (2014), *The Privatisation of Royal Mail*, London: National Audit Office. HC 1182, Session 2013–14, 1st April.

OECD (2011), 'Divided we stand: Why inequality keeps rising-an overview of growing income inequalities in OECD countries: Main findings', www.oecd.org/else/social/inequality. Accessed 10th May, 2014.

Office of National Statistics (2014), *Wealth in Great Britain Wave 3, 2010–2012-Chapter 2, Total Wealth, 2010/12,* London, www.ons.gov.uk/ons/dcp171776362809.pdf. Accessed 15th May, 2014.

Oxfam (2014), *Working for the Few: Political Capture and Economic Inequality*, London: Oxfam. Briefing Paper 178.

Picard, R. G., Selva, M. and Bironzo, D. (2014), *Media Coverage of Banking and Financial News*, Oxford: Reuters Institute for the Study of Journalism.

Piketty, T. (2014), *Capital in the Twenty-First Century*, Cambridge, MA: The Belknap Press of Harvard University Press.

Rethinking Economics (2014), *Portcullis House Press Release*, 1st March, www.rethinkingeconomics. blogspot.co.uk/2004/03/portcullis-house-press-release_1.html. Accessed 12th May, 2014.

Schlesinger, P., Murdock, G. and Elliott, P. (1983), *Televising Terrorism: Political Violence in Popular Culture,* London: Comedia Publishing Group.

The Economist (2014), 'A modern Marx', 3rd May, pp. 13–14.

Warren, T. and Mathiason, N. (2014), 'Unmasked: The city institutions given privileged status in the controversial royal mail flotation', *Open Democracy*, 30th April, http://www. opendemocracy.net. Accessed 12th May, 2014.

Wintour, P. (2014), 'New tax figures show boost to rich in recovery', *Guardian,* 14th May, p. 11.

Notes on contributors

John Corner formerly Head of the School of Politics and Communication Studies at Liverpool University is Visiting Professor at the Institute of Communication Studies at Leeds University. His recent books include as author, *Theorizing Media: Power Form and Subjectivity* (2011) and *Political Culture and Media Genre* (2012).

Aeron Davis is Professor of Political Communication in the Department of Media and Communications at Goldsmiths, University of London. His recent books include, *Political Communication and Social Theory* (2010) and *Promotional Cultures* (2013).

George DeMartino is Professor at the Josef Korbel School of International Studies at the University of Denver. His recent books include, *The Economist's Oath: On the Need for and Content of Professional Economic Ethics* (2010).

Monika Elsler, **Swantje Lingenberg** and **Anne Mollen** are Research Associates on the project 'The Transnationalization of Public Spheres in Europe: Citizens' (re)action', based in the collaborative research centre 507 'Transformations of the State' at the University of Bremen.

Jostein Gripsrud is Professor in the Department of Information Science and Media Studies at the University of Bergen. He is one of Europe's leading scholars of communication, and a former International Francqui Professor in Belgium. His recent books include as co-editor, *Media, Markets and Public Spheres* (2010) and *The Idea of the Public Sphere* (2011).

Andreas Hepp is Professor of Communication and Media Studies in the Centre for Media, Communication and Information Sciences at the University of Bremen. His recent books include, as author, *Cultures of Mediatization* (2013) and as co-editor, *Mediatized Worlds* (2014).

Nina Kvalheim is based in the Department of Information Science and Media Studies at the University of Bergen where she is exploring the relationship between multimedia news production and the role of newspapers in public debate.

Justin Lewis is Professor of Communication and Dean of Research for the College of Arts, Humanities and Social Sciences at Cardiff University. His recent books include,

The World of 24 House News (2010) and *Beyond Consumer Capitalism: Media and the Limits to Imagination* (2013).

Johanna Möller is completing doctoral research on the Europeanization of public spheres at the University of Bremen.

Graham Murdock is Professor of Culture and Economy in the Department of Social Sciences at Loughborough University. His recent books include, as co-editor, *The Handbook of Political Economy of Communications* (2011).

Anke Offerhaus is University Lecturer in the Department of Communication and Media Studies at the University of Bremen.

Anja Peltzer is based in the Institute for Media and Communication Studies at the University of Mannheim. Her recent books include, as author, *Identity and Spectacle: The Hollywood Blockbuster as a Globally Successful Identity Provider* (2011) and as co-editor, *Crisis, Cash and Communication: The Financial Crisis in the Media* (2012).

Helle Sjøvaag is a post-doctoral researcher in the Department of Information Science and Media Studies at the University of Bergen, where she is investigating the impact of structural changes in the media landscape on media ownership and its influence.

Richard Thomas is completing doctoral research in the Business School at Cardiff University.

Peter A. Thompson is Senior Lecturer in the School of English, Film, Theatre and Media Studies at Victoria University Wellington. He is currently developing his research on the operation of financial markets.

Catherine Walsh is completing doctoral research on financialization and the UK state at Goldsmiths, University of London.

Index